Strange Ways To Die in the Tudor Ages

Strange Ways To Die in the Tudor Ages

Emily Bush and Carrie Ingram-Gettins

First published in Great Britain in 2025 by
Pen & Sword History
An imprint of Pen & Sword Books Limited
Yorkshire – Philadelphia

ISBN 978 1 03610 873 1

A CIP catalogue record for this book is available from the British Library.

Typeset by Mac Style
Printed in the UK by CPI Group (UK) Ltd, Croydon, CR0 4YY.

The Publisher's authorised representative in the EU for product safety is Authorised Rep Compliance Ltd., Ground Floor, 71 Lower Baggot Street, Dublin D02 P593, Ireland.
www.arccompliance.com

For a complete list of Pen & Sword titles please contact

PEN & SWORD BOOKS LIMITED
47 Church Street, Barnsley, South Yorkshire, S70 2AS, England
E-mail: enquiries@pen-and-sword.co.uk
Website: www.pen-and-sword.co.uk
or
PEN AND SWORD BOOKS
1950 Lawrence Road, Havertown, PA 19083, USA
E-mail: uspen-and-sword@casematepublishers.com
Website: www.penandswordbooks.com

Contents

Introduction

Death, the last great adventure. Considered by many to be the one true equaliser, death is the one thing that links humanity throughout the ages as a unifying experience. While the fact that everybody must, at one point, face the consequences of their mortality, not everybody will face it in the same way or with quite the same level of dignity.

What we endeavour to do within these pages is to provide examples of when people have taken that final journey in less-than-ideal ways. Whether through misadventure, misfortune or quite literally missing the mark, we will shed a light on how souls from across the social spectrum met their end.

Some names you may know, others you will likely never have heard, but we hope that this book serves as an insightful, respectful but also sometimes incredulous look at how our ancestors removed themselves from the gene pool. Join us as we ask the question that must have crossed the minds of many historians at some point in their career – how are we not extinct yet?

List of Illustrations

Chapter 1

The Tudor Period: A Quick Tour

The period that we have focused on here is what is commonly known in the UK as the Tudor period; however, we are aware that this is a localised naming convention, and we have therefore tried to refer to the period as the sixteenth century wherever possible. This is a chunk of time book-ended by two major dynastic changes and marked by so many historical events that we're sure everybody alive was affected by the curse 'may you live in interesting times'.

On 22 August 1485 in a field near the town of Market Bosworth, a battle was fought in which the king, Richard III of the Plantagenet dynasty, was killed and the successful pretender, Henry Tudor, assumed the throne through right of conquest. This battle brought to an end a dynasty that had reigned since 1154 and was the final major battle in a civil war, the Wars of the Roses (also known as the Cousins' War) that had raged since 1455.[1] The Tudor dynasty was to sit on the throne of England for the next 118 years when, in 1603, the last surviving and legitimate heir of that line, Elizabeth I, died.

Elizabeth I never married, and, despite many rumours and conspiracy theories, she produced no legitimate heirs to inherit her crown, so she named her cousin James Stuart, at that point James VI of Scotland, as her heir and so the Stuart period began. This is the history that we grew up with in our native England and so it seemed sensible to start with this nicely packaged period. We are aware for the rest of the world it was not quite so clearly defined, however, and that has made research challenging but interesting.

The sixteenth century was a time of innovation, coming at the peak of the Renaissance and after the invention of the printing press. Information could now be disseminated on a much larger scale than before, but so could misinformation. As much as this was a period of artistic achievement and invention, it was also a period of turmoil. Religious reforms and mass hysteria destroyed alongside disease, famine and environmental factors. People turned their fear and lack of control over the outside world inward and it was a century of fear as much as it was of wonder.

While many of the deaths included in this book are those of the everyday people in the sixteenth century, there are honourable mentions of some of the most influential characters from the period, so we thought it prudent to give you a brief tour of some of the main players, starting with the Tudors themselves.

The Tudors

Henry Tudor came to the throne in 1485 by victory in battle against Richard III. At this point he made good on an agreement previously arranged to marry Elizabeth of York, niece of Richard and daughter of the former king Edward IV. By all accounts this became a genuinely strong and affectionate marriage and produced a few children, with four surviving to adulthood: Arthur, Margaret, Henry and Mary. Through a series of advantageous marriages, they and their ancestors helped connect the royal families of Europe. Arthur married Catherine of Aragon, daughter of Isabella I of Castile and Ferdinand II of Aragon, the rulers of Spain following the period known as the Reconquista. With the death of Arthur from sweating sickness in 1502, Catherine was later remarried in 1509 to his younger brother and by that point the king, Henry VIII.

The eldest daughter of Henry VII and Elizabeth of York, Margaret Tudor, was given in marriage as part of a treaty to James IV of Scotland. Together they had six children with only one surviving infancy, being the future James V of Scotland. Margaret remarried twice, first to Archibald Douglas, 6th Earl of Angus, with whom she had one daughter named Margaret, then to Henry Stewart, 1st Lord Methven, with whom she had no further children. Her first son James V had three legitimate children with his wife Mary of Guise, only one of whom survived infancy and became known to history as Mary, Queen of Scots, inheriting the throne from her father and later crowned at only 9 months old. Mary's married life would be a tumultuous one, with her first husband Francis II of France dying in 1560 after only two years of married life. Her second husband, Henry Lord Darnley, was the son of Margaret Douglas and the grandson of Margaret Tudor. Darnley was found dead under suspicious circumstances, possibly linked to the man who would be Mary's third husband, James Hepburn, 4th Earl of Bothwell. While Mary had no children with Francis II or Bothwell, she did have a son with Darnley who would go on to become James VI of Scotland and later James I of England, whose reign closed the Tudor period in England and therefore the period covered by this book.

The youngest Tudor child, Mary, married twice in her lifetime. Her famous good looks and slender frame made her one of the most desirable royals in Europe. She had the pick of the very best bachelors of the time, but her father needed to be clever. The first marriage was, as like her siblings, a strategic political move on her father's part, a betrothal to Charles of Habsburg, known mostly for his unfortunately deformed chin. However, fortunately for Mary and due to political alliances changing, at the beginning of 1514 the union was called off. A second treaty was made by Henry VII for Mary to marry King Louis XII of France, however her father died before the deal could be sealed, leaving her fate in the hands of her favourite brother, the now King Henry VIII. At just 18 years old, on the 2 March 1514, Mary arrived in France and was married to King Louis XII of France, who was 52 years old at the time, a week later, on 9 March. Luckily for Mary, the marriage was short-lived as the king died on 1 January 1515, just three months after the wedding due to health complications with his ongoing gout. Following the death of Louis XII, Mary married Charles Brandon, a close friend, confidant and member of the privy council of her brother Henry VIII. This marriage was based on mutual love rather than political strategy. They married secretly in France, without Henry VIII's permission, which initially caused a scandal. Henry was absolutely furious about this marriage but due to Mary being his favourite sister and some intercession by Thomas Wolsey, he relented and agreed to the union but imposed a hefty fine on the couple (which was never paid). Mary and Charles Brandon had four children: Henry Brandon, 1st Earl of Lincoln, Frances Brandon,[2] Eleanor Brandon and Henry Brandon, who died young. Their marriage was a happy one and lasted until Mary's untimely death on 25 June 1533 from health complications.

Last, but by no means least, was Henry Tudor and Elizabeth of York's third child and second son Henry Tudor or more commonly referred to as King Henry VIII. Condensing Henry VIII's marriages into a single paragraph isn't going to be easy, but we shall do our best. Henry VIII was married six times, and despite being on the cutting edge of the English Renaissance, extremely clever, cunning and athletic, it is what he is mostly known for. His first marriage was to his brother's widow Catherine of Aragon. The daughter of Ferdinand II of Aragon and Isabella I of Castile, this marriage was a love match but was also a clever political move. They married on 11 June 1509 and, nine pregnancies notwithstanding, only two children would be born alive, with little Henry only living for two months. Their surviving child, a girl Mary would grow to become Mary I. After twenty-four years, in 1533, Henry had his marriage to Catherine annulled, which led to a break from the Roman Catholic Church, the beginning of the English Reformation and Henry's second marriage, to Anne Boleyn. Married on 25 January 1533, Anne had been a lady-in-waiting to Catherine of Aragon and promised Henry she would shower him with male heirs. This did not happen, their first daughter Elizabeth (soon to be Queen Elizabeth I) a disappointment to Henry as she wasn't the son that was promised. Anne suffered a further three miscarriages before her execution for treason on 19 May 1536.

It is widely speculated that Henry was already courting Jane Seymour before Anne's execution, and lining her up to be wife number three, which she became on 30 May 1536. As before, Jane was also a lady-in-waiting, to Catherine of Aragon and Anne Boleyn (Henry clearly had a type). It is believed that Henry and Jane truly loved one another, with Henry stating on several occasions that Jane was his favourite wife; coincidently, Henry is buried next to Jane in the Chapel of St George in Windsor Castle. They had one child, a boy, Edward. However, due to complications in childbirth Jane died on 24 October 1537 leaving Henry devastated. After three years, it was decided that the king needed to remarry, so the search for wife number four was on. This time focusing on a political alliance, and after seeing a portrait of the Duke of Cleves's sister, a betrothal treaty was signed and Henry VIII married Anne of Cleves on 6 January 1540. This was not a happy union; Henry found Anne unattractive, stating that 'She looked like a horse' and the marriage was never consummated. Anne agreed to an annulment on 9 July of the same year and was given a generous settlement, living out her life in England as the 'King's Beloved Sister'.

Just three weeks later, Henry married his fifth wife, the young and beautiful Catherine Howard, on 28 July 1540. At only 17 Catherine's marriage to the 47-year-old Henry was driven by his infatuation. Court life wasn't what Cathrine had planned. Henry was away a lot, and she was bored. Catherine spent a lot of time with other courtiers and was, by all accounts, a bit of a flirt. She was arrested in late 1541 on charges of adultery and on 13 February 1542, Catherine became the second wife and queen to be beheaded under Henry's reign. To quote a TikTok trend, which doesn't sound like many, but it's strange it happened more than once. Lastly, we find ourselves with the queen who survived, Catherine Parr. A twice-widowed noblewoman, Catherine had been a part of the Tudor court for some time. An attentive wife during his final years, Catherine was instrumental in reconciling Henry with his daughters Mary and Elizabeth and played a key role in the education of Elizabeth. There were rumours of adultery, but these were quickly quashed. No children were produced from this marriage – not entirely sure Henry could have even had he wanted too. Catherine tended Henry's wounds and his many other health ailments before his death on the 28 January 1547. Catherine outlived him and remarried Thomas Seymour shortly thereafter.

Henry VIII's marriages were pivotal in shaping English history, particularly in relation to the religious and political transformations of the period. He died safe in the knowledge that he left behind a son and heir to continue the Tudor dynasty … right?

Edward VI was a sickly child, only being king for nine years and dying at the age of just 15. He didn't marry, so had no children for a legitimate heir. Not waiting to choose either sister to succeed him, Edward named Lady Jane Grey as his heir. She was instantly imprisoned and was executed on 12 February 1554, at the Tower of London.

Upon Jane's death, Henry's daughter Mary Tudor, also known as Bloody Mary, became Queen Mary I. She only had one marriage in her life and on her side at least it was a marriage of love, though for her husband, not so much. King Phillip II of Spain was the son of Emperor Charles V and heir to the

Spanish throne. The marriage was orchestrated to strengthen the political alliance between England and Spain, and to bolster Catholic influence in England. The marriage was deeply unpopular in England due to fears of Spanish dominance and the potential loss of English sovereignty. For Mary it was also an effort to restore Catholicism in England after the Protestant reforms of her father Henry VIII and her half-brother Edward VI. The union was formalised in the Treaty of Windsor, which stipulated that Philip would co-rule England with Mary but would have limited independent authority. Their lack of children is a sad story. Mary had multiple false pregnancies, which caused significant personal distress and public disappointment. Her stomach would swell, and she would have all the symptoms of pregnancy but no baby. It has since been theorised that she may have had stomach cancer which could cause the same symptoms. The marriage ended when Mary died in 1558 on 17 November. Philip was not in England at the time as he had already left in 1557 to attend to his duties in Spain. Which added to his unpopularity in England.

The last monarch in this dynasty is a formidable woman, who led England into a glorious period of history. Elizabeth Tudor was the daughter of Henry VIII and Anne Boleyn, and she never married. Known as the 'Virgin Queen', her decision to remain single was a significant aspect of her reign and political strategy. Elizabeth very cleverly used her unmarried status as a diplomatic tool, entertaining marriage proposals from various European princes and kings to foster alliances and keep potential enemies at bay. This strategy provided her with significant leverage in international relations. Elizabeth's potential suitors did however include both Protestant and Catholic candidates. Marrying a Catholic could and would alienate her Protestant subjects and vice versa. Elizabeth wasn't without a love though, a childhood friend and favourite of Elizabeth's, Robert Dudley, Earl of Leicester, was widely considered the queen's true love. Despite intense speculation and rumours, their relationship never culminated in marriage, possibly due to the political and social implications and the fact Dudley's wife Amy was found mysteriously dead at the bottom of some stairs. Moreover, Elizabeth's experiences with her father's tumultuous marital history and her mother's execution might have influenced her views on marriage. With no children, on 24 March 1603, Elizabeth died with no direct heir. She was succeeded by James VI of Scotland, who became James I of England, uniting the crowns of England and Scotland and beginning the Stuart dynasty.

The Valois

At the end of the fifteenth century France was ruled by Louis XII of the Valois-Orléans line and his first wife Joan of France. Their marriage was annulled without children by Pope Alexander VI in 1498 and the following year Louis married Anne of Brittany. From this second marriage came five children, of whom only two daughters, Claude and Renée, survived to adulthood. As the law at the time (Salic Law) prevented women from inheriting the throne, upon the death of Louis XII in 1515 the crown passed to his cousin and through marriage to Claude, his son-in-law Francis I who would have a somewhat tempestuous relationship with England's Henry VIII. Francis I and Claude together had seven children, with five surviving past infancy. Their oldest surviving daughter Madeleine married James V of Scotland but died before they could have children, aged only 17. Their eldest son Francis lived to be only 18 and so when Francis I died in 1547 the crown passed to their second eldest son Henry (Henri) II.

Henry II ruled France from 1547 to 1559 alongside his wife, Catherine of the powerful Italian Medici family. Together they had ten children, with an impressive seven surviving past infancy,[3] three of the male children going on to be successive kings of France in their own right, with Francis II (mentioned above as husband to Mary, Queen of Scots) being the eldest and first to accede to the throne. Their eldest daughter Elizabeth became the third wife of Philip II of Spain after the death of Mary I Tudor in 1558. Following the death of his brother, Francis, the second-eldest son Charles IX, was named King of France in 1560 and reigned for fourteen years. Upon his death, his younger brother Henry III took over in 1574 but was later assassinated, in 1589, being the last surviving son of Henry II and Catherine de' Medici. The throne then passed to their son-in-law, husband of Henry II's third daughter Margaret, Henry IV (who prior to this was Henry III of Navarre). He reigned until 1610 and has gone down in history as Henry the Great, so it can be safely argued that he had a pretty decent reign compared to some of his predecessors who oversaw conquest, assassination attempts (and successes) and religious turmoil, though Henry the Great's reign was far from a picnic.

The Spanish Contingent

From the Spanish side of the continent, this book opens on the joint reign of Isabella I of Castile who came to power in 1474 and her husband Ferdinand II of Aragon who came to power in 1479. Together they had seven children with five surviving past childhood. Their oldest two surviving children, Isabella and John, died within a year of each other in 1547–48 and without children, leaving their third child Joanna to inherit the throne of Castile upon her mother's death. Joanna married Philip the Handsome from the Habsburg family and together they had six children, two of whom assumed the role of Holy Roman Emperor, Charles V and Ferdinand I. Sadly Joanna would be betrayed by her husband, father and latterly her son with regards to her mental health and has gone down in history as Joanna the Mad.[4] The next youngest daughter, Maria, married Manuel I of Portugal who had previously been married to the eldest daughter Isabella, and together they had nine children, with all but two making it past infancy and who went on to marry their cousins or uncles – inbreeding was very much a Habsburg trait.

Ferdinand and Isabella's youngest daughter Catherine would go on to marry first Arthur, Prince of Wales, and then his younger brother Henry VIII and become Queen of England.

The combined branches of Castile and Aragon would go on to take the position of Holy Roman Emperor, the title belonging to the head of the Holy Roman Empire, also known as the Holy Roman Empire of the German Nation. This was a far-reaching and wonderfully complicated empire established in 962 by Otto I when he was crowned by Pope John XII and continued to grow in strength and size, reaching its zenith under Charles V in the mid-sixteenth century, stretching across much of Central Europe. The empire was finally dissolved in 1806 during the Napoleonic Wars. Towards the end of his reign, Charles V began to face increased opposition from

Protestant forces and from the growing Ottoman Empire to the east. This combined pressure led to him abdicating his various offices piecemeal to members of his family and the title of Holy Roman Emperor went to his younger brother Ferdinand I, leaving Charles to retire to a monastery in Spain.

Ferdinand I took over in August 1556 until his death in December 1562 when he was succeeded by his son Maximilian I. The Spanish royal family were part of the Habsburg Empire, a strong ruling family prominent in Europe from the mid-thirteenth century with King Rudolf I of Germany, and remained in power until 1918 when the final monarch, Charles I of Austria, was exiled and the monarchy of Austria abolished. While undoubtedly an influential and far-reaching family, the Habsburg dynasty is largely known in the public consciousness for their regular intermarriage and inbreeding, with many studies done on this, in particular around the 'Habsburg Jaw', a prominent feature in a number of family portraits.

While we understand that this is a lot of information to take in over a short period of writing, we will not be offended if readers have skimmed through. This is more here as a reference point should people want to skip back and orient themselves within a certain reign or period. We have also included a family tree in the images contained in this book to give a visual assist if that proves easier.

Chapter 2
Animal Accidents

Agriculture was the primary industry in Tudor England, with most of the land being given over to arable farming or livestock,[1] with the main animals reared being cattle, pigs and sheep and the latter becoming the largest contingent of livestock farmed across the country. Substantial areas of land were used by landowners for grazing pastures to support a growing sheep population. Despite the attempt by the government in 1533 to limit the number of sheep any individual was able to own, there was still an exponential increase and during the 1540s it is estimated that the average annual production of wool combined for England and Wales stood at over 50,000 sacks.[2] Efforts were soon taken to promote the English wool trade following a collapse in the price of wool exports. Elizabeth I had a law passed in the 1570s stating that all Englishmen except for the noble class were to wear a woollen cap to church on Sundays to boost the industry domestically.

Legal statute also required that other livestock be kept as well as sheep and it was decreed by the mid-sixteenth century that a minimum of one milking cow was required for every sixty sheep owned and one calf for every 120 sheep. All forms of livestock were taken to local markets to be sold for meat or breeding and farm animals such as cows, sheep and pigs were a common sight in rural areas.

Blood sports were also common, and people gathered en masse to see events such as bear baiting, dog fights and cockfighting as entertainment. Certainly not to most of our tastes today but considering that during this era public executions were considered a day out for all the family, the prevalence of blood sports is hardly surprising really. This did mean, however, that wild animals such as bears were a surprisingly regular sight in the Tudor period, even if those sightings didn't always end well for all involved. As anyone who lives or works with animals will tell you, there is always an inherent risk in their care and maintenance as much as there is to be gained from them. Here are a few cases, intentionally or otherwise, where our feathered or four-legged friends hit back.

Bullish Behaviour

It would not be hard to imagine that several deaths may have occurred historically in some way, shape or form thanks to cattle, and you would be correct. The exact number will likely never be known but even a quick search through coroner's reports and assizes will turn out a surprisingly substantial amount. While mostly docile, cattle are still powerful animals and, especially when startled or enraged, can do a great deal of damage to anything or anyone in their path.

For reference, assizes were courts that convened only periodically to deal with the most serious criminal cases such as murder. Visiting judges from London would preside over these sessions and were required to cover a large geographical area. As such, assizes were traditionally held twice a year, in summer and over Lent (the forty-day period in the Christian calendar that is the run-up to the feast of Easter). Because of the infrequency of assizes, as well as the severity of the cases that were heard there, sessions could last for several weeks at a time, making them quite gruelling for the legal teams involved, let alone the accused and any witnesses.

One such incident is the case of Mr John Skarborow (alternative spelling Scarborough) of Rutland, who on 18 October 1535 was leading a bull belonging to Mr William Radcliffe when they were attacked by a dog. The dog bit the bull, causing the injured animal to lash out in self-defence. We are not aware of what became of the dog in the mayhem that ensued, however we do know that poor Mr Skarborow took a decent amount of blunt force trauma from the bull to his genital region, causing his testicles to be crushed. The injuries he sustained were fatal, but the end was not quick for John, as the coroner's report shows that he was not declared dead until 15 November 1535, a full twenty-eight days after the incident occurred.

An ox[3] was responsible for the drowning of one Richard Cornishe in 1595 when they were both travelling by boat on the River Tamar in Cornwall. The ox did not want to be on the boat, however, and tried to jump over the side to freedom. The trouble was the ox was tethered by the legs to the boat and when this powerful beast took it upon itself to jump, the force of it caused the boat to pitch and take on water, leading to it sinking and Cornishe drowning.

A pair of oxen bulls were responsible for a fatal accident in Kent in 1560 when, while pulling a loaded dung cart under the watchful eye of John Prall, they passed through a gate and then decided that they really didn't want to be doing what they were doing. The oxen broke into a run, pulling the cart too close to the gate and causing one of the wheels to strike the gatepost, causing it to fall over with some force. The collision and sudden upturn of the cart threw John Prall and he landed with vigour against a nearby oak tree, breaking his neck. The oxen, however, survived just fine. This is not the only dung cart or even dung-related death to have occurred during this period; in fact there are that many we felt we had to devote a whole chapter, 'The Final Gong', to them. History really is a fascinating place.

In March 1557 a man was walking through a field in Hogsthorpe while on his way to Ingoldsmells in Lincolnshire, when he caught the attention of one of the cows grazing in said field. The reasons why have been lost to time; however, for some reason the cow, belonging to a William Cheills, became enraged at this rambling gentleman's presence and charged him down, goring him with her horn. The wound was fatal and he died that same day. The greatest irony of this unfortunate demise is that the name of the man who met death that day at the pointy end of a cow was none other than Mr Robert Calf.

There seem to have been a few instances in Tudor England where one could be going about their daily business and suddenly … cow. Take for instance the tale of Robert Rayner from Norland in Yorkshire who was spending time in his 'tenement'[4] when suddenly a bull appeared and knocked him to the ground, mortally wounding him. Death was instant, with the official cause cited as a 'wound to the right side of the stomach'. It is interesting to note that in a number of these cases, the coroner's report will often record the cost of the offending animal, though we doubt it would have been much comfort to the deceased as to whether the horns that pierced them were from a more expensive bull or not.

Sheepish Accidents

While it has been difficult to find records of deaths where sheep were directly involved in ending someone's life in the same way that cows or other larger animals were, there are plenty of recorded incidents where they were more indirectly responsible and watched on in a distinctly sheepish manner. One of the main causes of sheep-related death was drowning, whether this was from trying to rescue a hapless sheep that had wandered somewhere it shouldn't, washing the dirt of the day from their woollen coats, or from driving sheep home during a storm when a nearby river bursts its banks.

One such example is that of Walter Frost who, on 12 February 1507, was helping his master Richard Gyfford ferry sheep across the River Avon in Bodenham, Wiltshire. The endeavour was mostly successful; however, the boat had seen better days and while crossing the river to collect more, the wind picked up and the speed of the current increased. To steady the boat, Frost placed his oar in the riverbed and pushed down, using it like an anchoring pole. The current was too strong however, and the boat started to move away, causing poor Frost, who was still holding on tightly to the oar, to fall into the water where he succumbed to the current and drowned.

Another common way to drown involving sheep was when washing them, and on occasion it was not just the washer themselves who fell afoul of the water. In June 1551 in another incident occurring in Wiltshire, William Hancocke was washing the sheep he was tending at a point on the River Avon when one of the sheep strayed too far into the river. Hancocke went in to rescue the sheep but fell backwards into a whirlpool where he began to drown due to his limited swimming ability. Upon seeing Mr Hancocke in difficulty, one Alice Phenne tried to help but fell into the same whirlpool and also started to struggle. At this point another person on the scene, William Catour, saw that both Phenne and Hancocke appeared to be drowning and went in to save them, but alas he also fell into the whirlpool. Finally, Mr John

Catour jumped in to also assist but the whirlpool claimed him too and all four drowned together. The main tragedy was that the sheep belonged to William Catour Senior, so it is likely that two of the four victims were his family, with at least one potentially being his son. He does appear, however, to have kept his sheep, though he might have questioned the wisdom of letting any more members of his family, staff or indeed flock go anywhere near that particular river.

A similar event happened in Yorkshire in June 1560 when Alice Bonde was washing sheep and a young male sheep (known as a wether) jumped up and knocked her into the water where she was caught in a current and drowned. Seeing her sister then lying prostrate in the water, Catherine Bonde climbed in to help and was caught in the same current. So too was John Swinglehirst who came to the aid of both women. This was a slightly more direct way in which sheep claimed further victims, though we cannot assume premeditation on the part of the sheep. The inherent message here appears to be a warning to take care when washing a flock in fast-flowing water or, better still, do not do it at all, though apparently the sheep often seemed to get away just fine in these scenarios.

In one last story of sheepish stupidity, we have the case of William Hall, who frankly only has himself to blame when in 1574 he decided to engage in tomfoolery while he and some of his colleagues were busy washing a large flock of sheep in a nearby creek. Hall decided it would be a great idea to jump on the back of one of the rams and ride it across the creek. Once they were both in the water, however, Hall lost his grip on the back of the ram and fell into the water where the current caught him, and he drowned. So as much as care must be taken when washing sheep, riding them across fast-flowing water probably isn't the best of ideas either. Needless to say, dear readers, please do not try that at home!

Horses for Courses

While not as problematic as determined oxen and wayward cattle, or as unlucky as sheep proved to be for people, horses were still responsible for many deaths during the Tudor period. These were more through accident than carelessness or bad ideas but are still worthy of note. As could be expected, accidents were more prevalent when other animals or extremes of nature were involved. Such is the case with one William Gefferey of Berkshire, who was riding through the town of Wokingham on 14 May 1505 when a dog suddenly appeared and startled the horse. The horse bolted and Mr Gefferey was unable to maintain his hold, falling headfirst to the ground and sustaining a fatal injury that he took six days to succumb to.

Sometimes it was simply a case of the horse being a horse that was the danger, such as with John Halfe from Suffolk, who was working with a horse when he was kicked in the chest by the hind legs, leaving him with an injury, the physical trauma of which claimed his life within twenty-four hours. Or there was John Blakloke of Lincolnshire who was fatally wounded in 1538 while cleaning down his horse when the creature lashed out, catching Blakloke on the crown of his head with its hind leg, causing instant death.

Meanwhile, in Coventry in 1507 a poor gentleman named John was minding his own business standing on a somewhat narrow bridge at Bastellmyll when someone came over the bridge on horseback. Clearly overestimating the width of the bridge (or perhaps underestimating the width of the horse) they continued to cross and pushed poor John into the water below where he was then carried by the current under the waterwheel of the nearby mill. As with sheep, the combination of animal and water could be somewhat problematic, especially when it came to either crossing moving water or riding alongside water, as we have just seen.

It is considered good practice, not to mention common sense, when leading a horse to water for it to drink, to dismount for a moment otherwise things might go wrong. This advice was lost on William Gode of Worcestershire, when in March 1508 he took the horse he was riding to the edge of the River Severn with the hopes of giving it some water, but remained in the saddle … until he didn't. As the horse lowered itself to drink, Gode lost his balance and pitched forward, falling headfirst into the river, leaving his horse behind. A similar end befell John Brown of Rochester in August 1509 when, as he was watering a horse in a nearby river, the horse stumbled, and he was thrown into the water. Brown was able to hold on to the reins briefly, but his relief was short lived as they then snapped and he was washed away.

In much the same way as with cattle, it wasn't unknown for a horse to cause direct death or fatal accident while not actually being ridden or otherwise directly involved in the situation. In a tragic twist of fate William Hall of Gloucestershire was up a ladder repairing a roof when a horse that was for some reason running free down the road (the reason has been lost to time) knocked into the ladder sending both it and Hall flying, causing instant death upon landing. In another case of 'suddenly … horse', there was Anthony Coke who was fatally kicked in the head in Lincoln by the horse of Sir Thomas Heneage who was riding through the town. A day in town could be an exciting prospect at times, with potential new sights and experiences, however we would wager that getting kicked in the head by a horse was not really what Coke had in mind.

Blood sports were a very common pastime during the sixteenth century and one of the main spectacles was bear baiting.[5] On 4 June 1567 a mix of animals and excessive noise came together to create a perfect storm that ended in tragedy in Southwark. As part of a campaign to drum up business and excite potential spectators, a procession travelled through the streets of Southwark where a drummer was followed by a bull and a bear, which were to be baited by dogs. The cacophony of sound was too much for a nearby horse which bolted, pulling the cart it was yoked to with it and sadly running over and 5-year-old George Jeames in the process.

With deaths falling from horses or because of the powerful kick that a horse can inflict being fairly common, it is unusual to find an incident where the individual involved was a victim of both. Sadly, this was the case for John Bidwell of Buckinghamshire who died on 5 October 1537 when the horse he was riding threw him and then proceeded to kick him in the stomach. The kick was considered by the coroner's report to be the fatal blow, meaning he would otherwise have likely survived the fall; the horse just seemed intent on finishing the job.

Standing they are dangerous enough but a horse in motion is sometimes worse and considering the size and strength of a horse in comparison to the average person, it is unsurprising that incidents of being dragged by horses occurred. This is something that William Humfrey of Essex found out to his detriment while leading a horse belonging to one William Wynseley back to the house where his father lived. He was leading it by a halter that was tied to Humfrey's hand when the horse suddenly broke into a canter, yanking the unsuspecting man along, causing him to fall and be dragged, breaking his skull against the ground. A similar accident occurred to Willim Jylys of Cambridgeshire, who was pulled along by a horse whose halter was wrapped around his arm, dragging him for over a quarter of a mile (approximately 1,320 feet or 440 yards) during which time he was unable to free his arm and died because of his injuries.

Also considering the strength and size of horses, it is possibly ill-advised to mistreat them or act irrationally around them. John Jakson, also of Cambridgeshire, learned this lesson the hard way in October 1538 while driving a cart full of firewood when he struck one of the horses pulling the cart. The animal kicked back, catching Jakson in the genitals, causing him a mortal wound and leading to the horse being taken into the custody of the local constables, though we doubt there would have been a trial, unlike those that other animals had to face.

In a decided case of instant karma in 1581, David Morris of Shropshire found himself in the area we now call Powys, Wales, working for the household of one John Jones. One night he decided to play a prank on one of his master's mares by gathering some stinging nettles to torment her with. The plan worked and the nettles caused the horse to react, but she kicked back hard, right where Morris was standing and caught him square in the chest, killing him instantly.

People were not the only victims of wayward horses; sometimes they also took their own with them. One such case happened in Derbyshire in 1538 with Robert Boche riding a horse that was tethered to two others when they came to a bridge. While crossing, one of the horses stumbled and fell into the river below, pulling Boche and the other two horses in with it, leading to all four drowning together.

It wasn't just riding or standing innocently on ladders that could lead someone to have a fatal falling-out with a horse. Horse-related sports were very popular during the sixteenth century, particularly in the form of racing or the traditional jousting tournament. Races didn't often have the benefit of a large hippodrome such as the Ancient Greeks had for their chariot racing, and those wishing to engage in the sport had to make do with what was around them.

Such was the case for Henry Hedlam and Brian Newton in January 1540 when they were racing their horses in a garden near London. The problem with racing in gardens, however, is that you're a lot taller on horseback and there are often trees around. Brian Newton's horse carried him too close to an elm tree and Newton collided head-first with it, causing him to be knocked from the horse and break his neck. Whether the broken neck was from the impact with the branch or the ground is unclear, however poor Mr Newton passed away the following day. He was not the only rider to fall foul of a horse: take the lady by the name of Jane Jones in 1534, who was not the rider but instead a spectator. In an incident that would make Emily Davison wince, a horse broke ranks during a race and Jones was a little too close to the riders, leading to her being trampled and sustaining grave wounds to her check and legs that she succumbed to within five days.

The horse-related accidents continued to mount throughout the century, though in the case of Alan Wellard of Kent, it was the dismount that did it. Wellard was transporting a cart through the parish of Birling, riding on the first horse and using that to lead the others. As he brought the cart to a stop, his horse took the opportunity to urinate. To anybody who has never been near a horse when this happens, let us just say that it leaves quite a puddle. Wellard dismounted, ready to conclude his journey when he landed in the puddle of horse urine and slipped, falling under the horse who was subsequently startled and accidentally trampled his head, killing him instantly. Strangely enough, throughout all the deaths you will encounter in this book, being trampled to death in a pool of horse urine is not the most dignified way to go.

This final horse-related death is included for the narrative given at the end of the coroner's report, rather than for the death itself, though it was very much a tragic accident. Jane Clerke, aged 9, of Cambridgeshire (apparently a county that deserves renown for its murderous horses) was sitting on a mill wheel being pulled by a horse when she slipped and fell, landing between the mill wheel and a piece of wood that was attached to the house causing her to be crushed to death. The report from assizes then goes on to mention not only the cost of the horse and harness (2 shillings) and the mill wheel (5 shillings), but also mentions the cost of the piece of timber (4 pence), all of which was paid to the coroner. You cannot put a price on human life, however the instruments that end it can apparently be costed.

Avian Accidents

Birds, sometimes considered omens in certain beliefs and cultures, are not exempt from being the cause, directly or indirectly, of accidental death and misfortune. Many incidents occurred while trying to shoot birds with either guns or bows but sometimes the death was a little more unusual. Such is the case with one Richard Wolstanrrose of Shropshire who attempted in November 1596 to use a large net, known as a 'cockeshut' net, to catch a woodcock. In doing so he ended up running under a large rock when the net snagged, yanking him backwards and causing him to hit his head on the rock, resulting in instant death.

Meanwhile in Yorkshire, Alan Walton took it upon himself to climb the portcullis of Pontefract Castle to catch a bird for his daughter. He climbed onto a wooden part of the structure holding the portcullis and found out too late that the wood was rotten, whereby the board supporting his weight broke, and he fell to his death. In another falling incident in 1542, Isabel Philips of Herefordshire was attempting to rescue a cockerel which had fallen into a well when she fell in herself, striking the side of her head on the bucket on her way down, causing instant death in a classic case of no good deed goes unpunished.

Most deaths involving birds appear to relate to slips, trips and falls from height, which can be expected when your quarry has wings and knows how to use them. For example, Richard Alworth of Oxfordshire decided to climb onto the roof of his local church to catch pigeons, when the section of the roof on which he was standing broke and gave way, sending him plummeting sixty feet, leading to his death from crushing injuries. In another prime example of animal-related instant karma, John Coole attempted to destroy a kite's nest (the birds of prey being seen more as a pest at the time) in Rutland in

June 1560 when he stood on a branch that was too weak to take his weight and he fell approximately twenty feet to his death.

Many bird-related deaths appear to have occurred because of attempting to shoot them, whether with a gun or a bow, some of which will be explored in our chapter about weaponry, and the often-spectacular ways wielding a weapon could go horribly wrong, or horribly right.

Bearing Up

As is probably evident by now, the Tudor period was a touch risky where animals were concerned. Creatures regularly encountered such as dogs, farmyard animals and urban wildlife could turn on a knife edge and either directly maim and kill you or, in the case of rats, carry the means of destroying a large portion of the population. But what about the animals that you wouldn't normally expect to see in your everyday doings? To paraphrase Shakespeare, here are some people who exited life pursued by a bear.

Such was the case for poor Agnes Owens in Hereford, who was innocently asleep in her bed in September 1570 when a black bear being held captive by one David Northe managed to break free of the chain holding it and escape into the street. The reasons why are unclear, but the bear was for some reason driven to enter through a window into the house where Mrs Owens was sleeping and maul her, dragging her out into the street where she died of her excessive wounds. Nobody likes being woken up suddenly from a nap, least of all by a random bear in the bedroom.

It would appear that Tudor-era bears had something against certain names, as another Agnes fell victim to a grisly attack in 1563. While at the house of Lord Bergavenny in Birling in Kent, his bear broke loose and attacked one Agnes Rapte in the hallway, subjecting her to multiple bite wounds. Ms Rapte died six hours after the attack due to multiple wounds to her head, torso and legs. Lord Bergavenny ordered that the bear should be immediately shot and his servant John Washenes carried out the sentence.

Lord Bergavenny's bear was not the only animal punished for fatal attacks on humans, and some of the ways that the animals were destroyed is almost as bizarre as the events themselves. The revenge dealt to suspected criminal animals is covered in the chapter 'Crime and Punishment' and we would advise the reader to suspend disbelief for some of the cases mentioned.

Man's Best Friend?

As well as farmyard animals and beasts of the wild, one of the risks to human life in the sixteenth century came from the creature considered normally to be man's best friend, the dog. Here are a few ways in which that ancient friendship was called into question.

In February 1599 John Jervis of Kent was walking to an outbuilding to let out a dog of his that he had enclosed in there for the night. Jervis is recorded as having suffered from a fall a few weeks before this which had left him unsteady on his feet. As he was walking back to his house he had to walk past a pond, at which point the now-released dog tried to jump up on him, knocking him forward into the water. Due to his fall, Jervis did not have the strength to pull himself back out of the water and he drowned.

Sometimes the animals inadvertently join forces to create mayhem that ends in tragedy. This is what happened in the case of John Somer who in April 1526 was riding his horse accompanied by his dog through a field, also in Kent, when his dog spied a hare and took off after it. Somer attempted to turn his horse to call the dog back when he struck his head hard against the overhanging branch of an elm tree, instantly breaking his neck. While the coroner's report records the cost of the horse he was riding, there is no indication of what happened to the dog. A second incident of horse and dog versus man was that of William Kene who was riding through Leicestershire one day in 1536, carrying sheepskins, with his two dogs leashed to the saddle. A river blocked his route and Kene went to cross it, but though his horse was willing, the dogs were not. The dogs started to strain against their leashes and pulled so hard against their restraints that they broke the girdle on Kene's saddle, causing him to fall from the horse and into the river, the weight of the saddle and the sheepskins pulling him under so that he drowned.

Dogs seem to have a similar body count as sheep when it comes to interactions around watercourses, with the majority being tragic accidents or an overly affectionate dog not knowing their own strength. Though, in a potential example of poetic justice, the water struck back on behalf of the dog in the case of John Burry of Leicestershire who, on 15 January 1544, was trying to throw a dog into the nearby River Soar. The action of doing this unbalanced Burry and he fell into the river himself instead and drowned. It is not recorded but we hope the dog was able to swim ashore and survive. Burry was not the only person to fall victim to a dog and the River Soar. Richard Davye met a watery end there in 1545; he was crossing near a water mill when he saw a dog in the river. He tried to rescue the dog, but it wriggled in his arms and Richard lost his balance, falling into the river where the current took him and held him under.

On occasion it isn't even the animal that causes the death but another person attempting to assist with the animals. John Riche of Buckinghamshire met his fate at the end of a piece of wood wielded by William Thruston as the two were attempting to separate Riche's dogs from Thruston's pigs which had come onto his land and were rooting around, disturbing the soil. Thruston was using the stick to beat the dogs back when he swung it too wide and it connected with Riche's head, killing him instantly.

With the case of Juliana Streton from Kent (which would seem to be a rather risky county for animal owners), she was walking near a pond on land belonging to William Parrys, though he apparently did not notice she was there. Parrys was instead occupied with trying to drive off a dog that was chasing his ducks. The dog would not stop going after the birds, so Parrys picked up a clod of dirt and threw it at the dog to try and drive it away. His aim was not that good however, and the clod missed the dog entirely, instead hitting the nearby Ms Streton in the stomach, wounding her fatally and causing her rapid death thereafter.

While it is a rare occasion where the animals involved in this chapter actively meant to harm, let alone cause death, it would seem that the sixteenth century is certainly not a positive one when it comes to safe animal handling, or even being around animals at all really and if there is one thing we have learned it is that no matter where you are in this world, you are never truly safe from cows.

Chapter 3

Crime and Punishment

If you mention the Tudor period, along with the inevitable references to Henry VIII and that slight religious blip called the Reformation, the collective mind tends towards the violence of the era. We will cover some aspects of this and how weapons sometimes turned on their wielders in the most unexpected ways in the chapter entitled 'Weaponry Woes', but it also worth having a look at some of the more public violence that occurred in the form of torture and punishment. Beheadings are synonymous with the sixteenth century, particularly in England, but there was much more to the punishments meted out in this century that we felt they deserved their own space. Brace yourself for some ridiculous laws and deeply disturbing punishments which very much reinforce the viewpoint that the scariest thing that can happen to a human is another human.

The Tudor Court System

It is worth noting here that when looking back at the past, it is important not to look at it through a modern lens. What we see as socially acceptable or unacceptable now may not have applied to our ancestors and it is also important to recall that things such as religious doctrine and folklore were far more real and visceral to them than they may be to many of us. For example, the concepts of hell and purgatory[1] were perceived in a far more literal way and therefore could be quite terrifying in the sixteenth century than, it could be argued, they are in the twenty-first century. People's reactions to the negative actions of others, therefore, were accordingly more extreme, with execution sometimes being seen as the only way to save someone's soul from the dangers of literal hellfire.

Some of what we may consider more minor crimes would often receive harsher punishment and we have some examples in this chapter, as well as some of the more serious and oftentimes disturbing reactions. Swift retribution was seen as a necessity in some cases and punishments were regularly carried out in public with the more serious ones often bearing a symbolism linked to the crime itself. Imprisonment often tended to be used more as a form of detention until trial and then punishment.

Public executions were not a new concept and while we may be more sensitive to it in our current century, it does persist to a degree, for example with viewing galleries for executions in parts of the United States of America that have legalised capital punishment. It was a macabre form of entertainment to many, as well as a chance for them to react to people who had been deemed a public enemy and therefore keep an eye on public sentiment. It was also meant as a deterrent, though the continued supply of prisoners sent to execution would make you question how well that worked, or if other mitigating factors were just stronger than the fear a public execution could instil.

It may first be helpful to have a brief understanding of the court system in the sixteenth century, specifically the English legal system. Other countries across Europe had some similar systems but the punishments and severities differed based on cultural norms as well as the area's prevalent religion.

Court types such as the Petty Courts (also known as Magistrates Courts) and Manorial Courts could be called upon to issue fines. Manorial Courts held more feudal responsibilities such as land disputes that were dealt with by the steward or seneschal[2] of a manor on behalf of the landowning lord. They would often hear cases relating to the land and tenants, including incidents where tenants were implicated in assault or accused of criminal irregularities in the sale of goods at a fair price, known as the Assizes of Bread and Ale. The Petty Courts then had a wider net, dealing with minor thefts, public disorder and lesser civil disputes up to a certain amount. Once the crime exceeded a certain monetary value or was considered of a high enough severity then the case could no longer be dealt with at a Petty or Manorial level and would be referred to a higher court through the Assizes.

Legal representation was available for those who found themselves in need of it in the English system, with the legal profession already well established by the sixteenth century. Such representation could prove expensive, however, which allowed for members of the profession to gain wealth and respectability through successful cases, even being elevated to peerages and ending up as members of the royal court in some cases. There is evidence, however, that some legal counsel was available to the less financially fortunate, with the introduction of the Poor Person's Procedure in 1495. This legislation entitled poor persons to legal representation in certain circumstances where they might otherwise struggle to afford such, known as '*in forma pauperis*' or 'in the form of a pauper', though it was likely that the level of legal counsel available was dependent on the severity of the '*pauperis*' part of the sentence.

With that very brief whistlestop tour of the English legal system concluded, let us have a look at some of the cases, with minor crimes and misdemeanours up first.

Minor Crimes and Misdemeanours

Crimes such as minor thefts, vagrancy and moral crimes sat on the more lenient end of the punishment scale, though some of what the perpetrators were subjected to might raise more modern eyebrows. Fines were perhaps the most common form of punishment dealt in the sixteenth century, with the size of the fine dependent upon the severity of the crime and the locality in which it was committed. Fines were commonly issued in instances of theft where the items stolen were worth less than one shilling (a single coin value amounting to 12 pence).

Should the items or amount stolen come to more than a shilling, a more severe punishment was called for. This would often take the form of the pillory or the stocks, which are often inaccurately interchanged in the public imagination.

Stocks were designed to hold the feet of the offender, having them sit on a bench or bucket with their feet then secured in a wooden or metal device that locked their ankles in place to prevent escape. While incapacitated in the shackles, the offenders were at the mercy of the public. They would be left there for as long as their sentencing dictated (or relevant authority decided), exposed to the elements with the potential for passersby or those who just felt like going out of their way and head over to dole out extra punishment as they saw fit. This could take the form of kicking or slapping the offender, verbally abusing them or spitting at them, throwing rotten food or stones and in some cases even excrement depending on how angry they were, with the sole intention of causing further humiliation. The stocks were often used for crimes such as swearing, being drunk and disorderly or cheating at card games.

The pillory, on the other hand, was often a wooden frame with holes in to secure the hands and head of the offending person. Sometimes these were deliberately low to cause the offender to have to bend down and stay in a stooped position once secured in place, or they could be forced to kneel. Similar crimes warranted both stocks and pillories, with the public able to further abuse the offender as they wished, but with the added pain of standing or kneeling in a constantly stooped position for a prolonged period. The goal, once again, was to use humiliation as a deterrent while also giving the public the opportunity to do their bit and feel like they had been actively involved in the punishment process of the individual.

Additional punishments could also be handed out to those in the stocks or pillories depending on the crime, such as branding or avulsion (having all or part of the ear cut off).

The observant reader may have noticed the crime of swearing included in the lists above of what was punishable by public humiliation. While it is noted that bad language is by no means something new and unique to the modern era, our ancestors would apparently do more to try and curb its use in a public place than simply threatening to wash one's mouth out with soap. Surprisingly, a lot of words that we would consider profane now were simply descriptive then, whereas anything evoking the name of God was considered a blasphemous oath and would be dealt with sharply. The more extreme profanities were those that called the character of the person being abused into question, such as knave or harlot, as one's reputation was something to be defended fiercely.

Branding

Branding was a punishment reserved for certain crimes and the brand used would often depend on the crime committed. The Vagabonds Act of 1547, also known as the Vagrancy Act, laid out some of the branding punishments for certain crimes. Under this Act, gypsies or those designated as vagabonds (someone who was homeless and unemployed) would be branded with the shape of a large letter 'V' on their chest. This could also be given to those who were able-bodied but unable to find work for three days or more and was considered a mark of shame. If the vagabond or vagrant was found to have travelled far from their place of birth then, in addition to branding, they could also be publicly whipped and then sent back to where they came from. Children who were accused of vagrancy could be forced into service and for those in adulthood who were proven to be able-bodied, they would risk being sold into slavery for up to two years as part of their punishment.

Over time, distinctions were made between those who were not in work and those who were unable to work, a form of can't work–won't work idea, and institutions called Bridewells were established, which were an early form of poorhouse. The name Bridewell came from Henry VIII's palace in London known as Bridewell Palace that, upon the succession of his son Edward VI, was gifted to the City of London Corporation in 1553 for use as an orphanage and correctional facility for 'wayward women', with a notable claim to fame later on in the eighteenth century as the first of its kind to host an appointed doctor. The name Bridewell eventually became the generic term for such institutions in much the same way that its sister institution for the mentally ill, the Bethlehem Hospital, became synonymous with asylums, more commonly known in its shortened form of Bedlam.

As well as 'V' for vagabond or vagrant, an offender could be branded with other letters associated with their crimes. 'B' was for a blasphemer who was heard to take the name of the Lord in vain for example, or otherwise speak out in a minor way about the main religion of the time.[3] 'F' was reserved for fray makers, those who engaged in public brawling or fighting without the licence of a ring or scheduled fight, while perjurers could receive the letter 'P' on the forehead. Expressing discontent against authority could see you branded with 'SS' as a sower of sedition. An 'R' was reserved for rogues who, aside from being an intriguing or edgy Dungeons and Dragons class, were those who committed petty theft or fraud, but could also apply to those caught begging for food or money and was sometimes interchangeable with

'V' in that respect. Rogues and trespassers could receive further punishment from the hot iron by having a hole burned through their ears, or having the ears removed entirely. It seemed that, in the case of petty criminals at least, the sixteenth century really had a thing against ears.

Brands were also used for more severe crimes in addition to punishment as a form of further humiliation; for example, 'M' was for murderer and 'T' for thief. We will come back to the more severe punishments for such crimes later in this chapter. The main aim of branding or maiming was to further punish the offender beyond the immediate pain by marking them out as a criminal for the rest of their life. This would impact on their ability to work as well as their social lives and would therefore hopefully act as a deterrent to others considering such actions.

Loose Women

Women were subject to specific punishments for certain behaviours, with the definition of a 'loose' or 'immoral' woman being rather broad, and punishments geared towards the discouraging of certain behaviours that could end up being harmful to a latently patriarchal society. One such punishment was for women considered scolds, who nagged or were seen to scold their husbands or male relatives in public or were otherwise just thought to be excessively talkative.

One such punishment was the use of a ducking stool, that was also used in witchcraft trials, which will be expanded upon later in this chapter. The offending woman would be tied by her arms and legs, sometimes also across her chest, to a ducking stool (a chair or stool often attached to a pulley system or a long plank of wood) and submerged in a river or pond few times until her lesson was learned.

The Scold's Bridle was also implemented in such cases, as well as for women who were deemed to be gossips. This was a heavy iron cage that would fit around the woman's head, secured at the neck with a large, flat iron paddle that lay across the tongue, sometimes forcing the mouth to be held open, with the goal of forcibly stopping the woman from being able to speak. Other noises were still available to the woman in the bridle, however the wisdom of making them when there were other, harsher punishments available, would have to be questioned.

The Shrew's Fiddle was another punishment that had been available since the mediaeval period and later gained popularity throughout Germany and Austria. This consisted of a hinged wooden plank that resembled a violin, or fiddle, in shape with a hole for the head and two smaller holes for the wrists. The woman would have her head locked in place and then her arms likewise immobilised in front of her face.

Those accused of harlotry, or prostitution, were made to do 'penance in sheets', which constituted standing or being paraded through marketplaces or town halls, particularly outside or near churches, dressed only in a thin sheet, where they would be subject to the jeers and sometimes physical abuse of the public, receiving similar treatment to those in stocks or pillories. In addition, they could also be publicly whipped where the resultant wounds would likely cause more physical harm than the actual immediate pain of the punishment due to the oftentimes questionable medical practices available. It should be noted that women of higher social standing, sometimes known as courtesans, may have been spared some of the more common punishments but they were dependent on their benefactors and could easily fall into ruin and find themselves on a social par with their baser counterparts. When it went right for them, however, the social sky was the limit, though some of the lengths they went to to maintain their beauty and social status could be equally as punishing – for example, in the case of Diane de Poitiers as demonstrated in our 'Kill or Cure' chapter.

The crime of adultery varied in punishment depending on severity, with the more common punishments being public shaming, confiscation of goods or even in some cases banishment from the local area. For more high-profile members of society, however, the punishment could be more severe and in the case of royalty, adultery against the monarch was seen as high treason against the King's Majesty as it posed a risk to the line of succession. Two of the most infamous cases of royal adultery occurred in England in this era, with Anne Boleyn and Catherine Howard both being accused, tried, convicted and then beheaded for this crime against their joint husband, the infamous Henry VIII. The accusations against both women have been the subject of intense scholarly debate in recent years and is certainly worth a deep dive into as part of further reading, with the central figure of Henry VIII being equally as fascinating and divisive.

Execution

Breaking on the Wheel

Coming away from focusing just on England for a moment and widening our gaze to all of Europe, one might encounter a method of torture called 'the breaking wheel', also known as the Catherine Wheel. The goal of this method was to inflict as much pain and damage upon the victim as physically possible before death occurred, though that was not the end of the punishment.

In 1581, following being convicted of no fewer than 544 murders, German serial killer Peter Niers was sentenced to the wheel. He was, as the name would suggest, tied to a large wheel and, starting with his ankles and working their way up his body, his executioners delivered a total of 42 blows over two days, breaking and dislocating bones in such a way that it inflicted the most amount of pain without actively killing Niers. On the second day he was taken down from the wheel and quartered alive as the final part of his punishment, which by that point was probably more of a mercy.

Another example of the wheel being used as punishment was in Edinburgh, Scotland, in the case of Robert Weir, accused of murdering John Kincaid on behalf of the latter's wife Jean Livingston in 1600. Livingston (also known as Lady Waristoun or Warriston) was sentenced along with her nurse Janet Murdo to death by burning. Livingston's sentence was commuted to beheading but her nurse was not as lucky, neither was Robert Weir when he was finally apprehended in 1603/4. After sentencing, Weir was tied to a cartwheel and was struck repeatedly with the part of a plough known as a coulter, the part used for cutting into the soil. The bodies of those executed by wheel were often displayed on the instrument of torture for several days following their death, with heads sometimes removed and mounted on spikes. Those who did not expire from pain, shock or blood loss could be strangled or decapitated to bring about an end to their ordeal.

The origins of the wheel can be traced back in record to the days of Roman Emperor Commodus, in the second century CE. The alternative name of the Catherine Wheel comes from the fourth century CE and the execution of Christian martyr St Catherine of Alexandria who, upon refusing to renounce her faith, was affixed to the wheel for torture and execution. Legend has it that through divine intervention the wheel broke, though this did not save Catherine as presiding Emperor Maxentius ordered her to be beheaded. Oh, and yes, the circular whizzing firework that is responsible for many garden sheds going up in smoke is named after this torture device – though if that brings a new perspective to Bonfire Night, we recommend you look into the origins of that particular celebration too.

Heads Will Roll

Oh, come on now, you didn't honestly think we would talk about the sixteenth century without mentioning beheadings, did you? They go together like strawberries and cream, salt and pepper, Ant and Dec! We are sorry to say, however, that beheading was not actually as common as we would like to think and was often reserved for royalty or members of the nobility, being considered a cleaner form of execution than some of the others mentioned here.

Execution by beheading was often used as a punishment for acts of high treason, a crime outlined in English law under Edward III as part of the Treason Act of 1351. High treason is in relation to the 'unnatural' death of the monarch, being through assassination for example, and acts associated with this. That would include plotting and attempting as well as carrying out the act itself.[4] It also extended to members of the monarch's family and encompassed any perceived violation of the highest-ranking women in the royal family, being the queen and the wife of the heir. This included having an affair with the queen or heir's wife as that sort of action would call into question the legitimacy of the line of succession and therefore the stability of the royal family. It is for this aspect of high treason that the fates of Anne Boleyn, Catherine Howard and the men implicated with them were sealed.

Anne Boleyn

While two of Henry's wives met their end by beheading, one arguably overshadows the other due to the various events that led to her becoming Queen of England in the first instance. No shade on Catherine Howard, the demise of that poor girl is nothing short of tragic and she deserves for her story to be told; however, we do have a limited number of pages, and it is always a safe bet to go with the best known.

Anne Boleyn was the second daughter and youngest overall child born to Thomas Boleyn and Elizabeth Howard at Blickling Hall in the county of Norfolk (incidentally the county where this book is being written). Sent to the household of Margaret of Austria at approximately 12 years old, Anne received a good education and was reportedly well liked by her host. In 1514 Anne was sent by her father to be a maid of honour to Queen Mary of France, younger sister of Henry VIII[5] and her successor Queen Claude. By all accounts Anne thrived in the French court, and it was here she became interested in the concept of religious reform that was beginning to move through the continent.

Eventually in 1522 Anne was sent for by her family to return to England and make good on a marriage contract to her cousin James Butler. This contract fell through and instead Anne took up a position as lady-in-waiting to the English queen, Catherine of Aragon. It was while in this post that she caught the eye of Henry VIII. Anne initially resisted the amorous attentions of the king and declined to be his mistress, but when Henry eventually proposed to her, she agreed. The only problem was, he was still married to Catherine of Aragon. To cut a very long story short (one that we would strongly suggest you read up about as it has ramifications we feel to this day in the United Kingdom), Henry ended up breaking with the Catholic Church in Rome, establishing the Church of England over which the monarch was named Supreme Head, divorcing Catherine and marrying Anne.

The relationship was happy at first and the couple welcomed a daughter, the future Elizabeth I, in 1533, but it was promised that sons and heirs would soon follow as a daughter could not at that point inherit. However, a miscarriage late in 1534 started to cast doubts and cause issues within the marriage. Anne proved to be unpopular with the public who blamed her for the religious reforms underway and some refused to acknowledge her as queen instead of Catherine, who herself passed away in 1536. By this point Anne was pregnant again, but this was not to last.

Whether through the stress of her relationship with Henry starting to crack, his affair with her maid Jane Seymour becoming public knowledge or a jousting accident that almost killed the king, Anne miscarried a child believed to have been a boy. This was the last straw for Henry and whether independently or through manipulation and suggestion from advisors, he began to claim that he had been bewitched and seduced into marriage by Anne, a very serious claim for anyone, let alone a king to make at that time.

Other charges including adultery were added and Anne was arrested on 2 May 1536 and detained in the Tower of London, along with her brother George Boleyn who was charged with incest with his sister and treason against the king. Also detained on charges of adultery and therefore treason were the musician Mark Smeaton, Sir Henry Norris, Sir Francis Weston and Sir Willliam Brereton. Records indicate that Smeaton was tortured during his time at the Tower, while others were not due to their noble birth.

On 17 May 1536 Norris, Weston, Brereton, Smeaton and George Boleyn were all beheaded at Tower Hill on charges of high treason, using the traditional method of the axe. In an act of apparent mercy, Henry refused to let Anne die by axe as she was still a queen (although their marriage had at that point been declared void by Archbishop Thomas Cranmer, a one-time ally of Boleyn), so he requested that a professional swordsman be brought over from France to carry out the sentence.

Due to the swordsman coming from France, the execution was delayed twice, which must have been agonising for Anne, who at that point had all but resigned herself to her fate. However, on 19 May 1536 she was conducted from her rooms in the Tower to a scaffold outside the White Tower itself[6] where she was beheaded. Accounts indicate that she conducted herself with grace and dignity and when the time came, the execution was enacted in a single stroke. It may have been some small comfort to her spirit that despite her life ending for the failure to conceive a son, her daughter went on to lead her people through a golden age and is one of the most renowned monarchs in European history.

Margaret Pole

Life is a balance, so is death as it would seem. While the execution of Anne Boleyn was smooth and quick, others did not get the same mercy. Margaret Pole, Countess of Salisbury, was the daughter of George, Duke of Clarence and granddaughter to Richard Neville, Earl of Warwick, also known as the Kingmaker. When Henry VII assumed the throne after his triumph at the Battle of Bosworth in 1485, Margaret found herself in a precarious position as her brother Edward, Earl of Warwick, had a legitimate claim to the throne through the York bloodline and that made both siblings a threat. Edward was imprisoned in the Tower of London, where he would eventually be executed along with Perkin Warbeck, a young man who alleged himself to be one of the lost Princes in the Tower, Richard Duke of York. Margaret escaped imprisonment and was able to marry Sir Richard Pole in 1491, though she was later widowed in 1505 and left with their five children.

Margaret remained close to her cousin Elizabeth of York and after her death and the subsequent death of Henry VII, she remained in favour with her second cousin Henry VIII. She became governess to his eldest daughter Lady Mary and things seemed fine. However, when the issue around the marriage of the king to Catherine of Aragon arose, Margaret's son Reginald Pole, who was by then a respected member of the clergy, spoke out against the annulment of the king's marriage and made the very foolish historical mistake of putting it in writing.[7] He also then became involved with the Pilgrimage of Grace, a Catholic march on London calling for a return to Rome, which was treated harshly by the king.

Henry was incensed, but by this point Reginald had been made a cardinal and despite the break with Rome, he was considered untouchable by Henry – his family, however, was very much within reach. In 1539 Margaret Pole was imprisoned in the Tower of London, her titles and lands being stripped from her by a Bill of Attainder.[8] On 27 May 1541 she was scheduled to be executed.

Two versions of her execution exist, both of which are equally horrific though one has a dark humour to it that makes it memorable. In the first version, Margaret was led to her private execution which was conducted by an inexperienced executioner, as the Chief Executioner was not currently available. The first stroke of the axe missed her neck and instead cut her open at the shoulder. Repeat attempts were made, each as uncertain as the next and in the end, it took approximately eleven strokes of the axe to finally remove Margaret's head.

In the alternative ending, so to speak, Margaret managed to remove herself from the block and attempted to escape, being effectively chased round the block by the executioner who was swinging at her as he went. Both versions agree on the fact that it took eleven strokes to eventually fell poor Margaret Pole, a horrendous end for anybody, let alone a 67-year-old lady.

The Halifax Gibbet

The Halifax Gibbet, a cousin to and predecessor of the French guillotine, was a brutally effective execution method created by embedding an axe blade in a block of wood, suspended several feet in the air on a wooden frame. The condemned would be brought to kneel with their head and the top of their neck through the frame, after which the wooden block was released, letting gravity take it down and passing the (hopefully) highly sharpened blade through the neck, instantly severing the head.

According to the writings of William Harrison,[9] one could face the Halifax Gibbet for crimes such as theft if it was above a certain value.[10] He also suggested that people accused of stealing livestock such as cattle or horses should be executed somewhat ironically by the rope lifting the axe head being attached to the animal or one of the same species and then this being cut or untied to allow the axe to fall.

A device of this nature has allegedly been present on the green of Halifax, Yorkshire, since the late thirteenth century and it is from there that the execution method derived its name. A more permanent machine was created for use in the sixteenth century but was later taken down in 1650. A replica was created in 1974 and exists to this day on the now aptly named Gibbet Street, though as far as we are aware it has not provided anything more fatal than a splinter, unlike its predecessors.

Boiling Point

Moving on from the more traditional methods of execution, we come to one that is most definitely not for the faint of heart to read about, being boiled alive. While you may read in our chapter on 'Food Fatalities' of an incident where this happened in error, as an execution method it was most certainly deliberate and most certainly horrid.

In 1531 Henry VIII passed into English law that the crime of murder by poisoning should be classed as a form of petty treason (that is treason committed against someone in charge of you, such as your husband or master if you were a servant). The penalty for treason was death and in the case of poisoning it was decided that this would be in the form of being boiled to death.

The first to feel the wrath of this punishment was Richard Roose, accused of attempting to assassinate the Bishop of Rochester, John Fisher, by adding poisoned yeast to his porridge but failing and instead killing a member of the bishop's household and a beggar who had eaten the food instead while making several others seriously ill. Following Roose's arrest he was tortured on the rack to extract a confession.

After his sentencing, on 15 April 1532, Roose was taken to his place of execution at Smithfield in London where he was chained up and placed in a structure called a gibbet, in which he was lowered into and then out of a large vat of boiling water three times, taking approximately two hours to finally die. Contemporary descriptions tell of how he screamed loudly throughout, which is hardly surprising. For more details on Richard Roose and whether this punishment was justified, see our chapter entitled 'Food Fatalities'.

The practice of boiling alive was not exclusive to England and records show it being used in France and Germany for the financial crime of clipping coins, as well as further afield. In 1594 legendary Japanese outlaw Ishikawa Goemon (something of a Japanese Robin Hood as he stole from the rich and gave to the poor) was executed alongside his son for the attempted assassination of Toyotomi Hideyoshi.

There are several conflicting accounts about the life of Ishikawa Goemon, but contemporary sources are scarce, and as such there is much speculation around who he was, the earlier parts of his life and why he tried to assassinate

Hideyoshi in the first place. Whatever the reason, the attempt was unsuccessful and Goemon was captured and sentenced to death by being boiled alive in either water or oil.

As with Margaret Pole, there are two accounts of Goemon's death, the first being that he and his young son were sentenced to be boiled alive and when they were placed in the iron cauldron, Goemon held his son above his head and out of the boiling liquid and his son was then pardoned and allowed to live while Goemon died.

In the alternative version all Goemon's family were sentenced to be boiled and at first Goemon tried to save his son by holding him aloft but then eventually plunged him into the liquid and held him down to kill him quickly, holding the body up as an act of defiance until he himself succumbed to his fate. As a disturbing but not unexpected quirk, the type of large, round Japanese iron bathtub has become known as a *goemonburo* in honour of this execution, though we would recommend only having the water hot and not boiling.

High Stakes

Almost as popular an image in the collective consciousness as beheading, we have the execution method of burning at the stake. All forms of execution held some level of symbolism, but this may arguably be the most symbolic of all, as the act of being burned alive was meant to represent the fires of hell to which the condemned person's soul would surely be about to go. That is why this became a go-to punishment for heretics, people who went against the state religion of the time whether by subscribing to a different belief system or engaging in apostasy[11] and acts of witchcraft. Murderers were also often burned at the stake, as the crime of taking the life of another was a sure-fire fast pass straight to hell – pardon the pun.

One of the most notorious cases of burning at the stake in England was that of the Oxford Martyrs in 1555. We cover the reasons behind the executions a bit more in our chapter 'Ruthless Religion'; however, during the sixteenth century the national religion of England was on something of a pendulum, with successive monarchs swinging it to and fro with varying degrees of extremity between Catholicism and Protestantism, all as a result of Henry VIII breaking with Rome.

Those who refused to acknowledge the rightful religious observance at the time risked severe punishment, including torture and even execution if they refused to recant their beliefs. In 1555 England was under the rule of Mary I, daughter of Henry VIII and Catherine of Aragon. Mary had remained true to her mother's devout beliefs and stayed Catholic, seeing it as her duty to bring England back into the arms of the Church in Rome. Examples had to be made of those who refused to recant the beliefs that were considered heretical.

This was the case for Bishop Hugh Latimer as well as Archbishops Nicholas Ridley and Thomas Cranmer, all of whom were members of the Protestant Church of England. The three men were arrested and imprisoned in 1554 in Bocardo Prison, Oxford, where they stayed for nearly eighteen months before being put on trial. All three were found guilty of heresy and sentenced to be burned at the stake until dead.

Latimer and Ridley went first, being tied to stakes on 16 October 1555 and set alight while Cranmer was made to watch from the tower of the prison. Cranmer was able to try and appeal his sentence and in 1556 he recanted his beliefs and affirmed himself back into the Catholic Church; however, this did not save him from the wrath of Mary I, who was set on making an example of Cranmer for his part in the Reformation, her mother's downfall and how they were both treated at the time.

On 21 March 1556 Cranmer was burned at the stake in the same place as Latimer and Ridley. Legend has it that as the flames rose around him, Cranmer extended his right hand, the hand with which he signed the recantation of his faith, so that this would burn first. Interestingly, the marks of his death can be seen in the form of scorch marks on a pair of doors now hanging at Balliol College, Oxford.

It's a common misconception that burning at the stake was the way to get rid of witches, but this was more the punishment for the heretical side of their actions and, in fact, the majority of those found guilty of witchcraft were hanged.

Hanging Around

Next to beheading, hanging is probably one of the most widely known and commonly used form of execution, with places such as Tyburn becoming notorious for it and the punishment having been a cause of public spectacle since at least the Anglo-Saxon period.[12] Considering the traditional naming conventions of a lot of streets or parks over time, places like Gallows Green or Gallows Road just outside Bishop's Stortford in Cambridgeshire will give an indication where this kind of execution once took place.

Hanging is the act of taking someone and putting a rope about their neck and either lifting them from the ground or dropping them from a height. The rope will then either strangle them or, in the case of dropping from a height, potentially snap their neck. Some people were weighted down when hanged and it was not an unusual sight for someone to pull down on the legs of the accused so that they would expire faster. In many cases, once hanged a victim would be left there for several days as a visual deterrent.

It was a punishment that also came with an interesting deal of folklore to it. One of the common places where gallows were erected was at a crossroads. It makes sense from one point of view: when the bodies were left up for display afterwards, you wanted somewhere that had a lot of foot traffic exposure. Another, less corporeal reason was that crossroads were places of decision but also confusion and it was believed that the night after the execution had taken place, the spirit of the person would go to leave the body but would find itself trapped at the crossroad, unsure of which way to go to seek salvation or revenge. Being unable to choose, the spirit would be forced to remain in the body of the condemned until dawn, meaning that it was less likely that one of the demons presumed to be prowling the night would find the now-empty body and possess it to cause torment to the living.

Gallows were often temporary constructions that could then be taken down once the job was done, and in some rural places a tree sufficed. Tyburn had a more permanent installation that became known as the Triple Tree, three beams joined in a triangle shape and held up by wooden posts to provide the drop height. This structure was used to hang multiple people at once, twenty-four in one case. This was constructed in 1571 and remained in place until the mid-eighteenth century.

If a particular example was to be made of the hanged person, a gibbet could then be employed where the body was taken down from the scaffold and the clothing was removed so the body could be dipped in hot tar as a preservative.[13] The bodies were then redressed (for the sake of modesty) and placed in an iron cage called a gibbet. This was then riveted shut and displayed either from the gallows or from a position just outside town to dissuade potential visitors from certain misbehaviour. The body would often be left in the gibbet for months, or until it rotted away to a skeleton, at which point it would be taken down and either given an unmarked burial or put into a pit with other hanged persons, in theory forever preventing their soul from being able to reach heaven without the dignity of a proper burial.

Public execution by hanging continued in England until December 1867, though capital punishment itself was not officially abolished until 1969 but there were still some crimes, including treason, for which it could be administered. This was not amended until as recently as 1998 when the death penalty was abolished for all crimes.

Falling to Pieces

Finally, one of the most brutal methods of execution (which seeing the above, we know, is saying something) was that of being hanged, drawn and quartered. Practised as a form of execution since the fourteenth century, this punishment was reserved for acts of high treason, with the notion that the most severe crime should elicit the most severe punishment. If done correctly, the hanged, drawn and quartered method could see the accused still alive until the very last moment, drawing the maximum amount of pain and suffering from them and entertainment for the crowd.[14]

A few famous faces have met their equally famous end by this method, including William Wallace and Guy Fawkes. The sequence of the words is a bit misleading, as often the drawing was the first step. The accused would be taken, dragged either by hand using a rope or tied to the back of a horse and dragged; this is the act of being drawn and would end at the place of execution. Following this, the accused would then be hanged by the neck until nearly dead, which is where the expertise and sadism of the executioner came in, as they would ideally want the victim conscious, not just alive. If the accused died then so be it, the quartering would be quicker, but it would be much less entertaining.

In some instances, notably that of William Wallace, the accused would then be cut open and disembowelled (Wallace had his organs burned in front of him on a brazier) then finally, when death had occurred, the accused would be cut into pieces (that's the quartered part) and their head often displayed as a further deterrent with the disarticulated limbs being sent elsewhere to be shown off in relevant places on a kind of tour to let would-be rebels know what fate awaited them if they tried anything.

Thomas Wyatt was one rebel who in 1554 was executed for the crime of treason by being hanged, drawn and quartered. Wyatt's Rebellion was an expression of dissatisfaction with the proposed marriage of Queen Mary I of England to King Phillip II of Spain. Wyatt had spent some of his formative years with his father in Spain and had witnessed first-hand the actions of the Spanish Inquisition, giving him an immensely unfavourable view of the Spanish. In his mind, the proximity of a Spanish king to the throne of England could cause the Inquisition and its behaviours to spread to England as part of Mary I's drive to return the country to its prior state as a Catholic nation.

Wyatt organised a march on London to make his demands, supported by a makeshift army of approximately 4,000 men loyal to his cause, including some who had deserted from forces sent to oppose them. Upon reaching London and starting negotiations, Wyatt requested control of the Tower of London, as well as the handing over of the queen to his charge, both of which caused some unrest among his followers. Gradually, whether through desertion or direct conflict, Wyatt's supporters reduced, and this led to his capture and imprisonment in the very Tower of London that he sought control of.

On 15 March he was put on trial and subsequently sentenced for high treason and on 11 April 1554, he was beheaded and then quartered. His head was tied up to hang from gallows and his severed limbs were circulated and displayed around local towns as a warning. As it happens, his head only hung for six days before being stolen, ironically by people celebrating the acquittal of someone else accused of treason. We can safely say we've never yet been drunk or deliriously happy enough where stealing a head seemed like a good idea, but maybe we've just never had the opportunity.

In a rare case of dodging the executioner, we have the story of Humphrey Lisle who, along with his father Sir William Lisle and his younger brother Richard, was accused of misbehaviour along the border between England and Scotland. Border raids were a regular problem at the time, following a longstanding resentment exacerbated by the actions of Edward I, the so-called Hammer of the Scots. The raids were something that both sides engaged in and perpetuated the animosity through acts of theft, assault, looting, rape and sometimes going as far as to descend into skirmishes resulting in murder. The Lisle men had already been arrested previously for such behaviour and had been helped to escape, going on to terrorise the border towns, seeking vengeance. In January 1528, however, they apparently all gave themselves up peacefully to the Earl of Northumberland who was tasked, as warden of the East and Middle March, to monitor the northern border and stop such raids occurring on either side.

The trial took three months to conclude but when it did, Sir William Lisle and most of his followers were sentenced to be hanged, drawn and quartered for treason, with their heads and limbs being visibly mounted throughout Northumberland. Young Humphrey, who at this point was around 12, and his younger brother were spared execution and instead were sent to London where they not only received a pardon, but Humphrey was given over to the service of the Earl of Northumberland to help him keep an eye on the borders and stop the reivers. However, the adage teaches us that a leopard cannot change its spots and Humphrey Lisle once again pops up in historical record in 1535 as someone engaging in criminal acts along the border having fled the Earl of Northumberland, who was then looking for him to put a stop to his antics.

Person Pruners

While Henry VIII could undoubtedly be ruthless to those who conspired or acted against him, or even married him, with an impressive headcount (again, pardon the pun) of between 50,000 and 70,000 during his reign, he is not the only bloodthirsty monarch of the period. The Ottoman Empire was arguably at its peak during the sixteenth century following the successful martial reign of Sultan Mehmed II in the fifteenth century, leading to the capture of Constantinople and the defeat of one of the Empire's most troublesome enemies, the Transylvanian *voivode* Vlad III Tepes (yes, *that* one). Ruled from 1512–1520 by Sultan Selim I, the empire continued to expand. The concept of capital punishment was one that the people of the empire were very familiar with, although, unlike other countries, they did not have specially employed executioners for the task of dispatching the unfortunate accused. Instead, they had the *bostanci basha*, known as the head gardener. These were a crew of gardeners but they also added bodyguard, inspector and executioner to their CV. At the First Court of the Topkapi palace there was located a structure called the Executioner's Fountain, so called due to it being where the *bostanci basha* were said to wash their hands after they had just carried out an execution.

Unlike the rest of Europe, beheadings were a common execution method while strangulation was reserved only for members of the royal family. It was that fate which, on 15 January 1595 following his accession to the throne, Sultan Mehmed III ordered servants to carry out against members of his family that might have a rival claim. As royal blood was not allowed to be spilled, even in times of execution, bowstrings were used to assassinate his nineteen brothers and remove his potential threats. It might have prevented civil wars over the throne but must have made being at the top a very lonely place to be. The concept of family being one of the most important things in life clearly didn't quite spread to the Ottoman Empire, and in fact this kind of act was made legal by Mehmed III's predecessor, Mehmed II.

Honourable Mention

Here we have an execution that doesn't fully fit into the categories above but straddles several of them and is worth a mention just for the disturbing brutality of it. Now, having made it this far into the book, we would assume that you wouldn't necessarily need one of these, but here is your trigger warning for mention of extreme violence and forced cannibalism (yes, it's that bad).

Gyorgy Dozsa hailed from a noble family in Transylvania in the kingdom of Hungary and pursued a successful military career. He participated in the Turkish Wars and for his prowess and distinction in that conflict, was appointed to lead a new crusade against the Muslim Turk. His army consisted of thousands of peasants, but they were not given adequate supplies or armour and a rumbling of discontent soon spread through the army. Dozsa actually listened to the grievances of his men and instead of taking them forward on the crusade that they were assembled for, he instead turned them towards revolution, not just against the landlords who had failed to supply them, but against the monarchy as well, under King Vladislaus II at that point. As he is included in a section about executions, you can probably guess that this didn't entirely go to plan.

The peasant army managed to successfully advance for a while, taking and subsequently destroying a few fortresses belonging to landlords that they held grudges against, and slowly building on their limited supply of weapons. But they were not a trained military force and eventually this fact would catch up with them. In July of 1514 the rebels were beaten at the siege of Temesvar (modern-day Timisoara, Romania) and Dozsa was taken prisoner along with nine other rebels including his brother Gergely.

Dozsa was mocked for his ambition to take the throne, called King of the Peasants and his execution was disturbingly symbolic. A throne of iron was created and heated, with Dozsa forced to sit on it and restrained as a heated crown of iron was placed on his head and he was made to hold a rod of hot iron as a mock sceptre. Dozsa tried to plead for his brother's life, but to no avail as Gergely was cut into three pieces in front of him, yet this was not the worst part of the punishment. Readers with a weaker stomach, probably should take a break for this bit.

Pliers were heated in a brazier and when they were hot enough, they were used to pinch parts of Dozsa's flesh, instantly searing it. The remaining rebels were then forced to bite into and tear away the 'cooked' parts of Dozsa and made to swallow. Those who refused received the same treatment as Gergely, while those who obeyed were promised freedom – a promise that was surprisingly kept. The trauma and pain of the torture became too much, and Doza died. It is estimated that around 70,000 rebels were tortured following the uprising with far-reaching consequences that would make the surviving peasants' lives miserable for many years after.

Legal Animals

Having looked at some of the darker and more disturbing facets of crime and punishment in the sixteenth century, it would be easy to turn to something a little more light-hearted, though that may not necessarily be the right term as the suspects on trial in some of the following examples most certainly did not get off lightly, even if the crimes and the suspects themselves should raise an eyebrow or two.

While evidence of such practices is scant there are a few fairly reliable sources detailing animal trials and sentences during the mediaeval period. One such document is a treatise entitled *The Criminal Prosecution and Capital Punishment of Animals* composed by Edward Payson Evans and published in 1906, notably a good length of time after the trials are meant to have taken place.

Evans details two types of trials, being '*Thierstrafen*' which were tribunals often resulting in capital punishment for the animals, and '*Thierprocesse*' which were trials in ecclesiastical courts which could result in such actions as exorcism and excommunication. The cases tended to be larger animals in the former type of trial while smaller animals such as insects were left to the ecclesiastical courts.

An example of a *Thierstrafen* trial occurred in Paris in 1494 when a young boy was mutilated by a pig, causing severe damage to the face and neck. The pig was put on trial for its actions, prosecuted by Jehan Levoisier, a licensed lawyer who was also a grand mayor of the church at Saint-Martin de Laon, making him a well-respected gentleman in the local area. Monsieur Levoisier was clearly an effective prosecutor as the pig was found guilty and sentenced by the judge to hanging.

While we would view such trials as potentially ridiculous today, these were mostly treated seriously at the time, though the absurdity didn't quite escape everyone.

In an alleged example of *Thierprocesse*, a colony of rats were brought to trial at an ecclesiastical court in Autun, France, in 1522. The rats were charged with theft as their target was the barley fields of the region, causing serious damage to the harvest and therefore a risk of famine. It was felt that there was more at work than mere hungry rats and so this was brought before the religious courts.

The requested sentence was excommunication and anathematising (rendering unacceptable). However, the rats were defended by Barthelemy de Chasseneuz, just starting out in what would become a very lucrative legal career. De Chasseneuz was effective in defending the rats and his arguments effectively reduced the trial to a level of absurdity. Initially the rats did not attend court and conviction was set to continue *in absentia* until de Chasseneuz argued that insufficient time had been given to gather the rats and that to start the trial already would be unfair. As a compromise the trial was postponed and then systematically announced during mass at all churches in the bishopric.

At the second attempt, when the rats were again absent, de Chasseneuz argued that the rats were unable to attend due to the dangerous nature of the journey and requested that they be given safe passage through the province, particularly in respect of the local cat population. At this point the trial was ended, though in his retelling, Evans records uncertainty over whether this was due to the trial being terminated or the rats being acquitted.

In his series of legal documents, *Consilium Primum*, published from 1531, de Chasseneuz discussed various animal trials and associated precedents, while notably not mentioning the trial of the rats of Autun. While there are scholarly arguments against this trial ever having occurred, despite de Chasseneuz being a real person, it nonetheless makes for an interesting and somewhat unbelievably believable tale.

In some cases, the animals were put on trial and punished for the actions of humans, though the humans themselves did not get away with it either. We're talking, in no uncertain terms, of the crime of bestiality. One such instance was when in 1565 in Montpellier, France, a man and a donkey were both executed by burning alive for that crime, with the poor donkey facing an additional indignation of having its feet cut off as it was seen to be objecting to its circumstances. Sadly, this situation is one that was repeated across the centuries, with the poor animal receiving equal punishment for the crime.

Chapter 4

Extracting a Confession

As we graduate from general misdemeanours and minor crimes to more major ones, there is a growing need for proof of the crime through confession as well as evidence. This occurs in crimes such as treason, witchcraft or heresy where various methods could be called upon to extract a confession that not only proved the guilt of the accused, but also could implicate accomplices. Torture techniques, or advanced methods of persuasion, were used that were as varied as they were grotesque, proving that human innovation really does know no limits.

First things first, let us dispel a potential myth. As macabrely impressive as it may seem, the Iron Maiden is disputed as a medieval and early modern torture device. Instead, it is most attributed to the mind of Johann Siebenkees, a German philosopher who penned a description of the device in 1793. This does not mean, however, that similar devices did not exist, with descriptions seeming to indicate this, though some of the actual torture methods we know for a fact existed were oftentimes far worse.

Under Pressure

For those souls unwilling, or even sometimes unable to enter a plea of guilty or not guilty in court, a method called pressing could be employed to encourage them to find the right words. Pressing, also known as '*peine forte et dure*' (hard and forceful punishment) was an ordeal by which the accused would be lain down with a large piece of wood such as board or even a door placed over them, Heavy stones or metal weights would then be added one by one to the board, pressing down on the accused until either they relented and pled, or died from the crushing weight. Pressing could also be used as an execution method, where a stone would be placed beneath the accused, pushing into their spine so that as the pressure was applied, their back would break. Whether as a method or torture or execution, it was slow and excruciatingly painful to endure.

A prominent example of death by pressing was the case of Margaret Clitherow of York, who was arrested in March 1586 following a tip-off to authorities that she was harbouring a Catholic priest in her home on the Shambles in the city of York which led to the property being raided. This is an action that was made a capital crime by an Act of Parliament in 1581 that designated it as an act of treason, with a following law called 'An Act against Jesuits, seminary priests and other such like disobedient persons' passed in 1585. This second law made it an act of treason for a Catholic priest who refused to swear the oath required in the Act of Supremacy 1558 to remain in England on threat of imprisonment or even death.[1]

Many still tried to harbour priests to preserve their religion and many surviving properties in England from this period still have examples of 'priest holes' where the ministers were forced to hide in the event of raids. Margaret Clitherow was arrested for treason, accused of harbouring a Catholic priest and brought to trial at the Guildhall, where she refused to be tried, maintaining that she had committed no crime and therefore should not need a trial.

Despite being made aware of the consequences, Margaret continued to decline to be put on trial and on 25 March 1586 at the Ouse Bridge in York, Margaret Clitherow was laid out to be pressed. The ordeal took approximately fifteen minutes and in the end her body endured around 900 lb (approximately 408 kg) before finally giving out. Margaret's story has resonated with the Catholic faith through the centuries; for her steadfast adherence to her religion, Margaret was canonised as a saint and a martyr by Pope Paul VI in October 1970, and 26 March, the day after her execution, is a feast day in honour of her sacrifice.

Bit of a Stretch

Possibly one of the most iconic instruments of torture was the rack, used in several places including the infamous Tower of London. The rack took various forms, with the most instantly recognisable being a board of wood on which the victim would be laid with their hands and feet secured by ropes or cuffs to turning devices at either end. The principle behind it was that the cranks would be turned and the bonds would tighten, gradually stretching the person. In the first instance this would cause a great deal of pain and pressure on the joints. This would eventually escalate to dislocation of limbs and the joining bones being pulled from their sockets.

An example of the rack being used in England was in the case of Anne Askew, later named as a Protestant martyr for the accusations against her relating to her speaking the scriptures as a woman and denying the idea of transubstantiation.[2] Askew was arrested three times between 1545 and 1546, escaping the first time and being released the second.

It was on her third arrest in May 1546 that she was detained in the Tower of London and became one of only two recorded women to have been tortured there during her imprisonment. She was put on the rack and interrogated by Sir Richard Rich and Lord Chancellor Thomas Wriothesley, repeatedly pressured to renounce her heretical Protestant beliefs. They also tried to get her to implicate the queen, Catherine Parr, as the two were known to each other. However, despite twelve successive days of torture on the rack, Anne did not recant and did not implicate Queen Catherine. In the end, her execution was set for 16 July 1546, to be burned at the stake. Her torture on the rack, however, had been so extensive that she was unable to stand and had to be carried to her execution in a chair. At that point even a death as horrific as burning may have been a relief from the pain she was already in. She was the very definition of one tough cookie.

Sometimes variations of the traditional rack were used where spikes were affixed either to a roller device or to the rack itself, designed to penetrate the victim's back while they were simultaneously stretched. An alternative form of the rack was suspension, where a person was attached by the wrists to a pulley system that would then raise them in increments from the floor. In some instances, the feet were attached to the floor or weights were added to further add to the pressure to the joints. The body would then be exposed to further injury while the person was suspended.

This was further adapted into a form of torture prevalent in mainland Europe called strappado or corda, whereby the victim had their hands tied behind their backs and then affixed to another piece of rope which would see the victim lifted into the air. The weight of the victim's body would cause strain on the shoulder and arm muscles, leading to dislocation, tearing of the muscles and possible permanent paralysis of the arms due to an injury known as a brachial plexus.[3] In some cases, it would cause further internal damage, including strain on the chest cavity causing heart-related fatalities.

The impact of strappado could be further increased by a technique known as squassation, the technique reported to have been used on Italian writer and philosopher Niccolo Machiavelli who was arrested in 1513 for an alleged part in a plot to murder members of the Medici family, the ruling family of Florence at the time. Whist it was later proven that Machiavelli played no part in the plot, he was still subjected to torture by squassation whereby he was suspended using the strappado method and then dropped from a height until the rope pulled taut, yanking on his arms. This drop happened a total of six times and though there was no doubt lasting damage, it did not stop Machiavelli who was able to continue writing for the remainder of his life.

Smelling a Rat

Strappado was a torture technique utilised by the Spanish Inquisition, a group that we cover in our 'Ruthless Religion' chapter. However, it was not just the Spanish and English who had a penchant for religious persecution. It may not be a stretch to say that the Protestant Reformation, essentially a religious revolution, forever changed the religious and cultural landscape of Europe and had far-reaching consequences that echoed throughout the following centuries. Religious extremism started to take hold and persecution against perceived heresy was accepted and in cases like those seen above, it was actively encouraged. People began to get creative with their persecution methods however, and a great case in point is that of Diederik Sonoy and his potentially first recorded use of rat torture.

Fans of George R. R. Martin's *A Song of Ice and Fire* or the companion television series *Game of Thrones* may find that they are familiar with this particular torture and execution method. The recorded use of rats in torture can be traced back to the days of the Roman Empire, however their usage during the Dutch Revolt of 1566 to 1648[4] was particularly cruel to both the victim and the rats themselves. In a brief nutshell, the Dutch Revolt was a rebellion by natives of the Netherlands against the Spanish Empire, ruled over by the Habsburg dynasty under Phillip II of Spain. In the end the Dutch Republic was recognised as independent, though the Spanish did maintain a hold on the Southern Netherlands until the early eighteenth century. To read more on a turning point in the Eighty Years' War, there's an incredible story in 'Ridiculous Survival'.

Diederik Sonoy (born c. 1529) was one of the rebel leaders in the Dutch Revolt and it was during this time that he developed a reputation for extreme actions against Catholics. To extract information from prisoners, Sonoy would have them laid down on their backs and restrained. A domed cage was then placed on top of the prisoner's abdomen with rats inside. Finally, a tray was laid on top of the cage and red-hot coals was placed on the tray. The heat from the tray would distress the rats and, in an attempt to get away from the source of it, they would burrow through the softest part of their entrapment they could find, being the prisoner's flesh. The excruciating pain of this would last as long as the prisoner's will and sometimes just the thought of enduring this form of torture was enough to make a someone talk.

There is no documentation that we could find which indicated the fate of the rats used in the torture after they had done their work, but if Sonoy and his men were fine with doing this to fellow humans, we somehow don't think effective rodent aftercare would have been a priority to them.[5]

Contortion and Restriction

As demonstrated with the use of the pillory, effective forms of torture employed more than basic maiming and outward injury; pain caused through extreme discomfort was just as effective and the damage could last equally as long. Forcing the human body to bend or fit into a particular shape was one way this was achieved, for example with the 'Scavenger's Daughter'. Also known as the 'Spanish A-frame' this was an iron contraption in which the ankles and wrists of a prisoner were shackled and then linked together by a single iron bar, at the end of which was a collar. When locked, this forced the prisoner bent double but with their backs arched so the neck could lean forward, placing constant pressure on the spine and shoulders, leading to permanent spinal damage. A variation of this included an iron bar that went over the back of the prisoner, affixed to the bar holding their legs and a screw-type contraption on top that could be tightened, compressing on the person's back. One recorded use of this device was on Thomas Cottam, a Catholic priest from Lancashire, who was tried for treason and imprisoned in the Tower of London in 1581 where he was tortured and then later hanged for treason in 1582.

Spikey Endings

While mainly attributed to a certain person within a certain period just outside of the confines of this book, impaling had a wider usage for torture than the execution method nearly perfected by Vlad III Tepes. The Holy Roman Empire employed this execution technique for various reasons including adultery, infanticide and murder with stakes being driven into the accused as they were otherwise buried alive. Partial impalement, however, could also be used as an effective torture method. This was the case in the use of the Judas Cradle.

A simplistic device to look at, the Judas Cradle consists of a pointed pyramid block of wood (sometimes topped off with a capstone of iron) atop four long legs. The idea behind this implement is that the prisoner would be suspended above the pointed pyramid and then either slowly lowered or dropped onto it so that it would effectively penetrate the rectum or vaginal area. The accused could then either be moved around, lifted and dropped again, or could be weighted down to cause the spike to push further into the body. The tip of the cradle could also be oiled to allow for the victim to slip further down onto it and cause greater internal damage. This would be repeated for hours, sometimes even days and if the shock and pain did not kill you, then the infection from the repeated use of the device most likely would.

Magical Misdemeanours

It would be difficult to discuss the sixteenth century and the advent of the seventeenth century without referencing the fervour of the witch trials that swept across Europe, eventually travelling across the ocean and culminating in arguably one of the most infamous cases, the Salem witch trials. While the ordeals faced by the men and women accused in Salem, Massachusetts, between February 1692 and May 1693 are certainly some of the most well known, they regrettably fall outside the period covered in this book. A lot of the methods used in the 'investigations' and the executions were well established by this point, however, and while not as subjected to popular culture as their American counterparts, the European witch trials are no less disturbing.

While the execution of the accused by hanging and burning (the former being the more popular despite what Hollywood would have us believe) is terrible enough, the worst and often most degrading part of the trials was arguably how the confessions were extracted. The search in the trials was not just for the individual witch themselves, but for the implication by the accused of others who practised witchcraft in their area as part of a coven. This could lead to outbreaks of mass hysteria in what could often feel like a witchcraft plague.

Various ways to identify a witch, as well as proposals for how to deal with them, were put forth in the now infamous book *Malleus Malificarum*, translated as the Hammer of Witches, written by Heinrich Kramer (a Dominican prior from Alsace) and first published in 1486. While not initially well received, it took a while for the book to take off, which it did thanks to Johannes Guttenberg's invention of the printing press. The often-venomous anti-female rhetoric within those pages would make us inclined to ask Kramer were he in front of us now – who hurt you?

This book would be one of the foundation texts for witch hunters across the next two and a half centuries along with King James VI/I's *Demonologie*. Below are some of the methods used to identify or force an accused witch to confess, and you will probably see why a number did confess, mostly just to make it stop.

Just a Prick

It was a common belief that witches had made a pact with the devil or a lesser demon for their powers and that sometimes that demon or another would take the form of an animal or spectral entity to accompany and serve the witch, known as a familiar. To sustain this familiar, it was believed that a witch would suckle them from their own body, not from the chest in the way that a mother would, but from an often hidden 'witch's mark', thereby making it seem even more unnatural. This led to people who were accused being subjected to an examination with anything like a birthmark or particularly large mole being an object of suspicion – but how to test if this was indeed a witch's mark? One method was called pricking, where the person testing the accused would take a pin or other suitable sharp object and prick the area suspected of being a witch's mark. If the mark bled, it was just a mole or birthmark, if it did not bleed then that was conclusive proof that this was a witch's mark.

This led to industrious souls who were either overly zealous or were planning to make what could prove to be quite a lucrative living from the profession of witch hunting, using retractable needles (we're looking at you, John Kincaid)[6] that would, of course, retract on contact with the suspected mark and therefore the witch would be guaranteed not to bleed. This would then leave the poor 'witch' open to further investigative methods.

Ducking Stool

One of the tamer ways of finding out if an accused person was guilty of being a witch (tame insofar as it didn't intend to draw blood) was the use of the ducking stool. This was a method by which the accused person was affixed to a stool or chair at the end of a pulley or wooden plank (or just the plank itself in a budget version) and then 'ducked' into a local pond, lake or river. The act of ducking would then cause the accused to be completely submerged under the water.

Sometimes the ducking would be a repeated measure until the accused confessed, other times they would be submerged and held there for a length of time, usually around five to six minutes and then resurfaced. The belief was that if the accused was indeed a witch, then by the devil or their own power, they would survive the time underwater. If they were innocent then they would drown, but their souls would be welcome to heaven. For those who somehow survived their time underwater, execution was assured so it was pretty much a case of you're dead either way.

The witch trials of the sixteenth century were the beginning of a metaphorical landslide into mass hysteria fed by the perfect storm of famine, religious turmoil, disease, war and inclement weather. Books such as the *Malleus Maleficarum* and *Demonologie* fuelled the fire that led to some of the darkest episodes in human history, echoes of which are still felt today. While some of the worst episodes in the trials are outside the period on which this book focuses, they are no less a part of the wider narrative relating to the treatment of those society considers outcasts or other.

James VI/I had an almost obsessive level of interest in witches, the start of which is often attributed to an incident that occurred following his marriage to Anne of Denmark when storms made their journey back from Copenhagen to Scotland almost fatally dangerous.

A witch hunt was launched in Copenhagen, where fears of occult practices were already rife, and confessions were extracted that dark arts had been used to call up the storms that affected the king and his new queen. This had a profound impact on James, who had already seen the actions behind and impacts of some of the Danish witch hunts first hand. and he soon began to hunt witches in his own kingdom, even going so far as to question some of the accused himself.

Agnes Sampson

The first victim of his ire was Agnes Sampson, the woman whose arrest started the North Berwick witch trials. Sampson was accused of using an image of King James, allegedly given to her by the devil himself, to bring harm and attempt to bring death to the king.

Sampson was taken to the Palace of Holyroodhouse in Edinburgh where King James questioned her and where she refused to confess to the allegations put to her, causing him to in turn question whether she really was guilty. When it was clear that the questioning was getting nowhere fast, she was then arrested and tortured, starting with her head and body being shaved and thoroughly searched for the witch's mark. Sampson held up for over an hour under the examination and humiliation until an alleged mark was found near her genital region. Whether from the torture or to spare her the distress and indignation of having her intimate areas searched, Sampson confessed and was even made to implicate others.

On 28 January 1591, Agnes Sampson was taken to Castlehill, Edinburgh, where she was strangled by a garotte and then her body burned at the stake. It is said that her naked ghost now haunts the Palace of Holyroodhouse, the place where she faced up to a king and made him doubt her guilt, at first.

In 2020 a campaign was launched by a group called Witches of Scotland with the aim of asking the Scottish Parliament to issue a posthumous pardon to those killed in the Berwick Witch Trials. In 2022, the then First Minister of Scotland Nicola Sturgeon issued a formal apology to those accused as part of Scottish witch trials and asked that consideration be given in the Scottish Parliament to the call for pardons. As yet, the pardons have not been issued but this is certainly a positive step, and more developments may come with time.

Margaret Read

It would be remiss of us, writing this from Norfolk as we are, to not mention a legendary witch execution that happened right on our doorstep in King's Lynn. Margaret Read was a woman who lived in a cottage down one of the many alleyways in the town that lead to the River Ouse, having moved there from the nearby town of Grimston. Rumours began to circulate about Margaret, sometimes known as 'Shady Meg', and various misfortunes that she was alleged to have caused to her neighbours. It was also rumoured that people would visit her to assist with healing or sometimes darker practices that she did for them. An example used against her was that of Marion Harvey, who was pregnant out of wedlock (scandalous, we know) and the father had spurned her. She visited Margaret Read and shortly after, the father died following complaints of severe chest and abdominal pains. It is highly likely that Margaret may have been a 'cunning woman', the term for a woman who has knowledge of medicine and herblore, and that Harvey was visiting for advice and support with her pregnancy, or even for a natural termination. The father could then have died of completely natural causes, but it just happened to be a few days after Harvey's visit to Margaret. There were more than enough illnesses lurking around at the time to be responsible for this.

But logic is not strong in the face of fear and, along with other incidents that happened around her, enough of a case seemed to be building that the authorities were called. They conducted a search of Margaret's property and alleged to have found occult paraphernalia, including a poppet.[7] This was enough evidence to have Margaret arrested and it was decided that she should face what was known as a trial by ordeal, where she would face certain physical tasks that would either prove her innocent or guilty. Her ordeal was to be the ducking stool where she was bound by her hands and feet and thrown into the River Ouse. She initially floated, an apparently clear sign that she was a witch, but as her clothes became waterlogged, she started to sink. This was apparently not enough to exonerate her as she had initially floated, so she was pulled from the water by a rope around her neck and sentenced to death by burning. This is where the legend part begins.

Margaret was taken to one of the central meeting points of the town, known as the Tuesday Market Place on 20 July 1590 where a pyre had been constructed (even though she technically hadn't been found guilty up to that point). She was tied to the central stake and the wood around her lit. As Magaret burned, a sudden loud bang rang out as her screams abruptly stopped and something flew out from the fire, shooting directly, hitting the wall of a nearby building. Witnesses claimed that what they saw was actually Margaret's heart that had burst forth from her chest and the building it struck just so happened to be the house of the same magistrate who condemned her.

Now here's the caveat bit, it is a fascinating story and has been retold many times over the following centuries, and King's Lynn certainly uses the tale to entertain tourists on its famous walking ghost tours or even in stories in the local newspapers, but the actual origins of the story are debated. What we do know is that to this day if you take a walk through the Tuesday Market Place there is a large brick building that looks out over the square and above one of the central windows is a distinctly shaped carving, to commemorate it as having been struck by the heart of an executed witch.

Ursula Sontheil – Mother Shipton

Ursula Sontheil, better known as Mother Shipton, is another quite real historical figure whose legend looms large in the public consciousness, especially in regard to her apparent gift for prophecy, a lot of which appears to have come true. Born in 1488 in a cave just outside Knaresborough, Yorkshire, she was an illegitimate child, and her mother faced legal consequences for this but despite that, her father's name was never given. At a young age she was separated from her mother, who was sent to a convent, while Ursula remained in Knaresborough. She is said to have had features that are now considered stereotypical for a witch, a hunched back and hooked nose for example, which got her teased and ostracised from a young age by the locals – think the Wicked Witch of the West, only less green, less wicked and as far as we know not allergic to a bath. Ursula learned to live an isolated life and often returned to the cave where she was born. Here she learned how to use the herbs and flowers that grew along the banks of the nearby River Kidd.

Eventually she met and married Tobias Shipton from York but he died not long after in 1514 and they had no children together. People can be cruel, and after already alleging that the only way Tobias would marry Ursula is because she bewitched him, they then started to suggest that his death was something to do with her. Eventually, the attitudes of others drove Ursula to move away from the town again and back to the cave where she was born, making it her home. People still came to visit her, however, for her herbal remedies, her wisdom and the fact that she had the gift of seeing into the future. It turns out that people can be mean unless there's something that they want or need. Now known as Mother Shipton, she began to give readings of the future of locals and of the town itself, which seem to have proved frighteningly accurate. This made her popularity grow and eventually she started to branch out with her prophecies, predicting the future of the English monarchy and maybe even further afield.

It is believed that while others have added false predictions attributed to her in following centuries, Mother Shipton made accurate prophecies about the Great Fire of London, the fate of Cardinal Thomas Wolsey, and the rise of Elizabeth I and the fall of Mary Stuart (Queen of Scots). What is interesting is that Mother Shipton was making her prophecies at around the same time Nostradamus was also making his; we can only conclude there must have been something in the water.

One event that Mother Shipton did predict with some certainty, and which grants her entry into a book about strange ways people met their end, was the date of her own death and, unlike others in this chapter, she was fortunate not to meet a violent end. She fulfilled her own prophecy and passed away in 1561, at around 73 years of age. She was buried at her request near her cave but her grave has not been located to this day. The cave is now a tourist attraction and the story of Mother Shipton is told, along with some of the local folklore that has grown up around her. Interestingly enough, a mineral-rich waterfall called the Dropping Well flows not far from the cave which, over time, has the ability to petrify objects with its calcium content, and a lot of offerings have been left there by the public over time for this process to occur. There is something distinctly eerie about seeing partially petrified teddy bears hanging beneath a waterfall. Visitors to the site can also see a life-size sculpture of Mother Shipton near the mouth of her cave; however, this is a modern artist's interpretation and not the result of petrification of the woman herself, which is the fate that allegedly befell the so-called 'Witch of Wookey Hole' instead.[8] The United Kingdom may not have always been kind to our witches, but we certainly love to create vivid and fantastical folklore tales and traditions around them, plus they make for great Halloween costumes in a pinch.

Something 'Other'

People in the sixteenth century had more to fear from the supernatural than just witches though. With a belief in the literal existence of heaven and hell, not to mention a strong remaining tether to folklore, superstitions and stories from centuries past being used to explain events in the physical world around them, the other world was still a fact of life for many. With plagues, war, famine and roving cows being almost everyday hazards, it is not surprising that people turned to the supernatural for explanations and for aid. Superstitions and practices from the time are evidence of this, but so too are some of the trials and events that occurred in the century.

With population numbers of less than 20,000 across mainland Europe now,[9] the grey wolf (Canis lupus) is not really something we would see every day outside of a zoo. However, in the sixteenth century they were a much more common sight. Mass sheep farming meant that prey was not in short supply, bearing in mind that we are considering both the sheep and the shepherd in that category. This increased the view that wolves were an enemy but their nature and the fact that they lived in the wilderness gave them a more supernatural air. It is therefore not a surprise that wolves occupied a place in folklore and stories, even coming to mix with humans as spirits, familiars or maybe something more – perhaps learning to pass among us seemingly as one of our own.

Jean Grenier

Pierre de Lancre was a judge from the Bordeaux region of France who found himself linked in with the witch trials of the seventeenth century, writing three books on the subject of the supernatural, especially witchcraft and lycanthropy, a condition in which a person either takes on the persona of a wolf or, in some cases fully becomes one as a werewolf.[10]

In his book *Tableau de l'inconstance des mauvais anges et demons* (Account of the Inconstancy of Evil Angels and Demons) published in 1612, de Lancre recounts the story of the trial in 1603 of a young man also from Bordeaux called Jean Grenier, who proclaimed himself to be a werewolf.

The account tells how Grenier, to impress three young female cowherds, one day made claims about how he would run with a local wolf pack, wearing the skin of a wolf and essentially becoming one of them, even going so far as to declare that he had eaten human flesh. He also took responsibility for a recent wolf attack against a young woman called Marguerite Poirier, incidentally one of the ladies that Grenier happened to be bragging to that day.

The women reported these claims to their local prosecutor, and this led to Grenier's arrest, the situation likely exacerbated by recent wolf attacks in the village. On 2 June 1603, Jean Grenier was questioned about his claims and confessed to being a werewolf. The evidence was carefully arranged and examined and while the original documents have since been lost to history, de Lancre gives a full account of it in his work after speaking to the prosecutors and Grenier himself.

In his testimony, Grenier implicated his father Pierre Grenier and a family acquaintance named Pierre du Tilhaire, though both men were later released due to inconsistencies in his testimony. For his own confessed deeds, it was decided that Jean was acting under demonic influences, and he was sentenced to live out the rest of his days in a monastery.

There are several mitigating circumstances that might have made Grenier confess, not least of all the intense and repeated questioning, but also, he is described by contemporary witnesses as having had a fractious and troubled childhood through a negative relationship with his father. Some of the contemporary descriptions of Grenier, including de Lancre's after interviewing him, would suggest that he either had a low intelligence or what we might identify today as a form of learning difficulty. While we are by no means mental health experts, it might explain the outlandish claims and willingness to confess if Grenier was not able to understand the potential consequences of what he was doing and was easily led by those questioning him.

The Werewolf of Bedburg

In a segment that would combine this chapter with 'Crime and Punishment', the story of the Werewolf of Bedburg shows how the folklore and myth of lycanthropy combines with the darker side of human nature. Peter Stumpp earned the moniker of the Werewolf of Bedburg after being on trial for lycanthropy in 1589. In actuality, he was a serial killer active in Bedburg,

Germany, who was found guilty of the murders and partial cannibalism of at least thirteen children and two pregnant women, plus livestock over the course of at least twenty-five years.

At his trial, Stumpp confessed in disturbing detail to the murders, as well as to having an incestuous relationship with his daughter and consorting with a succubus.[11] The rack was employed to extract further confessions and at the end of his trial he was sentenced to death for his awful crimes. On 31 October 1589 (an ironically suitable date for this kind of trial), Stumpp was executed using the breaking wheel where pincers were heated and then used to pull the flesh from his body before his arms and legs were broken. He was then beheaded and his body burned on a pyre to prevent him from returning from the dead to cause more havoc.

Stumpp was not the only one punished. For the crime of incest and being complicit in his other crimes, his daughter and another woman, recorded as his mistress, were also put on trial and later flayed alive and then burned. Stumpp's head was displayed on top of the wheel he was broken against, along with the image of a wolf. When it came to making sure that examples were made, and to ensure that people like that didn't come back from the dead, the executioners could be a little bit over zealous.

As we can see, humanity is nothing if not creative when it comes to ways in which to inflict pain and suffering on one another. What better way then, to follow up stories of external pain than with those of internal suffering. Follow us now to a veritable buffet of bizarre endings as we look at the ways that food could sometimes prove fatal.

Chapter 5
Food Fatalities

Eating is one of life's greatest pleasures, don't you think? Chowing down on a nice, rare steak with chunky chips or mum's roast chicken dinner on a Sunday can involve some of the happiest memories but imagine if something so simple and enjoyable as eating could be your downfall, and in the most hilarious or undignified of ways.

Don't get us wrong, history has shown us how eating habits have evolved and what foods were available at different times. Did you know that Henry VIII never had a cup of tea ... we know, we were shocked too when we first learned that – just imagine how different things might have been had someone just made him one. During the Tudor period the wealthy would eat a diet that consisted mostly of rich meats and the recently discovered sugar, in quantities that are frankly quite alarming. The poor, however, would eat what they could grow so several vegetables, potatoes, pulses and grains made up most of their diet.

Food fatalities are, unfortunately, more common if you think about choking, for example, but to feature in this book of strange deaths, food has taken people out in ways you would not necessarily imagine. Poisoning was also not uncommon in the years 1485–1603, as a lot of household substances could easily be 'accidently' added to a meal to cause the unsuspecting eater to die and the murderer to (usually) get away with it by claiming blissful ignorance. However, in the same breath, a few household poisonings occurred genuinely accidentally as food hygiene was not held to the same muster as it is today.

Richard Roose

Richard Roose is known to have suffered one of the most brutal and horrific deaths ever due to treason It was the first of its kind and changed the law so everyone who was found guilty of this particular treasonous act would be executed this way – being boiled alive like soup, or porridge. Intrigued? So were we.

This is touching quite heavily on 'Crime and Punishment', but it is food related so it is being included in here but please read that chapter, honestly there are some absolute corkers in there as well as a more detailed account of exactly how Richard Roose was punished. The reason he is being included in this chapter is due to reasoning used by Henry VIII for this method of execution.

Richard Roose (also known by Rose or Cooke) was the cook to the Bishop of Rochester John Fisher, who in 1531 was an archenemy of the king due to the lack of support for his proposed divorce of Queen Catherine of Aragon. It is thought that Roose was hired by George Boleyn, brother to Anne Boleyn, to poison Bishop Fisher in the hopes of hastening said divorce proceedings.

On 18 February 1531, Roose prepared some porridge for Bishop Fisher and his fifteen guests, including Sir Thomas More, for lunch, in which he added some poisonous powder. All who ate the meal became ill, and one Bennett Curwen died. Bishop Fisher did not eat that day, and sources do not know why this was. Unfortunately for Roose, the bishop's brother Richard was in charge of the household and quickly arrested him for the attempted murder, which Roose naturally denied. He claimed that he did not know the powder was a poison, simply thinking it was a laxative to play a practical joke. After a lengthy time on the rack, Roose confessed to the poisoning, and it was down to Henry VIII to decide his fate.

The king was very paranoid, specifically about his food being poisoned. He would have a servant test all his meals before he was prepared to eat them. Because of this, he wanted to make an example of Roose and use his death as a deterrent. He decreed that poisoning a person, whether successfully or not, was treason and the punishment was to be boiled alive, like the manner in which they were trying to administer the poison.

The House of Lords accepted the king's new law and the public agreed with their great king about Roose's alleged depravity. On 15 April 1532 a crowd gathered in Smithfield, London, to watch the king's justice in action. Roose was placed on a gibbet[1] where he was hanged to the point of death, but ultimately kept alive, and then at intervals he was lowered three times into a pot of boiling water. Contemporary records show that it took approximately two hours for him to die. The punishment was intended to last as long as it took him to prepare the poisoned porridge.

Do you think he was innocent, having honestly thought he was giving laxatives, or was he really a cold-hearted murderer? Either way Richard Roose came to a pretty 'crappy' end.

Pope Clement VII

Pope Clement VII, whose birth name was Giulio di Giuliano de' Medici, (one of those powerful Medicis)[2] was born on 26 May 1478 in Florence, Italy. He was made head of the Catholic Church and ruler of the Papal States from 19 November 1523 until his death on 25 September 1534.

During his papacy, Clement VII was known as 'Pope Clement the Unfortunate' due to all the issues he inherited from his predecessor Pope Adrian VI as well as the ones brought forward by Cardinal Thomas Wolsey in late 1520s (you know, the little-known issue of Henry VIII's annulment). How he died has also been thrown into the mix, due to its curious and somewhat ironic manner.

Leading up to his death in 1534 the pope's health had been in decline, likely exacerbated by the stress and physical strain he endured during his papacy, particularly after the Sack of Rome in 1527, and the constant barrage from Henry VIII. It is known that he suffered from what we now know as liver failure due to his documented 'yellow skin', total loss of sight in his left eye and partial blindness in his right; it was not until a fatal meal in September of 1534 that the pope finally perished.

Two days before he died, Pope Clement sat down for a meal of meat and vegetables, standard fare for the day. A few hours after he had eaten, he called out and clutched his stomach in agony. He languished in pain for forty-eight hours before he took his final breath on 25 September 1534.

Who or what could possibly be the villainous culprit responsible for the demise of a sacred pope, you ask? The answer is … a mushroom. A certain type of mushroom, in fact, so potent with poison that its very name should be enough of a deterrent, namely because it has the word 'death' quite literally in its title – the DEATH cap mushroom.

Upon researching this death cap mushroom poisoning, we found that as many as 90 per cent of all mushroom poisoning-related deaths worldwide are due to the death cap mushroom. The issue with these mushrooms is that they can easily be mistaken for their edible cousins and are even said to be quite tasty. Eating as little as half a death cap mushroom contains enough toxin to kill an adult. Symptoms can take some time to manifest however, appearing approximately six to twenty-four hours after eating and including abdominal pain, diarrhoea, nausea and vomiting, followed by jaundice, delirium, seizures, coma, kidney failure, intracranial pressure and bleeding and finally cardiac arrest.

Death can usually take anywhere between six to sixteen days to occur. Pope Clement VII however, suffering already with poor health, died much faster. People were shocked at his sudden death at the age of just 56, but if you are going to eat something with 'death' in its name, you cannot be too surprised. In the immortal words of Alanis Morissette – isn't it ironic, don't you think?

Pietro Aretino

Now this food-related death is quite literally a laugh a minute. Dying from laughter is an extremely rare form of death, but it can and does happen. Usually, the resulting laughter causes either cardiac arrest (heart attack) or asphyxiation (suffocation), which has itself been caused by a fit of laughter. Though uncommon, death by laughter has been recorded as early in Ancient Greece.

Born in 1492 in Italy, Pietro Aretino was an author, playwright, poet and blackmailer who, unusually for the period, was openly homosexual. He wielded great influence on contemporary art and the country's politics, being one of the most influential writers of the time and an outspoken critic of the powerful. He was also known to be an unrepentant satirist, and is widely regarded as being the inventor of modern literate pornography.

This would usually be the beginning of a tantalising tale of conspiracy theories, backstabbing and political murder, it was the Tudor period after all … but dear readers that would not be ridiculous enough to be included in our book on death. Mr Aretino's death may seem boring in comparison, but trust us, it is a laugh.

There has been much speculation over how Aretino died, however this is the most believed reason and the most wonderfully bizarre. It is said that on 21 October 1556, Aretino was at a party in Venice when a guest told him a joke involving the writer's own sisters and the brothel where they were employed (it seems like an appreciation of the world's oldest trade ran in the family). So amused was Aretino by this joke, that he was unable to stop laughing. He laughed so hard that he fell over backwards from his chair and keeled over right then and there. Another similar version of the story has it that he died by falling into a fit of apoplectic laughter after hearing the joke, while yet another has it that his death was caused by suffocation from laughing so hard. Whichever version it is, all accounts agree that it was laughter that killed him, and the official coroner's report states 'death by laughter'.

Pietro Aretino's whole life seems to have been one long and often seedy adventure, so it was somehow quite fitting that he died laughing at a dirty joke.

Disastrous Dining

Poisoning could be expected in Tudor times, even strange table etiquette could be explained, but what about when you are just minding your own business, enjoying a nice meal and something unexpected occurs?

On 30 November 1525 in Staplehurst, Kent, Richard Frensshe, along with William Fermor and James Kyng, were having breakfast at William Scranton's workhouse. They were eating bread, cheese and other foods while sitting by the fire. The men were chatting, having a laugh and James Kyng playfully nudged William Fermor with his shoulder. Unbeknown to Kyng, Fermor was holding a knife in his left hand for cutting said food. This led to Fermor accidentally inflicting a wound on Kyng's left thigh. The wound in question was not just a scratch, mind you, it was in fact half an inch deep, hitting a major artery and killing James Kyng instantly. William Fermor fled the scene and sought sanctuary at St Martin's Le Grand in London. He was eventually found and tried for the crime, whereby the coroner was seemingly unaware of the details and quantities of William Fermor's goods and chattels. As with coroner's reports of the time, all goods at the time of death were catalogued and you will be pleased to know that the knife used to accidentally kill Kyng was valued at one penny.

Accidental murder is one thing but imagine being boiled alive due to your own stupidity. On 15 November 1538 in Cambridge, Christopher Franke and Richard Wolf were at Nicholas Springe's 'Berbruehouse' (a place where brewing, typically of beer or ale took place) in the parish of St Peter. Roger Vanwright, a miller from Cambridge, was also present. Roger was sitting on top of a vat called a 'lyquour lede' which was filled with boiling liquid, eating his supper from a plate balanced on his knees. You could be thinking that this was probably a bad idea, and you would be right. While cutting or tearing at his food, Roger moved his knees and, losing his balance, tipped over and accidentally fell backwards into the vat, where he was burned and cooked alive. The vat was worth 40 pence and, being too expensive to dispose of, remained in the hands of Nicholas Springe, a stationer from Cambridge.

On 16 January 1598 in Syston in Leicestershire, Barbara Gilbert, the 50-year-old wife of labourer Blaise Gilbert, passed away three days after she accidentally poisoned herself. January the 13th was a particularly cold day and Barbara was preparing a 'good and healthy meal' for her family using flour and milk, which were staples in most Tudor households. During the preparation Barbara mistakenly used rat poison ('rattesbane') instead of flour, so we can assume it would not have been a small amount involved. After consuming a portion of the meal, she became severely affected almost instantly. Despite her extreme suffering, she languished until 2 am on 16 January, when she finally succumbed to the poisoning. The case was subsequently brought before the authorities, with Thomas Warde and William Sayvill involved in the proceedings; following their investigation, no foul play was thought to have occurred.

Tycho Brahe

'Manners maketh man' is what Colin Firth and Taron Egerton would have us believe from the *Kingsman* movies, but what happens when man takes having good manners a little too far?

Tycho Brahe was born in Denmark on 14 December 1546 and was a famous astronomer whose work consisted of measuring and fixing the positions of more than 777 fixed stars and developing several astronomical instruments. This paved the way for many future discoveries, with his observations being the most accurate known before the invention of the telescope.

Brahe is also known to have had a prosthetic nose, made from silver, which he took to wearing after losing his actual nose in 1566 in a duel with Manderup Parsberg, his third cousin. He and Parsberg became good friends after this, but Tycho wore a prosthetic nose for the rest of his life.[3] On or around 20 October 1601, Brahe was invited to attend a banquet in Prague organised by Petr Vok, the Count of Rosenberg.

Everyone loves a dinner party, and there tends to be an unofficial etiquette that guests follow. Nowadays it is more things like *not putting elbows on the table* or *burping really loudly* (even though this particular notion was considered high praise in Roman times). In Brahe's case, it was said that a guest at such a party was unable to leave the table before the host, for any reason. We would have thought this meant when one had finished their meal, but Tycho took this a little too literally.

During the dinner Brahe drank a lot of wine, quite an excessive amount according to reports, and what happens when somebody drinks a lot of liquid? They need to go to the loo, of course. Unfortunately for Brahe, the dinner host did not share his need to relieve himself, so Brahe held it in. In fact, he held his wee in for so long that his bladder ruptured, and he died four days later.

Anne Wyffyn

This next story is as sad as it is disgusting. Intestinal worms were a common and distressing health issue in sixteenth-century England, affecting humans and animals alike. This was due to poor sanitation, limited medical knowledge and widespread poverty, which created conditions perfect for parasitic infections.

In June 1580, 14-year-old Anne Wyffyn from Lawshall in Suffolk took desperate measures to try and cure herself of intestinal worms. At the time, to say effective medical treatments were scarce would be a slight understatement. Health care was also heavily influenced by social status and wealth. The poor had limited access to professional medical advice, which unfortunately led to people resorting to dangerous homemade remedies.

Having intestinal worms would have been extremely uncomfortable and distressing. The symptoms and sensations vary depending on the type of worm and the severity of the infection. Generally, an infected person would experience symptoms such as abdominal pain, nausea and vomiting, diarrhoea or constipation, a loss of appetite and because of the last symptom, weight loss. A patient would also feel weak, fatigued, have itching around the anus, worms visible in the stool, anaemia and a general feeling of being unwell – because the other symptoms would not leave you feeling quite low enough. Also, the psychological impact cannot be ignored; knowing that there are parasites living inside your body can cause anxiety, stress and an overwhelming sense of self-disgust.

After weeks of feeling this way, you can imagine the lengths people might go to rid themselves of worms. Anne was at the end of her tether, and she needed a way, any way, to make them go away. So, she ground up ratsbane, the arsenic-based rat poison, into a fine powder and mixed it with ale, hoping to kill the worms but without fully realising the lethal effects it might also have on her. Arsenic is known for its extremely toxic properties and was commonly used in rat poison. Its use in medicine was not completely unheard of in Tudor times, but it was exceptionally risky and often poorly understood. Tragically, after ingesting the mixture, Anne fell ill and died two days later, though on the plus side, the worms died too.

Fatal Falls

On 24 November 1599, in Notton, Yorkshire, Robert Crowder passed away following an accident while collecting pears from a tree in William Brodhead's croft. On 11 September 1599, at around 3 pm, Crowder fell from the pear tree, severely injuring his buttocks. He sustained significant injuries and contusions from the fall. Despite the medical care available at the time, he languished until 4 pm on 24 November when he succumbed to his injuries. The case was recorded by Percival Woderoffe, the coroner, who valued the pear tree at two shillings and sixpence, having it placed in the custody of William Brasley, the constable of Notton. We are not entirely sure how the logistics of placing a pear tree in custody works, but there you go.

In Uppingham, Rutland, on 8 April 1539, George Randylson met his end after eating a meal under a haystack. On 7 April 1539 at around 9 am, part of the haystack, owned by one Robert Pakman, suddenly collapsed. The falling hay suffocated Randylson. Despite efforts to save him, George succumbed to the injuries caused by the accident.

On the evening of 21 November 1562, at about 11 pm in the village of Sonning in Berkshire, James Tusser, along with a group of friends, engaged in a traditional mediaeval nighttime activity known as batfowling.[4] This involved using nets to catch birds at night, often by startling them from their roosts with torches. The group decided to go to the common lake of Burwey, which is now referred to as Borough Lake and as they moved along the stream, Tusser spotted a 'teele' – a teal, a type of waterfowl – resting on the water. Feeling hungry and seizing the opportunity, he cast his net to capture the bird; however, in the process of reaching out to secure his net, Tusser lost his balance and fell into the water and drowned, marking a sorrowful end to what had begun as a fun evening with friends.

A servant's watch was ended after a strong sense of loyalty went slightly too far. On 28 July 1528 in Norton, Hampshire, John Benett, servant to John Twyn, died. John was ordered to watch over his master's fruit and grain in the area known as Farnham near Norton Wood. That afternoon, at around 3 pm, a severe storm broke that prompted Benett to seek shelter under four hurdles called 'fooldhordyll[es]' that were stacked together in a field. Fooldhordylls were pieces of wood woven together to create a sort of fence and collectively were very robust. The intense rain and wind were stronger, however, and caused the hurdles to collapse onto Benett, pressing him to death. His body was discovered at 6 am the following morning.

In Heathfield, Sussex, Richard Wyke drowned on 16 February 1502, after falling from an apple tree in Byxstrode garden. While climbing the tree to collect fruit, it appears that he lost his balance and fell into a pit or well beneath the tree. The fall, combined with where he landed, resulted in his drowning.

While 'death by bacon' may sound amusing or even appealing to bacon lovers, there isn't a specific historical account of someone dying exclusively from eating bacon because that would be a sacrilege. However, in the case of Elizabeth Bowne's demise, it was falling bacon that was the cause. Elizabeth was a widow in the service of Hugh Talmage of Bury, Cambridgeshire, when she met her untimely death on 16 February 1543. Elizabeth had unfortunately been sickly and was debilitated from childhood, resulting in a weakened body. After a long, hard day working in nearly freezing temperatures, Elizabeth was sitting by the fire in her master's kitchen to warm herself when suddenly, the rope holding four flitches of bacon in the chimney fell on her from a height. The flitches struck her hard, knocking her to the ground and crushing her head and body. Reports say that Bowne lingered on in a great deal of pain until 17 February before finally succumbing to her injuries. The bacon, which was estimated to be worth two shillings, was kept in the custody of the coroner who investigated her untimely demise. Yes, you did read that right, the coroner completed the investigation and then took the bacon home for a late-night snack … talk about perks of the job.

Speaking of late nights, imagine being asleep when out of nowhere you are attacked by a bag of flour. This is exactly what happened to Margaret Witton from Skipton in Yorkshire when, on 16 March 1515, she was in a bed asleep in the house of William Witton. Suddenly, a sack of flour fell from high above her, landing on her face and chest. The unexpected impact of the heavy sack, which would have been quite a shock at any time of the day or night, caused her instant death. Margaret's death is not the only time where flour has caused a person's unexplainable demise.

Ergotism or the Strasbourg Dancing Plague

Like all good plague stories, this one begins with supernatural omens. A star streaks across the sky in a mysterious manner, fields unexpectedly flood, extreme and bitter cold is followed by extreme sweltering heat, which in turn is followed by inevitable extreme hunger, especially in the early sixteenth century. But what happens when none of that actually matters because the rhythm just moves you?

Welcome to July 1518 where we are going to take you to Strasbourg, part of the Holy Roman Empire then but today part of France. It is a horrendously hot day in July and the streets are full of people trying to cool themselves when suddenly they notice a strange woman dancing, with no signs of stopping. Frau Troffea in fact cannot stop 'strutting her stuff' and she dances with no music or a partner. There was very little in the way of entertainment in Strasbourg, so it was fun … until it wasn't.

Troffea continued dancing for a solid week, seven days where she did not eat, sleep or drink. She eventually collapsed with exhaustion, but upon waking from her rest started straight back up again and by the end of the first week, over thirty other people had joined her, all seemingly similarly affected. Nobody knew what was happening but by September 1518 more than 400 people had succumbed to the 'dancing plague', with many dancing past the point of injury and with countless people dying.

Not knowing what had caused this strange phenomenon, the Strasbourg city council turned to the only possible cause of unexplainable illnesses in that day and age – religion – with the most likely culprit St Vitus, a Catholic saint who pious sixteenth-century Europeans believed had the power to curse people with a dancing plague. When you combine the horrors of disease, fear and famine, all of which were tearing through Strasbourg in 1518, the St Vitus superstition may have triggered a stress-induced hysteria that took hold of the city. Other religious theories have suggested the dancers were members of a religious cult.

In the hopes of wearing the dancers out and putting a stop to this plague, the Strasbourg city council decided to take the 'if you can't beat them, join them' approach, and built a stage, hired musicians and moved the afflicted into halls. Their theory was that St Vitus had given the dancers 'hot blood' that could only be cured by dancing it out. They even paid professional dancers to make the most exhausted people dance more. This was obviously an absolutely ridiculous idea, which merely encouraged more citizens to join the crazed dancers. At its height, some historical sources claim the dancing was killing up to fifteen people a day, and it seemed it would go on forever as nothing was having an effect. One day, the worst-afflicted dancers were taken away to a shrine, where they eventually stopped dancing. Without them, the remaining dancers slowly stopped as well. This only went on to 'prove' the point that it was a divinely sent illness and forgiveness had been granted. However, we have a more scientific and probable cause, and it is food related (hence why it is included in this chapter and not the one entitled 'Perils and Plagues').

Ergotism or ergot poisoning is caused by eating food that has been contaminated with a fungus called *C. purpurea*. This is most found in rye and wheat but can be found in other grains and grasses too. Rye flour was extremely common in the 1500s and used to make bread, a staple in almost every household. The freezing cold winters would be a perfect catalyst for the fungus to grow, before the hot summer weather then made it a breeding ground for the toxins to spread.

The Strasbourg Dancing Plague of 1518 remains as fascinating now as it was back then, serving as an historical example of how it is not always the best idea to dance to the rhythm of your heart. So next time you are out and dancing through the night with no intentions of stopping, maybe double check that cheeky burger you had before leaving.

Chapter 6

Kill or Cure

Since the dawn of time people have tried to evade illness and death. It is one of the very few things that most of humanity can agree on – we do not like to be sick and we do not want to die, always looking for ways to make ourselves feel better or to live forever. Even now in the twenty-first century, modern medicine is making such advancements that many diseases that were once fatal are now not only curable, but totally eradicated. However, for our doctors to get to where they are today, a lot of people came before them making a lot of discoveries but also, and more often, making a lot of mistakes. Honestly, some historical 'cures' are so ridiculous we genuinely do not know how the human population has not died out already.

Life expectancy in Tudor times was only around 35 (worryingly the ages of we authors as we write this) and was extremely difficult. You had to not only be tough, but you also had to be lucky to survive. There was a high infant mortality rate, with around 14 per cent of babies dying before their first birthday, and women had a shorter life expectancy than men due to the risks posed by childbirth. Sad, but true.

During the years 1485–1603, more commonly known as the Tudor period here in England, the streets were rife with contagious diseases as regular epidemics of dysentery, tuberculosis and influenza swept through the country. People would hang backwards out of their window to defecate and urinate directly onto the street – it really was a kind of dirty, perfect breeding ground for bugs and bacteria.

Tudor doctors had many different theories on what caused illnesses and how to cure them. They themselves knew and relied a lot on astronomy, believing that different zodiac signs ruled different parts of the body – for example, we are both Capricorns which is the sign that protects the knees, joints and skeletal system (more on that later in the chapter). However, they knew frighteningly little about how the human body worked – which will be demonstrated in this chapter in the way that they used unusual treatments such as attaching leeches to suck blood, giving out special coins or jewels as a cure, or even tasting the patient's urine to decide on their treatment.

Sweating Sickness

During the reign of Henry VIII, there was one illness that terrified him more than any other, and that was sweating sickness. The onset of the disease was extremely quick and without warning, usually last thing at night or first thing in the morning. The symptoms began with a general feeling that something wasn't right, a strange premonition of oncoming horror, followed by the onset of a violent headache, flu-like tremors and aching limbs. This was followed by a raging fever complicated by pulse irregularities and heart palpitations. The course of the disease was exceptionally violent and sometimes fatal within just a matter of hours. Queen Anne Boleyn suffered from sweating sickness and almost died, which probably didn't help the king's fear.

There were five outbreaks of the sweating sickness during Tudor times, and each came with more ridiculous ways to 'cure' it. One medical 'professional' of the time, John Kays, or more pompously known as Johannus Caius (he thought it made him sound more impressive) published *The Sweating Sickness: A boke or counseill against the disease commonly called the sweate or sweatyng sicknesse* in which he detailed what he believed to be the signs, symptoms and cures for the disease. Caius's cure advised people to avoid evil mists, rotten fruit and to exercise frequently. He also recommended that people who were afflicted with the sickness drink herbal concoctions, sweat as much as possible and avoid going outdoors. Not that his advice worked, mind you, as despite his alleged expertise most of Caius's patients still ended up dead.

Henry VIII was so terrified of the disease, that as soon as it was rumoured to be spreading, he would not sleep in the same bed for more than a night and moved his whole household to the countryside – which may have actually worked as there were less people to spread the illness.

Also, and probably not surprising, the illness was catalogued as a 'disaster by God' in that it was only targeting those seen as 'unholy' or 'unrighteous'.

The priests at the time said prayers for those afflicted to be healed. This did not really seem to have had the desired effect either. We cover more on notable cases of the sweating sickness in 'Perils and Plagues' later.

Pope Innocent VIII – First Recorded Blood Transfusion?

The way in which human bodies work and why we die has always been a topic of interest throughout history. In 460 BCE Hippocrates is credited with applying a brand-new idea to medicine – the four humours. These were based on the four elements: Air, Water, Earth and Fire but in context of the human body, being represented as the four vital fluids: blood, phlegm, yellow bile and black bile.

It was believed that any extreme excess or deficiency of any of the humours in a person could be seen as a sign of illness. Greek physician Hippocrates, in a theory then developed further by another Greek physician named Galen, suggested that a moderate imbalance in the mixture of these fluids produced behavioural patterns that made us ill. Extreme and usually painful methods were adopted to restore the four humours to make a person well again, such as bloodletting, warming the blood using herbs and enticing the patient to vomit to remove the bile. This idea led to the unnecessary death of three young boys as well as the death of a pope who is thought to have undergone the first ever 'blood transfusion'. Spoilers, this did not work.

Pope Innocent VIII's reign is not looked upon favourably by historians. He is considered unworthy to have held the position and has a controversial reputation that continues to this day. He is known to have taken bribes, used political power to oppress, called for a crusade against the Turks and was strongly against witchcraft. He appointed German inquisitor Heinrich Kramer (author of the *Malleus Maleficarum*), to whom he granted complete authority to prosecute suspects. This decree, or papal bull, was heavily abused – no surprises there.

Then in 1492, while Columbus was sailing the ocean blue in search of a direct route to Asia (but ending up on the other side of the world entirely), in Italy, Pope Innocent VIII was having a stroke. It was one of a list of illnesses that the ailing pontiff was suffering from and the best physicians at the time were trying to find ways to cure him. They believed that the stroke was probably caused due to the age of his blood. Blood was seen to not only pump and transport nutrients around your body, but it was also believed to be connected to your soul as well. At the time, Pope Innocent VIII was 60 years old, which meant his blood was too old to successfully continue to keep him well. There was only one option left: to replace his old blood with that of a child, well, three children to be exact. Thus, the first recorded attempt of a blood transfusion was undertaken. Now the idea of 'sucking the blood from a youth's arm for rejuvenation' was not exactly new, but a complete change of the blood was. The Jewish doctor (not important now, but at the time this fact was used to instil antisemitic ideals in Rome) acquired three 10-year-old boys and drained them completely of their blood, resulting in them all dying instantly. The Pope then drank a draught of their blood with the thought that his would therefore be replaced by that of the three boys. This, strangely, did not work and on 25 July 1492 Pope Innocent VIII died of the most terrible of diseases, extreme old age.

It was decided that the three boys would be classed as martyrs. After all, they had all agreed to the practice, knowing they would die as they were devoted to their pope and the Church.

Smallpox

Smallpox in Tudor England was a significant health concern that left a mark both literally and figuratively during that time, that also nearly robbed us of England's greatest monarch. It's a highly contagious and deadly disease caused by the variola virus. It spreads rapidly through close contact with an infected person or contaminated objects. Smallpox causes the patient to develop a high fever, fatigue and severe back pain with less frequent symptoms being abdominal pain and vomiting. Approximately three days later the virus produces a characteristic rash with bumps full of a clear liquid, which later fill with pus and finally develop a crust that dries and falls off, leaving scars.

Smallpox outbreaks were extremely common and often led to high mortality rates, especially among children and those with weakened immune symptoms. The disease could cause severe scarring, blindness and even death in most cases. England at the time did not have the medical advancements we have today, so treating smallpox was challenging and led to some bizarre treatments.

One of the most well-known Tudor figures who suffered from the smallpox disease was Queen Elizabeth I. On 10 October 1562, 29-year-old Queen Elizabeth was taken ill at Hampton Court Palace with what everyone thought was just a bad cold. However, the cold quickly developed into a violent fever, and it soon became clear that the young queen actually had smallpox. Just a week later it was feared that she would die, which would push the kingdom towards a succession crisis as she was (and would remain) unmarried and without children. There were several possible candidates for the throne and her advisors were divided as to who might be the best option. Elizabeth, by this point, had lost all power of speech and her fever was dangerously high. Of course, the most highly educated of doctors were consulted, and one was brought in, a German physician called Dr Burcot, who subjected her to something called the 'red treatment'.

Developed in Japan, the 'red treatment' had been in use in Europe since the twelfth century and involved wrapping the patient from the neck down in red cloth and hanging red cloth around the patient's bed. It was believed that the cloth would prevent severe scarring of the skin as well as the colour changing the composition of the illness. This was of course ridiculous, and the colour of the cloth did very little to help the queen in any respects.

In addition to the red wrapping, Elizabeth was moved closer to the fire and, whether through actual medical knowledge or sheer dumb luck, her fever broke and within a few hours not only was she conscious, but she was also able to speak. By 25 October Elizabeth was able to resume some of her royal duties, though she remained removed from public view for a while. In the end, she survived but it left her with terrible facial scarring that plagued her all her life. It would make her extremely self-conscious which led to her wearing extensive makeup and only allowing one portrait of her to be painted. The lady-in-waiting who nursed her, Lady Sibley, caught smallpox while caring for Elizabeth and while she also survived, she was terribly scarred and disfigured. The queen's survival was seen as a miracle from God and boosted the public's confidence in her reign.

The sad side effect of the scarring for both was that they tried to cover up any markings by using a makeup known as Venetian Ceruse made from lead paint and vinegar. It might have worked at first, but the long-term effects were hair loss, skin discolouration and even death. The price of beauty never was cheap.

To combat the spread of smallpox in Tudor England, various measures were taken. Isolation of the sick was common to prevent further transmission of the disease – and you thought Covid was the first time people were forced into isolation. People also used herbal remedies and traditional practices to try and alleviate symptoms, although these were broadly ineffective.

One significant development during the Tudor period was the practice of variolation, a precursor to vaccination. Variolation involved deliberately infecting a person with a small amount of the smallpox virus to induce a milder form of the disease and provide some kind of immunity. While risky, variolation was sometimes successful in protecting individuals from the more severe smallpox infections.

Overall, smallpox was a constant threat during this period, causing widespread fear and devastation. The disease had a profound impact on society, affecting people of all social classes. It was not until the eighteenth century that the first smallpox vaccine was developed, by Edward Jenner, leading to an eventual eradication of smallpox worldwide in 1980.

Diane de Poitiers – Drank Gold

What is the price for eternal youth and beauty, and would you pay it if it meant death? A contradiction in itself, we know, but it was the price ultimately paid by the mistress to King Henry II of France, Diane de Poitiers.

Beginning their decades-long affair when Henry was 15 and she 35, Diane de Poitiers was basically untouchable. The king was not at all discreet about his love for Diane, regularly stating that he preferred her to his actual wife, giving her the Crown Jewels of France and a château that his wife Queen Catherine de' Medici was desperate to have for herself. Diane helped raise Henry's children, advised him on political matters, and even answered correspondence for him, signing the letters with a mash-up of their names: 'HenriDiane'.

After Henry II died in 1559, Diane's influence vanished overnight. The queen was able to act on her true feelings and Diane was sent into exile. Already 60 years old, Diane lived for a further six years in d'Anet then in 1565 she suffered a fall from a horse for which Ambroise Paré treated her for a broken tibia and fibula, but from which she never fully recovered and died at age 66 in 1566.

During her tenure as mistress, Diane was comfortable in her position but was always aware that Henry was twenty-five years her junior. Perhaps that age difference is one of the reasons Diane de Poitiers seems to have sought a certain elixir of youth from apothecaries. Unfortunately for Diane however, said apothecaries held to the alchemical principle that gold is the immutable and perfect element. If you want to retain your youthful perfection, therefore, ingesting some form of gold would seem to be the way to go.

Drinking gold wasn't completely uncommon at the time and wasn't attributed to her death until 2009 when her body was rediscovered and tested by French scientists. Having analysed tissue and hair remnants they found an extremely high concentration of gold, 500 times greater than in a lock of hair from her younger days preserved at the palace.

As she was not royalty, Diane did not wear crowns or gold fabric every day, so the gold was not externally applied. They also found that her bones were very fragile, which was unexpected for an athletic woman who swam and rode horses daily. They also found her hair to be thin and brittle. Both are symptoms of gold poisoning, which would have impeded her recovery and led to her eventual death.

Gold has also not been proven to enhance life expectancy or beauty when consumed, however a nice pair of gold earrings with a matching necklace can make you feel *bonita*.

Tuberculosis/Consumption

Tuberculosis (TB) or as it was more commonly known as in the Tudor era, consumption (it 'consumed' the victim), is one of the diseases that is still around today, however it is no longer the death sentence it once was. However, because of the poor health conditions in the Tudor era, TB was very common and, unfortunately, always deadly. It is the illness that is believed to have taken the lives of two Tudor monarchs – Henry VII and Edward VI, the latter at just 15 years old.

Tuberculosis is when the lungs fill with fluid and begin to deteriorate. It can be spread through air easily, if an infected person coughs. The patient's weight would drastically drop as the disease progressed with symptoms including chills, fatigue, fever, loss of appetite, night sweats and, as the disease finally took over, coughing up blood.

Doctors were at a loss as to how to treat this disease, and would try the usual herbal remedies, bloodletting with leeches, praying and mass for the sick, however none helped. It could take up to three years for an infected person to succumb to consumption; it was not quick and painless. It was not until 1946 that Selman Waksman, Elizabeth Bugie and Albert Schatz developed streptomycin, the antibiotic that is now used to cure TB.

Henry II of France – 'Wait and See' Method

Henry II of France was king from 1547 until his untimely and unfortunate death in 1559. He was best known for his ruthless persecution of Protestants, for which he favoured burning at the stake and cutting tongues out of people for 'spouting herecies'. He was also known for having a rather infamous mistress, whose name you may recognise from earlier in this chapter – Diane de Poitiers (clearly, they were into each other for their intelligence).

On the day his accident occurred, King Henry was in the midst of throwing a jousting tournament in honour of a peace treaty between France and Spain that was to last several days. The king was to enter the lists and compete before a huge array of lords and ladies from all over France and Spain, including his wife Queen Catherine, Diane de Poitiers and his new daughter-in-law Mary, Queen of Scots. The queen tried to persuade him not to enter as he had suffered recently from giddiness after some physical exertion. The king would not hear of it, however, and sporting Diane's colours as usual, he entered the joust. He had insisted that the young Count of Montgomery be his opponent, although the count did his best to refuse. However, if history has taught us anything it is that refusing the king is futile.

Lord Montgomery saddled up and with lance in hand hurtled towards the king, hitting him in a way that would eventually prove fatal. Montgomery's lance struck the king's helmet and a long splinter pierced Henry's eye and penetrated his brain. On closer inspection there was also a rather large slice of wood piercing his throat.

We have a rather sweet anecdote to interject with here. Montgomery, upon seeing the king in such a way, knelt before him and begged the king to take his head and hand in punishment, but Henry is reported as saying magnanimously that 'it was not his fault and he had carried himself bravely and well'. This does not have much significance in relation to the king's death, but we thought it worth including it.

The royal doctors removed all the wooden shards from the king, and they hoped losing his eye would be the only injury, though this was obviously not the case. The famous royal surgeon Ambroise Paré was joined by another celebrated medical man of the time, Andreas Vesalius, sent from Brussels by King Philip II of Spain; however, Henry's condition grew worse. They could not work out why he was not getting better, apparently the well-practised medical treatment of 'wait and see' turned out to not be that effective – shocking, we know.

It took the poor king eleven days before he finally died, on 10 July 1559. His death was, most likely, inevitable but we cannot help feeling that doing something may just have been better than nothing.

It's Written in the Stars … Apparently

Astrology played a significant role in Tudor medicine, deeply influencing both the diagnosis and treatment of illnesses. The belief was that the positions and movements of celestial bodies[1] had a direct impact on human health and behaviour. This idea stemmed from the broader philosophical view that the universe (macrocosm) and the human body (microcosm) were interconnected. Physicians would cast astrological charts or horoscopes for their patients, to determine the position of stars and planets at the time of the patient's birth or at the onset of illness. They would then use this to help decide on the best time for treatments or surgeries and what remedies to use. Astrologers would also be known to advise their patients on lifestyle changes and preventative measures based on their horoscopes. This might include dietary recommendations, exercise routines and other health practices aligned with the patient's astrological profile.

Each of the twelve signs of the zodiac was believed to control specific parts of the body. For instance:

- Aries: head and face
- Taurus: throat and neck
- Gemini: shoulders, arms, and hands
- Cancer: chest and stomach
- Leo: heart and back
- Virgo: digestive system and intestines
- Libra: kidneys and lower back
- Scorpio: reproductive organs
- Sagittarius: hips and thighs
- Capricorn: knees and bones
- Aquarius: ankles and circulatory system
- Pisces: feet

While the zodiac signs were believed to control specific parts of the body, the planets of the solar system were thought to exert their own kind of influence over different bodily functions and fluids. These were:

- Sun: vitality and the heart
- Moon: emotions, fluids, and the brain
- Mercury: nervous system and communication
- Venus: reproductive system and kidneys
- Mars: blood and muscles
- Jupiter: liver and growth
- Saturn: bones and ageing

This information would be collated and referenced against the patient's birth and the current ailment they were suffering from. For example, if a patient had a headache and the moon was in Aries, this connection might confirm the diagnosis, and the doctor could then suggest specific treatments. A lot came down to timing for medical astrology. Certain planetary alignments were considered more auspicious for performing treatments or surgeries. To give a couple of examples, procedures might be scheduled when the moon was in a favourable sign to reduce the risk of complications. Even in modern times there are still myths circulating around Accident & Emergency departments in hospitals being busier when there is a full moon. Which herbal remedies to give was also somewhat down to astrology, for example marigold is associated with the Sun and was used for heart conditions, whereas lemon balm was associated with Jupiter and used for liver and digestive issues.

For better understanding, let us walk through a hypothetical Tudor medical case study together. Imagine a Tudor physician treating a patient with a persistent cough. First the doctor would cast the patient's horoscope, starting from when the patient first noticed a cough. They check the charts and realise that Mercury, associated with the respiratory system, is in a challenging aspect with Saturn, which could indicate chronic or difficult-to-treat conditions. Using this information to diagnose and treat the patient, the physician determines that the cough might be related to issues governed by Mercury (lungs and airways). He prescribes herbs that are associated with the planet like coltsfoot to help soothe the respiratory system. The physician advises the patient to avoid cold, damp environments, as Saturn's influence might exacerbate these conditions. The treatment is scheduled to begin when the moon is in Gemini as that governs the respiratory system, to enhance the effectiveness of the remedies.

Astrology was so important that it was integrated into the medical curriculum of universities during the Tudor period. Physicians were expected to understand and use astrological principles in their practice. This included studying classical texts like Ptolemy's *Tetrabiblos* and incorporating astrological knowledge into their medical training.

Horoscopes were taken so seriously, in fact, that Henry VIII had his horoscope read at birth and his astronomical clock is still visible at Hampton Court Palace. It was said that he would be intelligent, athletic and be someone of great renown but would also have a violent temper … sounds pretty apt, don't you think?

Tudor Treatments

Tudor medicine is such a fascinating subject that, even though this book is concentrated on the ways in which people shuffled off this mortal coil, we would feel remiss if we did not include some of the most ridiculous treatments for common inflictions.

Headache – To cure one of the pains in the head, the patient should drink a medicine made up of a mixture of lavender, sage, marjoram, roses and rue. This could actually have worked well due to the antiseptic properties of some of these herbs. Although another common remedy that involved pressing a hangman's rope to your head was probably not that effective.

Rheumatism – A variation of arthritis that affects the joints and tendons, rheumatism was treated by making the patient wear the skin of a donkey. As horrendous as this may seem, the warmth of the animal's fur may have helped alleviate the symptoms. (Other animal furs are available, though not particularly advisable and frankly good luck trying to get some of them.)

Gout – Is also a variation of arthritis that affects mainly the feet and legs (Henry VIII was a known sufferer). The treatment was to apply to the affected foot a mixture made from worms, pigs' marrow and herbs all boiled together with a red-haired dog.

Deafness – Mix the contents of the gallbladder of a hare with grease from a fox. Warm the resulting concoction and place it in the ear. This may not help with permanent deafness, but in fairness it could remove a build-up of ear wax.

Head lice – Yep, even in Tudor times these pesky little annoyances were around and just as spreadable. The cure – pour tobacco juice onto the scalp. This would have been rather effective, but not great smelling.

Jaundice – A condition where the skin or whites of the eyes turn yellow can indicate a serious liver condition. Tudor physicians would prescribe swallowing nine lice mixed with some ale each morning for seven consecutive days.

Baldness – Seems a little counterproductive but, shave the head and smear onto the scalp the grease from a fox. If that didn't work, an alternate cure was to crush a garlic bulb and rub it into the scalp and then wash the scalp in vinegar. These may have had some success, though walking around smelling of garlic, vinegar or fox may not be the best idea – but hey, you do you!

Plague – Yes that one. The treatment during the years 1485–1603 was to put herbs on a windowsill near the patient or burn leather to produce smoke as it was believed that smoke would kill off the plague.

Fainting – Get the head of a criminal, dry the skull and feed the powdered scrapings to the patient. Cover live spiders in butter and feed them to the patient (definitely not recommended). A potent mix of marrow and sweat could be used to bring a patient round to consciousness. Another remedy was fustigation – beating the poor patient with a cudgel or bat until they are well again.

Asthma – Find a dead frog and place it in the windpipe (caution, this could cause choking) or, if you are suffering particularly badly, eat live spiders. It was suggested to cover them in butter to help them slide down more easily. For those of us with severe arachnophobia, however, the asthma seems like the better option there.

Toothache – It would be common practice for someone suffering with toothache to visit a barber surgeon and have the infected tooth removed, but before enduring such agony there was a religious ritual people would try. Write on a piece of parchment, 'Jesus Christ for mercy's sake, take away this toothache' three times before saying the words aloud and then burning the paper.

Scurvy – A very common illness in pirates and seamen, thought to be due to lack of vitamins and nutrients that are hard to take on long sea voyages. The treatment was vitamin C and a lot of it. Mostly though citrus fruits such as lemons and oranges, in herbs like watercress and other leafy greens, or a drink called spruce beer which was made from boiling spruce needles, which contains a high amount of vitamin C.

This chapter really highlights the Tudor era's approach to medicine. It was a precarious balance between rudimentary knowledge and burgeoning discoveries, painting a vivid picture of a society on the cusp of medical revolution. While many of the treatments and methods seem barbaric or even daft by our modern-day standards, they were usually the best and only options available at the time for pain-riddled people, rich and poor alike.

Onthoofding van Lady Jane Grey te London, 1554. Jan Luyken (1698). (*Rijksmuseum. Etching*)

Portrait of Thomas Cromwell, Earl of Essex. Jacob Houbraken, after Hans Holbein the Younger. (1737–39). (*Rijksmuseum. Engraving*)

Portrait of Sir Thomas More. Jacob Houbraken, after Hans Holbein the Younger. (1740). (*Rijksmuseum. Engraving*)

Tudor daggers – Lynn Museum, King's Lynn. (*Carrie Ingram-Gettins (2024). Photograph*)

Tudor daggers – Lynn Museum, King's Lynn. (*Carrie Ingram-Gettins (2024). Photograph*)

Front façade of Pentney Abbey, Norfolk. Esther Wild (2024).

Front façade of Pentney Abbey down pathway, Norfolk. Esther Wild (2024).

Front façade across moat. Middleton Hall, Tamworth. Carrie Ingram-Gettins (2024). (*Courtesy of Middleton Hall Trust. Photograph*)

Side aspect of main hall. Middleton Hall, Tamworth. Carrie Ingram-Gettins (2024). (*Courtesy of Middleton Hall Trust. Photograph*)

Tudor 'barn'. Middleton Hall, Tamworth. Carrie Ingram-Gettins (2024). (*Courtesy of Middleton Hall Trust. Photograph*)

Interior hall and Willoughby Exhibit. Middleton Hall, Tamworth. Carrie Ingram-Gettins (2024). (*Courtesy of Middleton Hall Trust. Photograph*)

Henri II (1519–1559), King of France. Workshop of Francois Clouet. (*The Metropolitan Museum of Art. Painting, oil on canvas, transferred from wood*)

der werlt Blat CCLXI

ſtöꝛlichkeit. von der tödlichkeit zu der vntödlichkeit. vō der vngerügſamkeit zu der gerügſamkeit. Dem nach ha- ben ettlich nicht vnſchickerlich gemaynt das der tod nit allain nit böße ſunder aller güter ding das gröſt ſey. vnd wañ vns nw weder der tag noch die ſtunnd vnßrer außfoꝛdrung von hynnen bekant iſt ſo iſt vns haylper in dē willen gottes zeleben ſeine gepot zehalten vnd alſo alweg berayt zeſeyn vnd mit beraytung nicht zeuerzichē. dañ wir haben vil geſehen die in hoher geſuntheit des leibs bey ganntzen kreften ſich nichtz ſolcher ding beſoꝛgende mit dem tod gehling hingezugkt woꝛdē ſind. Hinwiderumb ettlich die bis zu verzweiflung d' ertzte ſiechennde ge- ſuntheit erlangtē. So nw diſe ding alle allain in gottes gewalt vñ macht ſteen ſo gepürt vns nichts anders wen zehandeln dañ das wir (als voꝛgemeld iſt) den gepotten gottes in allem vnßerm leben bis in das end gehoꝛſam ſeyen. Wir glawbon alle feſtigclich das got nach ſeiner pildnus den menſchen gemacht hab. was mag vns nw leichtlicher begegnen deñ diſen kötigen irdiſchen leichnam den ſundenſack zelaſſen vnd zu dem wider zekeren der nicht verſchmaht hat vns nach ſeiner gleichnus zemachen das der gaiſt des menſchen mit dem gaiſt gottes erfül- let als taylhaftig der gotheit vnnd irer ſeligkeit zwiſchen den engelnn vnnd chören der heilligen ewigclich leben ſöll.

'Dance of Death', leaf from *The Nuremberg Chronicle*. Michael Wolgemut (1493). (*The Metropolitan Museum of Art. Woodcut with Letterpress text*)

Erasmus of Rotterdam. Hans Holbein the Younger. (c. 1532). (*The Metropolitan Museum of Art. Painting, oil on panel*)

The Spanish Armada off the English Coast in 1558. Cornelius Claesz van Weiringen. (c. 1620–25). (*Rijksmuseum. Painting, oil on canvas*)

Scene of a Spanish Inquisition. Cooper Hewitt. (c. 1885). (*Smithsonian Design Museum. Etching*)

Field armour of King Henry VIII of England, Italian, (c. 1544). (*The Metropolitan Museum of Art. Photograph*)

Lance head for the Joust of War, German. (1475–1540). (*The Metropolitan Museum of Art. Photograph*)

Grave of Otani Yoshitsugu. *Rikita*. (2009). (*Wikicommons. Photograph*)

Statue of Gráinne Mhaol Ní Mháille, County Mayo, Ireland. Suzanne Mishyshyn. (2013). (*Wikicommons. Photograph*)

The Preaching of John Knox. George Thomas Doo, after David Wilkie. (c. 1816–25). (*Rijksmuseum. Etching*)

The Famished People after the Relief of the Siege of Leiden. Otto van Veen. (1574–1629). (*Rijksmuseum. Painting, oil on panel*)

Iohanna Seymour Regina Henri (Jane Seymour, Queen of Henry VIII). Wenceslaus Holler, after Hans Holbein the Younger. (1648). (*The Metropolitan Museum of Art. Etching*)

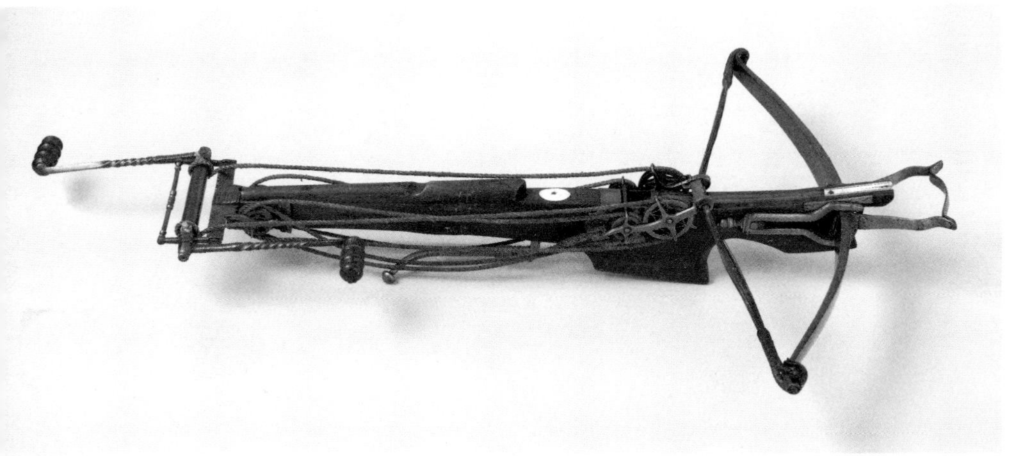

Crossbow. Anonymous. (c. 1500–1600). (*Rijksmuseum. Cutting*)

Henricus VIII Angliae Rex etc. Wenceslaus Holler, after Hans Holbein the Younger. (1647). (*The Metropolitan Museum of Art. Etching*)

Gravestone of Hans Steininger. Church of St Stephan in Braunau am Inn. (*Gerd Eichmann.* (*n.d.*) *Wikicommons. Photograph*)

Potret van Niccolo Machiavelli. Friedrich Wilhelm Bollinger, after Santi di Tito. (1818–32). (*Rijksmuseum. Sketch on paper*)

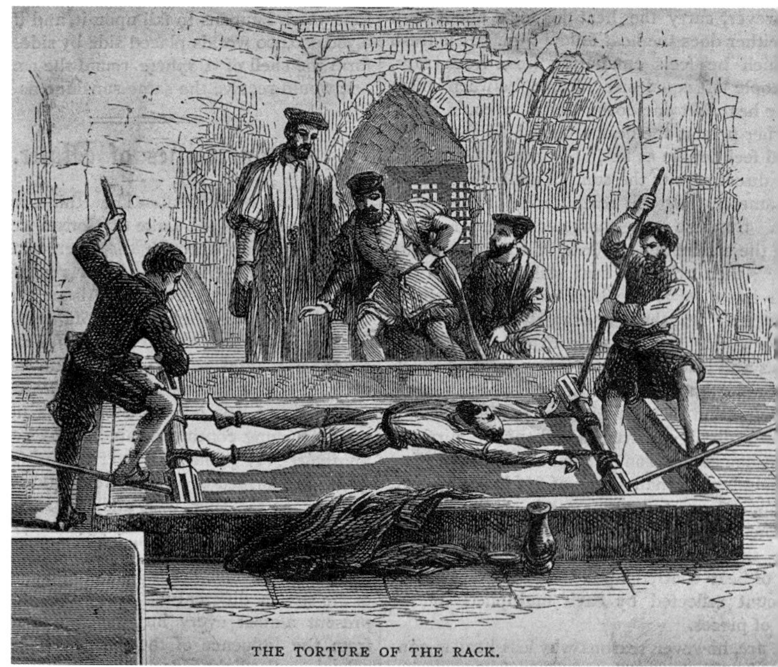

A man tortured on the rack. Unknown. (n.d.). (*The Wellcome Collection. Wood engraving*)

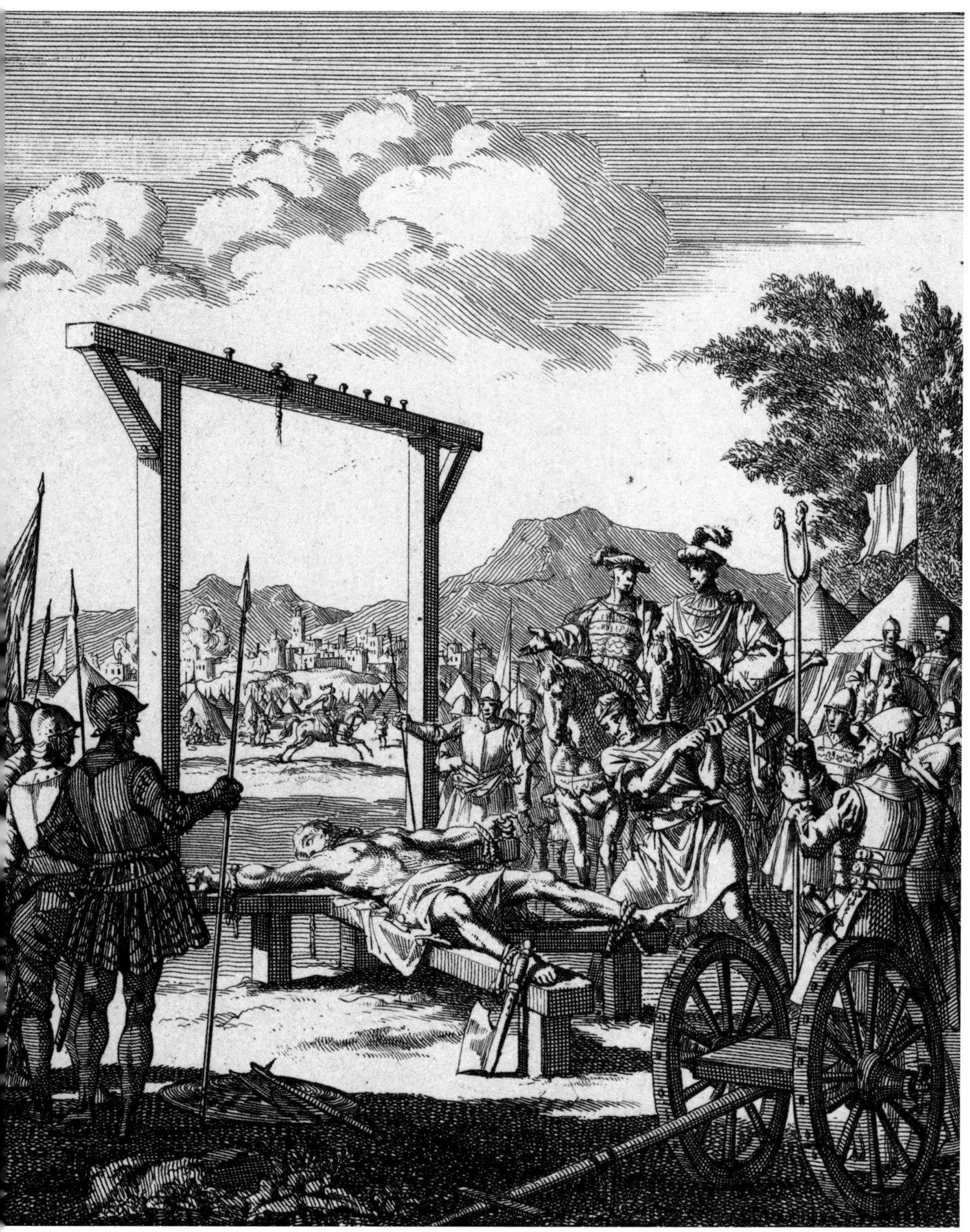

Georg Petersson, gunstelling van koning Erick, wordt geradbraakt, 1517. Jan Luyken. (1698). (*Rijksmuseum. Etching*)

Rear façade, Tudor building. St Fagan's National Museum of History. Emily Bush. (2024). (*Courtesy o*, *Amgueddfa Cymru: St Fagan's National Museum of History. Photograph*)

Chapter 7

Perils and Plagues

So far we have covered fatal misadventure through animal mishandling, questionable eating habits and dodgy feats of arms. Now it is time to turn our eyes towards some of the larger-scale issues that people, and indeed countries, faced during the sixteenth century. While we have tried to take a more light-hearted approach to the various ways that our ancestors met their demise in previous chapters, it needs to be stated that this one will have something of a more serious tone in parts, though there are some sections that are intended to cause readers to raise the eyebrow of disbelief.

We have already discussed both dysentery and ergotism, their cures and some of the more notable occurrences, so now let us look at some of the other perils and plagues that faced our ancestors in the sixteenth century. Mass migration from rural to urban areas occurred following the outbreak of the Black Death in 1348 and the sudden and drastic decline of the European population because of the pandemic.[1] This led to overcrowding in urban centres such as towns and cities. Coupled with poor hygiene, developing (and sometimes questionable) medical knowledge and the prevalence of migration through trade and pilgrimage across Europe and Asia, the conditions were a perfect storm when it came to pandemics.

Influenza

While a few historic plagues and agues are now theoretically extinct thanks to modern immune systems and medical practices, one is a persistent pestilence due to its incredible ability to continually mutate at a sometimes-alarming rate despite our best efforts. This is, of course, influenza.

Influenza, caused by the virus of the same name from the viral family *Orthomyxoviridae*, typically manifests with minor symptoms like muscle pain, sore throat, headaches, coughing and fatigue. More severe symptoms such as fever, vomiting and diarrhoea can also occur in some cases and can greatly exacerbate underlying conditions such as asthma or pre-existing cardiovascular concerns. In such cases, even in modern times, a case of influenza can sometimes prove fatal.

Influenza is commonly categorised into four types named A through to D, with Influenza A (*Alphainfluenzavirus*) being the variant most believed to have been prevalent in the sixteenth century, though this is a best guess based on the symptoms described in contemporary sources. This is the variant widespread in birds and mammals, including humans. Influenza B and C are found primarily in humans and are responsible for the seasonal epidemics that have become a regular part of modern life. We feel we can safely assume most of our readers will likely have come into contact with 'the flu' at some point in their lives – we most certainly have and even when mild it is never a pleasant experience. Transmission of influenza occurs in humans through respiratory droplets (i.e. coughing and sneezing) in the main, however transmission can also occur through contact with contaminated surfaces.

While there have been an estimated fourteen severe pandemic-level outbreaks of influenza since the start of the 1500s,[2] this century is our focus. The first, most notable outbreak was that of 1510, starting in Sicily where the disease was known as coccolucio due to the cap worn by the sick covering their heads. It is believed to have originated from the island of Malta, travelling over to Sicily and from there it spread across the Mediterranean and then north to modern-day Germany and the Baltic nations. Eventually all Europe was covered and while the death rate is unknown, it is believed to have been less than 1 per cent of those who contracted the disease.

Influenza struck again in 1557 where a strain emerged in Asia, then spreading across Africa and Europe and even to the Americas throughout 1557 to 1559. Europe was already struggling with rival outbreaks such as plague and smallpox so immune systems were questionable and therefore perfectly weakened for influenza. It is estimated that around 2.5 to 5 million people succumbed to the 1557 pandemic, approximately 10 per cent of those infected. With a global population at the time estimated to be between 430 to 500 million, therefore approximately 10 per cent of the upper estimate of the global population fell ill, with 10 per cent of those cases being fatal.

While the disease itself and underlying health concerns due to already depressed immune systems may have been the combined causes for the deaths that occurred in the 1510 and 1557 influenza pandemics, we cannot forget that many may have also died from the attempts to cure them. The belief in the balance of the humours (see our chapter 'Kill or Cure') led to treatments such as purging and bloodletting as a way of cleansing the body of the disease and bringing the fluids in the body back into balance and thereby curing the patient. Bloodletting was done either with leeches, or through the more simplistic method of opening small wounds in strategic areas of the patient's body and allowing the blood to flow out for a monitored period. You would likely not be surprised to know that infection was not really a thing at the time – sure it was roughly known about – but it was not high on the list of medical priorities.[3]

Purging would involve the use of emetics such as mustard seeds to induce vomiting, or purgatives such as rhubarb or senna leaves which have laxative effects. Enemas were also used in cases where the patient may have been deemed too weak to clear their own bowels without assistance. In some cases, these treatments may have worked but we highly doubt that any person suffering with the flu would welcome something stuffed up their rectum as a cure, although we admit it may have served as a distraction, albeit an unpleasant one, from some of the other symptoms that patients were experiencing. That said, it would have been a small mercy at best if this then went on to cause your death instead of the flu itself. At the very least it would have made one heck of a mess.

Due to the ability to live with and, in most cases, fully recover from influenza in the modern day, it is often overlooked as a serious illness of the past. It lacks the glamour (if that is the right word) of things like the plague but was no less important and concerning to those who suffered from it at the time, least of all because of the ever-present threat of the local physician. Perhaps that is why several people died falling from apple trees – an apple a day keeps the doctor away, after all, though best to leave the tree-climbing to the experts.

Leprosy

Leprosy has a long and troublesome history as a disease, with mentions in the Bible and notable cases such as that of Baldwin IV of Jerusalem in the twelfth century. It is unclear when or where leprosy first originated and a lot of study has gone into the origins and causes of the disease, as well as its treatment. From the bacteria *Mycobacterium leprae* it causes degenerative damage to much of the facial organs and tissue as well as extensive nerve damage, skin discolouration and ulceration across the body. The nerve damage can result in unnoticed injury to the infected person which could lead to further, more serious infections as well as permanent physical deformity.

While leprosy was prevalent during earlier centuries in Europe, by the sixteenth century it had reached a peak and was beginning to decline, though nobody is entirely sure why. It could be due to a gradual development of immunity in the uninfected population, and studies are ongoing to try and understand more about this debilitating disease and why it started to vanish. The bacteria responsible was identified in 1873 by Norwegian physician Gerhard Hansen, which is where the disease gets its more modern, alternative name – Hansen's Disease.

Treatments for leprosy in the sixteenth century seem to have loaned themselves more to care and relief from the symptoms rather than an attempt to cure. From the eleventh century special hospitals called leprosaria were used to house and care for the infected where they could live away from society but still have a decent quality of life in what were effectively small, mostly self-sustaining communities. Greater isolation was introduced in the aftermath of the Black Death as fear over contagion and further pandemics spread; however, the use of the leprosaria declined with the cases of the disease and eventually the hospitals were repurposed for other medical needs.

Otani Yoshitsugu

As a figure in Japanese history and folklore, Otani Yoshitsugu looms large, even featuring in the modern video game *Nioh* as a powerful 'boss' to conquer in a mission named after his actual final battle, as well as having a character in the popular HBO series *Shōgun* based on him. Born in 1565, he experienced firsthand the unification of Japan under daimyō Toyotomi Hideyoshi. He rose to become lord of Tsuruga[4] and oversaw an increase in the prosperity of that city. He distinguished himself as a brilliant military strategist and was by all accounts a great asset to Hideyoshi, even engaging directly in battle on the front lines and proving an effective warrior.

It is during a military engagement aimed at putting down an uprising in Osaka in 1586 that Yoshitsugu is said to have become infected with leprosy.[5] This did not seem to initially impact his military career, and he continued to support Hideyoshi and his armies towards several notable victories. Accounts then differ as to how quickly his illness progresses through the following years, which would make sense as this was a powerful warlord and effective military tactician so there needed to be an element of legend around him to not undermine him. What is clear is that, despite whatever level of physical debilitation his illness may have caused him from time to time or through gradual decline, he remained a prominent figure up to and past the death of his leader, Hideyoshi.

We do know from records that Yoshitsugu was blind by around 1599 as he attended a meeting with fellow and then later rival warlord Ishido Mistunari at his base of Sawayama Castle, north-east of his home in Tsuruga. Shortly after this meeting, despite initially planning to ally himself with soon-to-be Shogun Tokugawa Ieyasu, Yoshitsugu defected to the rival army.[6] Nobody is really sure why he did this and, again, a number of stories have grown up around the reasons, all worth reading into as the politics of this era in Japanese history are as fascinating as they are complex. His final battle was at Sekigahara and Yoshitsugu was present, though due to his advanced illness he was unable to directly engage and instead controlled movements from afar, receiving updates on how things were progressing from his closest retainers.

Despite the best efforts of Yoshitsugu and his men, the battle did not go to plan and due to a defection of troops led by one Kobayakawa Hideaki, as well as the loss of many of his own troops, Yoshitsugu was told that the battle was lost. In response, and likely bearing in mind the advanced state of his illness, Yoshitsugu chose to preserve his honour in the best way he could and committed the ritualistic suicide form *seppuku* involving self-inflicted disembowelment followed by beheading, just to make sure. It is said that Yoshitsugu's last wish to his faithful retainer was that his head be safely removed and protected away from his body. Otani Yoshitsugu is buried beneath a stone monument, next to a grave that is believed to be that of his son Otani Yoshikatsu, who also honourably took his own life in the wake of the defeat at Sekigahara. Although it wasn't the leprosy that killed Yoshitsugu, he is still worthy of being included in this book to show that people in this century lived with, and often lived despite, this debilitating illness. Yoshitsugu not only rose to legendary status in his own lifetime, but a cursory online search will show that the man, as well as his achievements and tactical skill, are still very much alive in popular culture.

Smallpox – the Red Plague

In our chapter 'Kill or Cure' we discussed the treatments used when Elizabeth I of England fell ill, leading to her remarkable yet scarring recovery. However, the disease that nearly claimed her was not just rampant in her kingdom: it killed nearly half the population of the continent. This was, of course, smallpox, caused by the variola major of the viral family Poxviridae and one of a family of pox viruses that still exist today, even if this particular strain was classed as eradicated in 1980.

Evidence of smallpox has been found in remains that date as far back as the seventh century in Northern Europe and is characterised by the emergence of fever, headaches and back pain that then progresses into the characteristic pustules across the skin that gave the variants their name – pockmarks or pox. Those who survived the disease could expect to be heavily scarred or even blinded because of it, though it is believed as much as 30 per cent of victims did not survive, with the young and elderly being almost guaranteed not to.

Smallpox in the Americas

Smallpox continued its rampant spread across Europe in the sixteenth century and, as the European population spread outwards from the continent engaging in both trade and colonisation, they brought their diseases with them, sometimes by accident and other times not so much.

Portuguese settlers had already brought smallpox to parts of western Africa in the fifteenth century and now it was the turn of the Americas. In 1519 Hernán Cortés[7] arrived on the shores of what is now Mexico with the goal of exploring the area and subduing the native population, whom we know today as the Aztecs.[8] It took less than two years for Cortés and his men to topple the Aztec empire but the main element of destruction was the diseases that the Spaniards brought with them for which the native population had no natural immunity. Contemporary sources including from victims and members of Cortés's retinue tell of how the population of the capital of the Aztec empire, Tenochtitlan, was reduced by nearly half in a year.

The disease itself seriously dented the population, with knock-on effects of disease from the large number of dead remaining unburied and the continued attacks from the Spanish and their native allies adding to the growing list of concerns. A similar fate would befall the native Mayan and Incan populations, with the latter losing most of their population to the disease, as well as their emperor, which led to massive civil unrest.[9] A later, additional epidemic of salmonella followed closely on the heels of smallpox, causing further tragedy though it is not confirmed that this came over with the invaders.

To give a more statistical slant on what happened, it is estimated that up to eight million people died in Mexico alone during 1519 and 1520, with a further epidemic in Chile in 1561 claiming upwards of 130,000 lives. With weakened immune systems, the population of Mexico then fell victim to what has become known as the Cocoliztli epidemic of salmonella in 1545 lasting around forty years and claiming the lives of nearly 80 per cent of the native population at the time.

Tuberculosis – Consumption

Tuberculosis, or TB as it is more colloquially known, is a disease that is possibly one of the oldest pathogen companions to humanity, with evidence found in skeletons as far back as 5000 BCE and the existence of the bacteria even further back than that in other forms. Caused by the bacterial strain *Mycobacterium tuberculosis*, symptoms of this highly contagious disease include fever, significant weight loss, persistent fatigue, painful swelling in the joints and lymph nodes and the most common symptom of all, a persistent cough that often involved haemoptysis or the coughing up of blood. A common name for the disease prior to the bacterium being identified was consumption considering how it effectively consumed the internal organs before death. It does seem that a lot of the diseases rampant in the sixteenth century presented flu-like symptoms, including the flu itself, so misdiagnosis and mistreatment would hardly be a shock.

In the Middle Ages through to the Renaissance period a suspected variant of TB characterised by excessive swelling of the lymph nodes,[10] known as scrofula, emerged with a rather unusual treatment. It was called the 'King's Evil', and it was believed that a single touch from the monarch could cure it. Coins and charms that the monarch had touched were passed out among the infected in the hopes that these trinkets had become imbued with their divine healing power. This was common practice until the reign of George I in England in 1714, though in France it continued for a further century. We don't know about you, but queueing for hours to see the king of England even with a minor headache would be a bit much, let alone a potentially fatal bacterial infection!

Lucrezia de' Medici

Known as the Duchess of Ferrara, Lucrezia de' Medici was the daughter of Cosimo I de' Medici and part of the powerful Italian Medici family, a colourful bunch who loom large in the history of Renaissance Europe, not least of all on the banking scene. Her marriage to Alfonso d'Este in 1558 was part of peace negotiations between Ercole II d'Este, Duke of Ferrara (Northern Italy), and King Philip II of Spain, when Lucrezia was aged only 13.

The marriage was not a happy one and Lucrezia spent the first part of it at the Palazzo Pitti, isolated from her husband until the death of Ercole II in 1559 when she and her husband became the new Duke and Duchess of Ferrara. When Lucrezia was finally transported to her duchy, however, she was already quite unwell with a fever, consistent weight loss, a regular nosebleed and a persistent cough. On 21 April 1561, three years into the marriage and aged only 16, Lucrezia died. An autopsy was carried out due to suspected poisoning and the ruling was given as 'putrid fever', a diagnosis based of the idea of the balance of the humours.

Tudor TB

Consumption was rife in the Tudor court of England, and it is known to have impacted at least five major members of the royal family or close associates, if not more, which would lean towards a lack of hereditary immunity in the family.

Henry VII is the first of these, with his death in 1509 following an emotionally and politically turbulent time for him with the death of his wife Elizabeth of York (see the section below on puerperal fever), his son Arthur (see the section below on sweating sickness) and a somewhat fractious relationship with his remaining son and heir, the soon-to-be Henry VIII. His death was kept secret for two days so that news could reach the young prince of what had happened and that preparations could begin for a handover of power. That part, at least, went more smoothly than some other aspects of the next king's reign.

Consumption seemed to bypass Henry VIII, though he had his fair share of medical difficulty later in life owing to a leg injury and a suspected concurrent head injury from a particularly unfortunate jousting accident. One of his mistresses, Elizabeth 'Bessie' Blount, however, became increasingly ill and died of what is commonly believed to have been consumption in mid-1540, outliving the son she had by Henry VIII, known as Henry Fitzroy, Duke of Richmond, who died aged 17 on 23 July 1536 of consumption.

King Edward VI, Henry's legitimate son and half-brother of Henry Fitzroy by the king's third wife Jane Seymour (for her fate see below section on puerperal fever), died aged 15 on 6 July 1553 of consumption following a rapidly advancing six-month illness and leaving behind a slight succession crisis that ended in one queen being beheaded after the shortest reign in English history, and the other earning the moniker of 'Bloody Mary'. The Tudors were not known for their straightforward reigns, you see.

Finally, Lady Jane Seymour (no not that one, a different one), first cousin to King Edward VI through his uncle Edward Seymour, 1st Duke of Somerset, died in 1561 aged 20 of consumption. You can probably tell by now that both the wider and nuclear Tudor family were either very sickly as a group, or very, very unlucky.

Plague

This is the big one, the disease that gets a lot of near-celebrity attention for all the wrong reasons and which put rats on the deadliest creatures list as arguably the animal with the highest body count in human history. When people generically refer to the plague, this traditionally means either the Black Death of 1346 or the Great Plague (London 1665 or Vienna 1679). The bubonic plague, however, is a much wider-ranging disease with multiple pandemics that, although treatable, is still known to resurface today.

Caused by the bacteria *Yersinia pestis*, the bubonic plague is only one of three plagues associated with this particular bacterial strain. It is characterised by initial flu-like symptoms (yet again) and a swelling of the lymph nodes which result in the characteristic buboes that give the plague variety its name. The first known pandemic-level outbreak is the Justinian Plague that struck in 541 CE and claimed up to 100 million victims. Given the estimated global population at the time, this would have been a devastating number and is cited as the beginning of the First Pandemic, while the Second Pandemic began with the Black Death in 1346 which wiped out around 60 per cent of the population of Europe and just over 30 per cent of the population of the Middle East at the time.

The second plague pandemic was prevalent throughout the sixteenth century, surfacing in London in 1563 and spreading across Europe thanks to improved trade links and migration traffic. As with influenza, purging and bloodletting were regular treatments, as well as lancing the buboes which involved using an instrument like a poker, heated to press against the buboes in the hope that this would kill off the infection in the area. By the time the infected person had reached the stage where lancing was needed, the pain involved in lancing would likely have been the least of their concerns.

Some of the plague treatments surprisingly enough made sense, such as cleaning down the house of an infected person with a mixture including chloride of lime, a derivative of which is used in modern swimming pools so it does have disinfectant properties and would therefore have gone some way towards helping. So too would the action that the majority of the twenty-first century world is now aware of – quarantine.[11] The Plague Orders set out by the Privy Council in 1579 confirmed that the quarantine period should be six weeks and should be for both the infected and any seemingly healthy members of the household. While this might be effective in stopping the spread of the illness to other houses, it might sadly condemn members of the household who otherwise might not have caught the plague. Food was provided, but outsiders were prevented from entering the infected household and in some cases, guards were posted to make sure that this did not happen. Some people did speak out against the Plague Orders, most notably in 1603 when the preacher Henoch Clapham was very vocal in condemning them, claiming that the plague was the judgement of God. Not surprisingly, he was arrested and locked away as quickly as possible to prevent him from doing further harm.

Herbal remedies and poultices[12] were also used on both the patient and the person treating them as it was believed that the plague could spread through inhaling 'bad air' or miasma. Some herbs would have helped to an extent, however they would not necessarily have helped prevent the spread, neither would prayers or religious rituals, though the psychological impact cannot be discounted. The popular image of the plague doctor emerges during the sixteenth and seventeenth centuries. The presence of these sometimes woefully unqualified plague doctors in their Hazmat-type suits would have frightened as well as comforted, as it would have been known what they were there for, with the characteristic beaked mask being used to hold strong-smelling herbs and spices, called posies. Having seen some examples of the suits, we understand why some people would rather have taken their chances with the herbs.

Sweating Sickness

Sweating sickness was a peculiar illness, the origins of which remain a mystery, mostly as it appears to have been confined predominantly to England during the sixteenth century with only a brief later entrance into continental Europe. Many causes have been offered for the epidemic, not least of all the conquest of Henry VII and his Lancastrian forces over Richard III to close out the conflict known as the Wars of the Roses, involving the use of French mercenary forces. Many believed that the sweating sickness was a judgement on the people for the deposition of a king in battle. While it is a convenient addition to the narrative, it is highly unlikely that bacteria and viruses take much note of the legitimacy of kings.

In a letter to the personal physician to Cardinal Wolsey,[13] Dutch philosopher Erasmus gives recommendations on how properties could be constructed to help with the prevention of the disease by having rooms with exposed walls on at least three sides of the building and more windows to allow for proper ventilation. This is a contrast to the method used to treat the illness in many cases that involved closing the windows and curtains to prevent the introduction of bad air from outside and lighting a fire in the room where the infected was placed (if this could be afforded) to ensure they were not cold at any point. In the case of a disease where sweating and dehydration were the main symptoms, perhaps intense heat was not the best option for a cure.

One of the most notable cases of sweating sickness was that of Arthur, Prince of Wales, son of Henry VII of England and first husband of Catherine of Aragon. At his seat of Ludlow Castle along the Welsh and English border, both Arthur and Catherine fell ill during an outbreak of sweating sickness at the end of March 1502. Catherine recovered; however, Arthur died on 2 April 1502, barely five months into married life and just six months shy of his sixteenth birthday. His death led to his younger brother becoming heir to the throne and eventually being crowned King Henry VIII. How different would the future of England have looked had Arthur survived?

Henry VIII was to have yet another brush with sweating sickness when an outbreak started in June 1528. Henry was known to be paranoid of falling ill, which is understandable because he had no legitimate surviving male heir at this point and that his death would spell the end of a dynasty that had begun only forty-three years prior. He fled the overcrowded court in London and did not remain in one place for long, taking his personal physician with him.

Meanwhile the woman he was then courting, Anne Boleyn, fled to Hever Castle, the Boleyn family home in Kent, to quarantine through the outbreak. The disease came to her doorstep anyway and she became ill. Fearing for her, Henry sent William Butts, his second-best physician (the best had to remain with the king, of course) to tend to her. Anne would go on to recover, but there was still a heavy death toll, including Sir William Carey, her sister Mary's husband as well as Elizabeth Wyckes, wife of Thomas Cromwell and two of their children, Anne and Grace. The illness would again hit the Cromwell household when, in 1551, eleven years after Cromwell's execution, his remaining child Gregory also succumbed aged 31.

Puerperal Fever

In a more sombre tone than other deaths, we turn now to puerperal fever. Also known as childbed fever, this is more of a peril than a plague but is one that women throughout human history have risked as part of the natural course of childbirth, even to this day. Puerperal fever is a form of postpartum infection located in the uterus following the removal of a child either through birth or abortion/miscarriage. The hygiene level of the procedure and surroundings undertaken during the birth often contributed to the likelihood of infection and several potential organisms responsible have since been identified, however this knowledge was not available at the time. While this is something that would have affected all women regardless of class, the examples we have below are royal ones, as we have confirmed records of these deaths.

Elizabeth of York

Queen of England, wife to Henry VII and mother to Henry VIII, Elizabeth of York was the descendant of the royal house of York and her marriage was one of the unifying components that ended the Wars of the Roses. By all accounts the marriage between Elizabeth and Henry was a happy one and together they produced seven children, with four surviving to adulthood (though we have already seen the fate of one of those four, Prince Arthur, in our section on sweating sickness above). It was her final child Katherine, that proved fatal for Elizabeth. On 2 February 1503 Elizabeth gave birth to a stillborn daughter, Katherine. Following the birth Elizabeth became ill with her condition worsening until on 11 February 1503, incidentally her thirty-seventh birthday, she succumbed to childbed fever and died, her death sending her husband Henry into deep grief whereby he secluded himself from everyone but his mother Margaret Beaufort for several days. Peurperal fever would be a condition that would go on to haunt her youngest son Henry VIII.

Jane Seymour

Jane Seymour was the third wife of Henry VIII and the one next to whom he is buried at the Chapel of St George in Windsor Castle. In a tragic echo of his mother's death, the loss of his wife sent Henry VIII into a deep depression, though the child produced did survive the birth.

Jane was the daughter of Sir John Seymour and occupied the position of maid-of-honour (a junior version of a lady-in-waiting) to Catherine of Aragon, the first wife of Henry VIII. When the marriage between Henry and Catherine ended and he married Anne Boleyn, Jane and her sister Elizabeth entered the service of the new queen.

Around the time of Anne Boleyn's downfall, Henry began to show an interest in Jane and on 20 May 1536, the day after Anne Boleyn's execution, they were betrothed and then subsequently married on 30 May 1536. While proclaimed queen, an outbreak of plague in London incidentally prevented her from having an actual coronation. In 1537 Jane fell pregnant with the future King Edward VI, giving birth to him on 12 October 1537 at Hampton Court Palace. It is suspected that Edward may have been in the breech position; simply put, he was facing the wrong way for birth, which caused complications and a very difficult labour for Jane. In addition to the usual complement of highly experienced midwives, Henry also ordered a handful of male physicians to attend to the queen, an unusual request as childbirth at that time was the domain of women and men were seldom allowed in the birthing room. It has been queried as to whether their presence contributed to greater difficulties during and after the birth. While she attended Edward's christening on 15 October 1537, reports indicate that the queen was very unwell at this point.

On 24 October 1537 Jane Seymour died at Hampton Court Palace. Accounts are conflicting as to whether it was directly because of puerperal fever or if there were other complications such as a retained placenta or further infections. Either way, her death emotionally devastated Henry VIII, though the pressure of succession and securing his kingdom would eventually lead to him looking for a fourth wife, and a fifth, and eventually a sixth – we assume most of you know how that particular story goes, it's a fairly popular and often problematic aspect of his reign.

Catherine Parr

Needless to say, the fourth and even fifth wives did not really work out for Henry VIII and eventually he married his sixth and final wife Catherine Parr, already twice widowed herself by the time of their marriage, having formerly been wed to Sir Edward Burgh (died 1533) and John Neville, 3rd Baron Latimer (died 1543).

Parr's marriage to Henry was initially content but this was not to last, with religious turmoil ongoing in the country being a cause for a warrant for her arrest being drawn up in 1546. Catherine, unlike two of her predecessors Anne Boleyn and Catherine Howard, was lucky and through her quick thinking and eloquence was able to reconcile with Henry VIII and prevent her being sentenced, not to mention the children's rhyme of 'divorce, beheaded, died, divorced, beheaded, survived' having to be changed for generations to come.

Following the death of Henry VIII in 1547, the now Queen Dowager Catherine remarried Thomas Seymour (incidentally the brother of Jane Seymour). Parr fell pregnant in 1548 but on 5 September 1548 she died from complications in childbirth, attributed to puerperal fever. Her daughter Mary Seymour would survive the loss of her mother and her father's execution for treason in 1549, however she seems to disappear from record after the age of 2, so it is unknown if she survived into adulthood.

Syphilis

An often, though not exclusively, sexually transmitted disease, the treatments proposed for syphilis were as much of a peril to sufferers as the plague itself.

Some of the earliest known cases of syphilis originate from the end of the fifteenth century when it appeared in French troops during the siege of Naples in 1495 and in less than a year it had spread across Europe. Symptoms included aches, fevers and sores that could leave a person permanently disfigured if they survived.

Known initially as *morbus gallicus* (the 'French Disease'), the term syphilis would gain popularity in later centuries following a description of the disease in the story of syphilis, of an unfortunate who angered the Greco-Roman god Apollo and was punished for this with a disfiguring disease. The story poem is attributed to Italian physician Girolamo Francastoro and is called *Syphilis sive morbus Gallicus*, or 'Syphilis or the French Disease'. It is unlikely that the French were overly pleased with the name.

Venereal syphilis is caused by the bacterium *Treponema pallidum* and starts with the growth of lesions in the genital region which are largely initially painless, though probably quite awkward. Other symptoms then appear including those listed above, but can fade just as quickly as they appear, though the infection itself remains and symptoms can resurface. The infection remains transmissible for a long time after the initial symptoms subside, so even if you are feeling fine, it would probably be risky jumping back into action.

The most dangerous stage is known as tertiary syphilis and is responsible for most of the lasting damage. The lesions are worse in this stage and can impact the internal organs as well as the skin, and a form of dementia can develop as damage to the brain and nervous system occurs. Treatments, however, could exacerbate the condition and could often end up being fatal in their own right. The continued use of such treatments speak to the desperation and suffering of those who contracted the disease in seeking any potential cure.

Initially concoctions using resin from the guaiacum plant were used; however, as this is a form of treatment known as 'purging', causing the patient to suffer vomiting or diarrhoea on top of their other symptoms, it was widely considered that perhaps this was not the best course of treatment. What they came up with, however, was much more questionable and the phrase 'one night with Venus, a lifetime with Mercury' may give a clue as to what this treatment was.

Mercury was already an existing remedy prescribed for some diseases, including leprosy. This would be used in a skin ointment, in elixir form, as an injection or even inhaled as a vapour in specially designated mercury steam rooms. There is some evidence that mercury did help and that would have increased its widespread usage. However, mercury is a heavy metal and as such is highly toxic, causing internal organ failure, tooth loss, nerve damage and skin ulcers.

One of the most recognisable side effects of Mercury poisoning, however, was the effect it would have on the mind of the person being treated. *Erethismus mecurialis*, known also as Mad Hatter Syndrome, is a neurological disorder resulting from prolonged exposure to mercury. It earned its nickname as it was allegedly used by hatters in the creation of varieties of top hats to help them hold their shape. The consistent use and exposure would eventually cause behavioural changes including but not limited to depression, delirium and memory loss. This is where the phrase 'mad as a hatter' originated and indeed the character of the Mad Hatter from Lewis Caroll's novel *Alice's Adventures in Wonderland* is a literary portrayal of this very condition.

Mercury poisoning was the risk that one ran for the potential relief from and treatment of syphilis, though in the long term it would have done more harm than good. This is just one of many bizarre treatments that, although they may have appeared miraculously to work some of the times, certainly have us questioning how we have remained the dominant species on this planet for as long as we have. Has this piqued your curiosity? Good, as we have more to say on this in our chapter 'Kill or Cure'.

Fatal but Not Illness

As well as those who either survived or succumbed, there are those who struggled with their respective illness and showed little sign of recovery, though it was not the illness itself that took them in the end. This is the case with Henry Kente, oddly enough of Kent, who in 1512 had been suffering from a debilitating illness for several days and was so convinced of his impending death that he had been given the last rites by the local priest and was actively preparing himself for the end. As the days passed and his condition showed no signs of improving or worsening, Kente decided to take himself out to get some air one night when sleep refused to come, taking care not to wake the people who had been looking after him. He went out from his house and kept walking until eventually he found himself falling into a pit filled with water. The illness had sapped his strength and so he was unable to pull himself out and he drowned. The sad thought is that he very well may have gone on to make a steady recovery had he not gone for that late night walk. A similar fate befell John Eke of Staffordshire in 1516 when he had a break in his fever and decided to go for a walk, falling into the nearby River Blithe where he was found a few hours later by his brother Richard.

As you may have spotted from the above plagues, several of the symptoms were consistent with what we would think of as a bad cold or flu, at least at first. Initial issues such as coughing, fatigue, muscle ache and fever would have people scrambling to establish what the disease was, which they would not know until more definitive symptoms appeared. This gave rise to generalised umbrella terms such as quotidian fever,[14] which refers to a type of fever that could happen on its own due to underlying health conditions, but also be linked to the likes of malaria or tuberculosis, even manifesting as a side effect to some medications prescribed. It was this type of fever that Dorothy Cawthorn of Lincolnshire was suffering from in October 1559. The illness severely dehydrated her but also caused a form of delirium that may have led to her not fully understanding her actions. That is why, in the early hours of 20 October, Dorothy rose from her bed and, walking to the kitchen of the house where she worked and lived, she is said to have broken through the wall, going out through the hole into the garden beyond where she promptly fell into a pit and drowned. We can only imagine what the owner of the house, one Mary Evers, would have thought when she awoke the next morning to find her servant gone and a Dorothy-shaped hole in the kitchen wall.

Looking back through coroner's inquest reports from the sixteenth century it appears that there was a fair correlation between people with a fever and falling into nearby water courses. It might have stopped their suffering but can't have been a good thing for the local water supplies.

Chapter 8

Ruthless Religion

Across Europe the sixteenth century was a time of turmoil and religious upheaval, with various sects of Christianity battling it out for supremacy following the onset of the Protestant Reformation in 1517. Religion in England alone began from the reign of Henry VIII to operate on something of a pendulum between Catholicism and Protestantism, beginning with the establishment of the Church of England and continuing in parts of the United Kingdom to this day.

For those unwilling to recant and convert to what was deemed the true religion at the time, a regime of torture or even execution for heresy was prescribed, with many notable figures falling foul of both, as well as everyday members of society.

Sir Thomas More

Possibly one of the most influential political figures of his time, Thomas More was a trusted friend and advisor to Henry VIII throughout his youth and the early part of his reign. More was a highly educated man and in his role as Lord Chancellor presided over several appeals cases in the Star Chamber, as well as overseeing legal matters in the royal household. When the Protestant Reformation began to gain ground in Europe, More became an outspoken advocate for the sanctity of the Catholic Church in the face of what he saw as heresy.[1] However, religious dissent had already reached the English court, as Henry VIII used the arguments presented around the king being God's true representative on Earth instead of the pope as part of his seeking an annulment from first wife Catherine of Aragon to marry second wife Anne Boleyn. We admit that the whole situation surrounding Henry VIII, his second marriage to Anne Boleyn and his break from the

Catholic Church in Rome is far more nuanced than that simple sentence suggests, however for the sake of brevity, it sums it up well enough for our purposes here.

More remained a steadfast Papist (supporter of the pope and the Catholicism) and refused to put his signature to a letter asking the pope to grant the annulment of the king's first marriage. When a royal decree was issued in 1531 requiring members of the clergy to recognise the king as the Supreme Head of the Church in England, More also refused to sign this.[2] He shortly thereafter resigned from his position as chancellor and a rift emerged in his once-close friendship with the king.

Multiple charges were brought against More in the following years, with attempted allegations of treason, however his prudent nature and reputation for strong moral integrity led to these charges being dropped. However, his refusal to sign yet another decree, the Oath of Succession in 1534 which aimed to confirm Anne Boleyn as the rightful queen and her children with the king as the legitimate heirs to the throne, as well as the buried clause of repudiating the authority of the pope, finally sealed his fate and he was imprisoned in the Tower of London.

Despite multiple pleas and pressures, More refused to admit his guilt or to sign the oath. His trial was held on 1 July 1535, with three of the presiding judges being Thomas Howard, 3rd Duke of Norfolk and the uncle of Anne Boleyn, her father Thomas Boleyn and her brother George Boleyn. With such a jury there was little hope of things going in More's favour, despite testifying on his own behalf that he did not explicitly deny that Henry VIII was the Supreme Head of the Church. A testament from Richard Rich was provided that conveniently contradicted this and despite More trying to refute the validity of the new evidence, he was found guilty after only fifteen minutes of deliberation and sentenced to the usual punishment for treason: being hanged, drawn and quartered.

The king, in a last show of affection towards his old friend and mentor, commuted the sentence to decapitation and on 6 July 1535 Thomas More was beheaded at the scaffold on Tower Hill, London, with his severed head then being taken and displayed on a spike over London Bridge for a month as was standard practice as a deterrent to others. His body lies in a grave at the chapel of St Peter ad Vincula within the Tower of London, not far from Anne Boleyn as it happens, while his head is reported to either rest with his family in Canterbury, or in a tomb in Chelsea Old Church.

Deadly Pilgrimage

While several people chose to speak out against the change in religion and held to their values despite the inherent danger, some chose to make their concerns known by more visible means. Riots and uprisings occurred and were just as swiftly put down, but one gained a fair bit of momentum before finally being ended. This uprising began in October 1536 and thanks to a lot of surviving documentation about this event, we know a good deal about what happened from both sides.

Initially the uprising started in Louth in Lincolnshire on 2 October 1536 to protest the dissolution of religious houses there.[3] This uprising was alarming to the powers immediately surrounding the throne at the time, as nobles were seen to join in with the general discontent as well as the peasants, that made this a legitimate and concerning threat. An estimated total of around 40,000 marched on Lincoln in a surprisingly organised manner and were met with welcome by the city, but Henry VIII had already started counteraction. Charles Brandon, the Duke of Suffolk, was dispatched with a force to put down the rebellion and at word of this, a number of the higher-ranking supporters sought to withdraw themselves from the rebellion, potentially realising at this point that they had too much to lose by opposing the king in a battle they were very unlikely to win. The rebels that remained were given the opportunity to leave peacefully in the knowledge that their grievances would be brought to the king for consideration, and many took Suffolk up on this, dispersing quickly. Those who chose to remain in Lincoln to oppose the king's men paid the ultimate price as Henry VIII was very keen to offer no mercy to those who sought to oppose the crown in open rebellion – to be lenient with that sort of behaviour was to risk setting a dangerous precedent and Henry was a lot of things but he was far from being a fool.

With the rebellion in Lincoln dealt with, Henry VIII's eye turned north to Yorkshire where another uprising was forming that would prove to be a far bigger danger to him. The rebels had set up base in the city of York and had nominated for their leader the prominent lawyer Robert Aske. Aske was a highly educated man and instilled strict principles in his followers, ensuring that their behaviour met a certain standard so that they could not be classed as a mob. It was Aske's belief that the king was not at fault over the Reformation, rather it was the work of advisors that he described as evil influences on an otherwise good and just man. If the advisors could be removed and the king reasoned with, Aske felt that Henry VIII could then be persuaded to return the country to the companionship of Rome and stop the shameful treatment of the religious houses and his fellow Catholics. To set it apart from a simple rebellion, Aske coined the name the Pilgrimage of Grace for what he and his followers were planning to do, emphasising both the hope for a peaceful resolution as well as the religious ideals underpinning their cause.

Aske was able to gather an army of around 30,000 to his cause and on 21 October 1536 they took Pontefract Castle in Yorkshire without bloodshed. Seeing this for the true threat that it posed, Henry VIII ordered the combined powers of the dukes of Suffolk and Norfolk as well as the Earl of Shrewsbury north to respond. The problem was that, despite being sent by the king, the army was woefully underprepared. Their supplies and equipment were of a poorer quality than those of the Pilgrims and they were mostly men from the land such as farmers with limited knowledge of battle, not to mention the fact that they were also greatly outnumbered. On the other hand, many of the Pilgrims were accustomed to fighting due to generations of border skirmishes with the Scots along the north of England.[4]

Robert Aske maintained that he did not want to initiate a conflict; his goal was peaceful persuasion, but that force would be used if no other choice was given. The Duke of Norfolk seems to have provided him with a choice, however, meeting Aske at the site of Doncaster Bridge on 27 October to start negotiations. Norfolk persuaded Aske to disband the rebels and gather a small party of trusted men to travel to London, with Norfolk providing an escort, to speak to the king directly. Aske himself remained in Yorkshire to oversee the rebels on the off chance that things in London did not go to plan, but it looked like a promising and potentially bloodless victory for the rebel Pilgrims, which is exactly what Aske had wanted.

Henry would not be so easily beaten and, when physical strength and arms failed him, he fell back on his considerable intelligence and tried the path of diplomacy. Receiving the rebels as promised, Henry asked what their grievances were and soon found out that the main goal was not to overthrow him as king, but it was instead to stop the rollout of the Reformation and Dissolution of the Monasteries, as well as discuss the concerns around consistently high taxation to fund expenditure and foreign conflict, which was having a disastrous effect on the economy of the north of England.[5] The king agreed to consider their demands; however, he delayed giving a response for several weeks. During this time, he asked that the rebel envoys draw up a formal list of detailed demands as he claimed that he needed further clarification on some points. In truth, Henry was stalling for time in the hopes that cracks would start to show in the rebel ranks and that Aske would be unable to keep all his men together. To be certain, Norfolk was given the command to end the rebellion by any means necessary.

The rebel envoy returned to Pontefract Castle where they worked together with Robert Aske to come up with a document called the '24 Articles', outlining their demands.[6] This list was presented to the Duke of Norfolk on 6 December 1536 and he agreed that these would be given to the king and a Parliament convened to discuss them. It was additionally agreed that anybody who had taken part in the Pilgrimage would receive a pardon for their involvement, which was welcome news and Aske felt that his men were victorious. Henry further requested that Aske travel to London to discuss the general feelings of the people so that they could work together to prevent this kind of thing from happening again.

When Aske returned to Yorkshire in January 1537, he was an outspoken advocate of the king, extolling his sound judgement and good will towards his people and all seemed well. A small uprising in Cumberland in February of that year seemed to be the catalyst of negative change. Fearing retribution from the king in dealing too softly with the Pilgrimage of Grace, Norfolk dealt harshly with the second rebellion and sought to place blame for this on the Pilgrims, though they were not involved in the incident. Henry used this smaller uprising as an opportunity to go back on his promises and, with most of the followers having disbanded on the promise of pardon, the Pilgrims were now a much easier force to deal with. Fifteen men were arrested, including Robert Aske and in May of 1537 they were put on trial in Yorkshire.

In a cruel but clever twist, the trials took place in Yorkshire with the juries consisting of people that knew the accused well and could even have formerly been counted as friends. The charges were treason, and the Yorkshire courts had to decide whether a verdict could be given there or if the trials should be moved to London instead. As it was basically a certainty that a London court would find the accused men guilty of treason, the Yorkshire contingent felt that they had little to no choice other than to do the same. The majority of the now-convicted traitors were moved to London for sentencing, but Robert Aske was later sent back to Yorkshire in June 1537 and being the figurehead of the Pilgrimage, Henry decided to use his death as an example of the price to pay for those who would conspire to rise up against their anointed king.

In hindsight, Aske did not really stand a chance. If that rebellion itself did not get him, then other reasons would have been found to accuse him of treason. Thomas Cromwell, one of the chief advisors to Henry VIII during this period, was able to gather statements from his fellow rebels that appeared to implicate Aske in other plots. In the end he was found guilty of high treason and his sentence was carried out on 12 July 1537.

Aske was bound and dragged through the streets of the city of York towards Clifford's Tower.[7] Once there he was taken to a scaffold erected next to the tower, wrapped in heavy chains and hoisted so he would hang, the chains weighing him down to cause an agonisingly slow death. His body remained on display and in chains for several days following his execution as a visual reminder of consequences and the inability of one man who, in his hopeful naivety, had faith and followers but still could not outwit a king.

Persecution in the Far East

We have already briefly made mention to the sixteenth-century Japanese warlord and feudal daimyō Toyotomi Hideyoshi, who in 1592 successfully unified his country after years of conflict. However, aside from his tactical cunning and military prowess, Hideyoshi was also known for violent persecution of Christian mercenaries.

Christianity had begun to set down roots in Japan in the mid-sixteenth century with the arrival of Jesuit missionaries and the establishment of a mission in Kagoshima. Ships began to arrive from Portugal with goods to trade, opening up the sale and transport of goods to the Japanese. While some were welcoming or at least tolerant to the missionaries (and the improved trading links that may come with them), others were less so. It seemed that they had a right to be, as Pope Gregory XIII issued a papal bull in 1575 granting the land of Japan to the Portuguese Diocese of Macau. One can safely assume that the Japanese were not actually consulted about this at the time.

The suspicious element was further vindicated when, on 19 October 1596, a Spanish galleon[8] called the *San Felipe* was found shipwrecked on the island of Shikoku. The Spanish and Portuguese, despite having a fractious relationship at this point, had been joined together when the latter entered the Iberian Union[9] and so shared a common monarchy. After the crew of the *San Felipe* had come ashore, they were met by Mashita Nagamori, a commissioner who served under Hideyoshi. He entered conversation with the pilot (navigator) of the ship, Francisco de Olandia, who told him that the Spanish would further conquest by first sending missionaries and then the conquistadors. Nagamori then discovered the close ties between Portugal and Spain … and put two and two together to equal trouble.

Hideyoshi was informed of this intelligence, and it added to his growing concerns over the rising tide of Christianity in the country being a method by which outsiders could undermine and then usurp control of Japan. An example had to be made, and quickly. In January 1597 a total of twenty-six missionaries – four Spanish, one Mexican and one Portuguese Franciscan monks, three Japanese Jesuits and seventeen Japanese Franciscan friars – were arrested, along with three altar boys. They were forced to march through villages across Japan for several weeks in between sessions of torture, so that their punishment would serve as a visual warning as well as a reminder of the power of the daimyō. They were offered the chance of freedom if they recanted and renounced their Christianity, but all declined.

On 5 February 1597 they were taken to a hill outside the city of Nagasaki where they were crucified and then, to make sure, were impaled with lances. They were not the last to be executed in Japan for their Christianity and Nagasaki would later see a greater massacre of fifty-five Christians in what became the Great Genna Martyrdom in 1622. It seems that no matter what side of the Catholic/Protestant divide you fell on, there was somebody somewhere in the world who was willing to persecute you for it.

Religion Under the Ottomans

While one of the most tumultuous religions in the period, Christianity was not the only faith that was divided within itself to bring innocent people strife. In the Ottoman Empire[10] the main religion was Islam, split into sub-branches, the two main ones named after the doctrine they follow, the Sunni and the Shi'ite Muslims. From 1512–1520, the empire was ruled by Selim the Grim, who was a Sunni Muslim, and he took brutal steps to try and stamp out the Shi'ite population in the rival kingdom ruled by the Safavid dynasty, in modern-day Iran.

Selim sent a decree ordering that a list be compiled of all Shi'ite Muslims in the Safavid region of the empire between the ages of 7 and 70. Once this list was compiled, he then proceeded to order the execution of every person on that list, irrespective of age. The majority were executed by beheading, the preferred execution method for the masses in the empire, and this became the largest massacre in Ottoman history to that point, a title that it held for the next 300 years. This was not the only nefarious act for which Selim the Grim is remembered. Upon acceding to the role of Sultan he had five of his nephews and two of his brothers strangled, the youngest of these being only 5 years old.

In 1514 he ordered an attack on the kingdom of Shah Ismail, head of the Safavid Empire. This involved the massacre of over 50,000 Shi'ite Alevis[11] as enemies of the Ottoman Empire, with the final defeat of Shah Ismail coming at the Battle of Chaldiran. Two years later, Selim launched a campaign against the Mamluk Sultanate of Egypt, ending in defeat for the Mamluks and the beheading of around 800 people captured by the Ottomans. The heads of these were placed on spikes around Selim's camp but the corpses were thrown into the nearby River Nile as a mark of disrespect.

It is always worth looking around at other conflicts during the sixteenth century as it is very easy to get entrenched in the Protestant Reformation and overlook the religious upheavals being experienced by other faiths. So, what if there was a group that didn't discriminate – they just persecuted everyone else? Arguably one of the most infamous instances of religious persecution in European history was the creation and activity of the group known as the Tribunal of the Holy Office of the Inquisition, established by Ferdinand II of Aragon and Isabella I of Castile in 1478 and more commonly known as the Spanish Inquisition.

The Spanish Inquisition

The Iberian Peninsula in the fifteenth century was a very multicultural area. Originally a Moorish territory (a mediaeval term for followers of Islam), this was taken back by the Spanish and Portuguese Catholics during the period known as the Reconquista.[12] The continued presence of a large Moor and Jewish contingent, however, came to breed resentment from the Catholic population and antisemitic views were beginning to grow. England and France had previously expelled their Jewish populations in the fourteenth century in one of a few bouts of frankly inexcusable antisemitic behaviour, so these sentiments were nothing new in mainland Europe. Riots broke out in parts of Spain, some with fatal consequences. Facing increased pressure and threat of violence, nearly a quarter of a million Jews outwardly converted to Christianity.

Over time the numbers of those converted grew and, now able to avoid the legal restrictions that were increasingly being placed on Jews and Muslims throughout Spain, they were able to build and sustain successful businesses. The success of these converts led to increased concern that they had not abandoned their previous religions fully after all. Concern led to whispers and whispers led to suspicions. Eventually these suspicions found their way to Queen Isabella I of Castile and her husband Ferdinand II of Aragon and the decision was made to set up an inquisition to ferret out who was guilty of the heresy of secretly maintaining or practising their old religion when they had been baptised into Christianity. On 1 November 1478, Pope Sixtus IV signed a papal bull giving official permission from the Church for Isabella I and Ferdinand II to put their plan into action and so the Spanish Inquisition was born.

The Inquisition at its heart consisted of a tribunal of three members, the Inquisitor General, a secretary and a third member, all appointed by the monarch. The Inquisition was reformed several times over the successive three centuries, officially being disbanded in 1834 and travelling as far as the Spanish colonies in the New World, but they are often grouped under the same umbrella title and follow a similar format.[13] The first Inquisitor General was Tomás de Torquemada, commencing his role in 1483.

The Inquisition, in short, operated through fear, though they only actually had jurisdiction when it came to prosecuting Christians; they had to deal with the Jews and Muslims in other ways. Much like the Gestapo of Nazi Germany or the Cheka of Bolshevik Russia, the Inquisition pitted neighbours against one another, utilising information provided to gather evidence and make arrests. While this is an effective technique for promoting a continuous flow of information, it can be problematic when it comes to neighbourly disputes or unreliable information. Suddenly any odd habit drew suspicion, all comments and conversations were carefully analysed, and even one's own home was no longer safe. It must have been a very stressful time.

Once there was enough evidence, though what was considered 'enough' or permissible evidence might not match our current understanding of the same, the individual under suspicion would be taken by the Inquisition and detained pending questioning. The Spanish Inquisition, like other Inquisitions before, was authorised in the use of torture to obtain confessions and further information, though they were not as liberal in the use of it as popular culture would have us believe, often choosing instead to implement torture following careful construction of a case as an additional avenue of evidence. In our chapter 'Extracting a Confession' we have discussed some of the torture methods common during the sixteenth century, however there were some that the Spanish Inquisition employed that we have saved for this section.

Finally, following the evidence gathering and torture process, the accused would be involved in the auto-da-fe (act of faith), a ritual ceremony where a public mass would be heard, after which the accused were brought before the Inquisition tribunal where their sentences would be read out and they would be turned back into the hands of the civil authorities for the punishment to be enacted. The last auto-da-fe is known to have taken place as recently as 1850, which shows the enduring power and presence of the Inquisition.

It is estimated that the Spanish Inquisition arrested and prosecuted around 160,000 people in just over three centuries before being officially disbanded, with around 5,000 deaths estimated to have occurred. While the Inquisition held the power to authorise the use of torture, they themselves could not give a sentence any harsher than life imprisonment, therefore any execution requests were left to the civil authorities where the accused lived. The secondary job of expelling members of the Jewish and Muslim communities from Spain was equally as effective, with over 250,000 from the Muslim community alone being forced to leave their homes. This was done through a civil tribunal, or by trial before the crown and considering the alternative was remaining and potentially being burned at the stake for heresy, many not surprisingly agreed to leave or convert.

Here are some of the reasons why the Spanish Inquisition might detain a person, as well as some of the notable cases in which they were involved.

The Articles

As mentioned, Tomás de Torquemada was named as the first Grand Inquisitor of Spain and as part of his role, he felt it necessary to set out the terms of reference on which the new Inquisition would operate. These were named the 28 Articles and were established in 1484 as guidelines for inquisitors identifying and prosecuting heretics. The focus of the Articles was to root out those who had recently converted from Judaism to Christianity, known as *conversos*, as the suspicion was that they had not fully abandoned their former faith. Many of the Articles therefore directly related to Jewish practices, such as observing the Jewish Sabbath or following the dietary laws known as the Kosher laws, or even giving children Hebrew names.

Secret meetings were also featured in the 28 Articles as a way of trying to conceal potentially heretical activities from the authorities and those suspected of meeting in secrecy or any other form of concealment were swiftly investigated, so planning a surprise birthday party was very much not advised. If someone under investigation or arrest were then to resist the Inquisition or others were found to be speaking out against their purpose or authority, this would also be grounds for investigation and possible arrest, as the authority of the Inquisition came from the combined agreement of the crown and the pope and was therefore not to be questioned or resisted.

Agustin de Cazalla

In a good demonstration of when the Inquisition went above and beyond for punishment, we will give you the story of the former chaplain to Holy Roman Emperor Charles V, one Agustin de Cazalla. After serving Charles V, de Cazalla found himself drawn away from more traditional Catholic beliefs and towards more Protestant beliefs, which were considered heretical. He and a group of other like-minded individuals met in what they believed to be total secrecy to practise and discuss their beliefs, meeting at de Cazalla's childhood home. Eventually they were discovered and de Cazalla was brought to trial at the auto-da-fe in his hometown of Valladolid on 21 May 1559, along with other heretics, including members of his family. All were accused of heresy and were sentenced to be burned at the stake, as a symbolic representation of the very literal fires of hell that they were believed to be condemned to for eternity for their sins, which is not at all dramatic.

The accused were offered a chance to recant and denounce their heretical ways, to save their souls for heaven before they died. Those that did recant were given the mercy of a death by strangulation before they were burned; those that didn't died by the fire. De Cazalla, one of his brothers and one of his sisters were all condemned to die. We can surmise that de Cazalla recanted before death as it is recorded that he was strangled before he was burned. Two of his other siblings were also put on trial but were not executed, and instead were sentenced to life imprisonment. It was what happened to his mother and the family home that then goes the extra mile.

As the meetings, or *conventicles* as they were known, were held at the house owned by his mother Leonora de Buiero, it was decided that retribution was to also be taken against her. The problem was that Leonora de Buiero was already dead by this point, but on paper the building was still in her name, and she was therefore the legal owner. So, the Inquisition did no more than exhume her body and throw it onto the fire, thus denying her the chance to reinhabit her body come Judgement Day, condemning her to an eternity in hell or purgatory instead of heaven. They also took their wrath out on her property, pulling it down and erecting a stone column in its place with an inscription that forbade anything to be built again on that site and threatening excommunication to anyone who was tempted to try. We will admit, a house committing heresy is a new one on us. In more recent times the column was replaced with a memorial stone to Agustin de Cazalla, who is now considered a martyr in the Protestant faith.

Nicholas Burton

It was not just those living in Spain at the time who fell foul of the Inquisition; it turned out to be a danger for some to even visit the country. Nicholas Burton was an English merchant's trader who was delivering freight to Andalusia when someone came on board claiming to be delivering a message to him. In fact, it appears that the messenger was working for the Inquisition with the goal of stalling Burton until the sergeant was available to come and arrest him. They refused to tell Burton of the charges against him, and he was taken to Cadiz where he was detained for fourteen days. During his imprisonment, Burton took time to preach his Protestant faith to the other inmates, seeking to convert them to the English belief system. In a Catholic prison and detained by a strict Catholic Inquisition was perhaps not the best idea, but he chose his hill, and he was prepared to die on it, literally.

As a result of his actions while incarcerated, Burton was taken from the prison to Seville and placed in solitary confinement where he could not continue to preach his religious doctrine. Then, on 20 December, he was brought with several others before the auto-da-fe in Seville for trial. To prevent him from speaking out, his tongue was forced out of his mouth and a stick tied to it, stopping him from pulling it back in. The sentences were pronounced and, still without knowing why he had been arrested and what he was even accused of in the first instance, Burton was sentenced to death as a heretic.

Burton, along with the others condemned to death on that day, were taken from the place of the auto-da-fe and the sentence of execution was carried out by burning. The issues against him did not end with his death however, as his goods were seized by the Spanish; this forced the merchant's solicitor to travel to Spain to try and get the goods released, a man by the name of John Fronton. Fronton was, after around four months of discussion, dismissed on claims of insufficient evidence, at which point he returned to England and gathered further information to come back with.

Fronton returned to Seville with more evidence, exhibiting this before the Inquisition. The matter was referred to the local bishop but was then referred on to others, Fronton being passed from pillar to post while evidence was gathered against him. Fronton was tricked into visiting the jail in Seville under the guise of speaking to a prisoner, ostensibly to help with the release of his employer's goods. While there, he was arrested and detained by the jailer. Fronton was later charged with heresy and the decision was taken that all the goods were to be formally confiscated and would not be returned, and Fronton was to be held in prison for a year. From a sceptical viewpoint, it is possible that the goods that were seized and later kept may have weighed heavily in the decision to arrest and then effectively dispose of Burton, with his preaching in jail just playing into the hands of his captors.

Methods

As previously mentioned, despite their reputation, the Spanish Inquisition were heavy handed with their doctrine but a little cannier when it came to employing torture. This is not to say, however, that when torture was employed, it was not brutal. We have already discussed the method called strappado where a victim would have their hands bound behind their back and then be lifted by their wrists and sometimes dropped repeatedly. This, public whipping, the stocks or pillories and the rack were all used by the Inquisition along with other equally disturbing techniques.

An item of furniture called the Iron Chair was known to have been used in which a victim was strapped down onto a chair covered traditionally in iron or wooden spikes, with the restraints forcing them onto the rough surface, causing great pain and discomfort. While detained either in the chair or in other restraints, hot coals or irons would be pressed against areas of exposed skin on the victim, causing burns that varied in severity depending on how hot the item was and how long it was pressed against the skin.

Another method was *interrogatiroi mejorado del agua*, known in the modern world as waterboarding. This was where the person being interrogated would be either held or strapped down and water forced down their throat, simulating the act of drowning, causing the person receiving this torture immense distress and panic, as well as a great deal of pain both from the effects of the water entering the body and from trying to free themselves from the restraints to escape it.

A milder punishment, not so much of torture but more of humiliation and to teach a lesson, was the forced wearing of a hair shirt, basically a piece of clothing made from animal hair that would be meted out as a punishment due to it being an irritant against the skin of whoever wore it. It was a form of penance and could be given out following a confession to remind the person wearing it of the need to humble themselves in the name of their faith. The length of time for which the shirt was worn tended to be dictated by the severity of the person's sin, or the leniency (or lack thereof) of their judges. This could range from a matter of hours to several days and, to those who had been physically marked by other tortures such as whipping or the use of hot coals, it would actively prolong the pain and potentially lead to an infection of any open wounds they may have sustained. There were also those who wore hair shirts by choice, simultaneously suffering for their beliefs and becoming fashion victims in one fell swoop.

The Navarre Witch Trials

Witches and witchcraft have been a prevalent in folklore and society in various forms for millennia, as has the public reaction to them, but the sixteenth century saw the beginnings of what would become mass hysteria and persecution that would continue to ring through the following centuries.

We cover the various witch trials in the chapter 'Extracting a Confession', however due to the links with the Spanish Inquisition, we are crossing over briefly here to discuss the trials that occurred in the Kingdom of Navarre in 1525.

Following a commissioned inspection into the Navarre region of the Pyrenees Mountains on the Spanish border, two young girls, both sisters, were employed for abilities they allegedly possessed that allowed them to detect witches. They proved decidedly effective as a total of thirty people were accused of witchcraft and handed over to the Inquisition for punishment. The Inquisition were concerned and surprised by the numbers being found among such a lightly populated area and decided to oversee the ongoing trials in the region. In what might be seen as an unusual injection of common sense in these types of proceedings, the Inquisitors realised that a lot of the evidence being presented as genuine acts of witchcraft were spurious and could lead to people being executed unnecessarily. In response to this, in December 1525 guidelines were issued as to how witch trials were to be conducted and what evidence was permissible, stating that only the Inquisition were able to bring suspected witches to trial and that property belonging to the condemned could no longer be confiscated, thus taking away a potential reason for someone to be accused.[14] The Inquisition stated that the main goal for bringing accused witches to trial was to bring them back to the Christian faith and re-educate them rather than simply seeking to punish.

In 1527 an inquisitor by the name of Avellaneda returned to the Navarre valley region to resume the search for and punishment of witches believed to still be operating in the area. Under Avellaneda's eye around eighty executions by burning were conducted against persons convicted of heresy. Another round of trials would begin almost half a century later, starting with the arrest of approximately fifty people accused of witchcraft, though following another intervention by the Inquisition, this time on the side of moderation, only one woman, Maria Johan, was executed.

This is not the last time that the witch trials would scar the Basque region due to the Inquisition. In 1609 the Inquisitors would return to the area to initiate one of the last witch hunts that they themselves were directly involved in, but which is also one of the most infamous European witch hunts of the period.

The sixteenth century, marked by its ruthless approach to religion, was a time of intense upheaval and persecution across Europe. Monarchs and political leaders wielded religion as a tool of power, enforcing drastic shifts between Catholicism and Protestantism. This led to widespread fear, suffering and the execution of those deemed heretics or traitors. The relentless enforcement of religious conformity, driven by political and doctrinal motives, created an atmosphere of intolerance and brutality. The legacy of sixteenth-century religious policies is a stark reminder of the dangers inherent in the fusion of absolute power and doctrinal rigidity, highlighting the profound impact of religious strife on societal stability and human lives.

Chapter 9

The Final Gong

Warning – we would not recommend reading this chapter at dinner time or immediately post-dining. It is, however, the perfect chapter to read on the privy.

To paraphrase Jane Austen, it is a truth universally acknowledged that everybody must die. If you have made it this far through the book you have realised this small fact, and you have likely also realised that it can sometimes happen in weird and wonderful ways. It can also happen in disturbing and distressing ways. It is also a truth universally acknowledged that people must vacate themselves of the things they eat and drink – what goes in must come out, so to speak. But what if the two were combined in the most unfortunate of ways? This is where we turn our eyes and our noses in this chapter, to look at those poor souls whose expirations were linked to their expulsions in one way or another.

Souls like poor John Decker of Somerset, who on 5 March 1600 sought to relieve himself in the cesspit at the rear of his property. As he was doing so, Mr Decker caught his foot on a stone near the pit, causing him to lose his balance and fall in where he subsequently drowned.

Or perhaps we should consider the demise of Mr James Bakon who entered the garden of Geoffrey Michells in Norwich on 9 April 1542 when he fell into the cesspool and drowned in the liquid within. One can only assume it was either late and therefore dark, or Bakon could not see what was about to happen; either way it was a less than pleasant end.

Mr Wiliam Fryshe of King's Lynn in Norfolk lost his life while relieving himself, though it was not in the traditional cesspit or latrine. Mr Fryshe decided instead to do so into a well belonging to Edward Martendale, though with the well described as old in the report of his death, one would hope that it was no longer in use, especially as the hapless Mr Fryshe sat on the well to conduct his business, lost his balance and fell backward, drowning in the water. In a darker twist, it took twenty days from 9 to 29 February for his body to be discovered.

We should also bring some balance by mentioning a female victim named Agnes who, being poor and without means, found herself begging for food near her home in Jesus Lane, Cambridge, in December 1534, when she slipped and fell into a ditch used as a latrine deposit and suffocated on the smell.

Meanwhile, in January 1531 one Richard Foster of Cambridge found himself fighting a fever and, having the urge to empty his bowels, took himself to a nearby ditch. Due to the weakness of his body brought on by the fever, Mr Foster fell backwards into the ditch and drowned. While up in Yorkshire in 1565 young Robert Appilton found himself playing in his father's garden when he lost his balance and fell into the family cesspool, drowning in the muck therein.

It seems that one does not need to actually fall in the pit to be a victim of it, as John Dunkyn also from Cambridge found out when, more than a few drinks into his evening, took himself outside to relieve himself, lost his balance and fell backwards where the smell suffocated him, and he died on 2 June 1523.

There is also the case of Vicar William Whalley from Dunstable who on 2 August 1547 went to the toilet while at the house of one John Denton. It is not recorded whether the bench covering the cesspit was rotten or simply broken, but either way it gave under Mr Whalley, causing him to fall backwards. His hose managed to catch on something which prevented him from falling headlong into the pit, however he was then left suspended, head pointing down towards the waste, causing him to suffer death by dangling.

Drunkenness and cesspits did not go well together, as evidenced by the case of James Harvie who, while very drunk on the night of 21 August 1565, woke from the middle of the street where he was apparently trying to sleep some of it off and decided he needed to relieve himself. Staggering to a nearby ditch, he undid his trousers but lost his grip and the trousers fell to around his ankles. Harvie bent down to pick them up but lost his balance due to his drunken state. Trying to stand back up, he staggered around a bit until, now facing the pit, he stumbled forward and pitched face first into the filthy liquid. Due to his drunkenness and the fact that his pants were still around his ankles, he was unable to get himself out and drowned.

These are a few examples of unfortunate death by drowning in excrement. It was a danger having such pits around, but surely it was better than having it lying in the street? But what goes in must come out and as cesspits were filled there was a need to have them emptied regularly, for hygiene as well as aesthetic reasons.

That is where the role of the gong farmer came in and trust us, it isn't as cool as it might sound. A gong farmer, sometimes also known as a nightman, was someone who removed human waste from cesspits. The work was considered too unseemly for the public to observe so a lot of the work was carried out at night, hence 'nightman'. The term gong farmer or gong scourer was coined in the sixteenth century, but there is evidence of the profession existing throughout the mediaeval period, as well as evidence of the perils of the job.

Once he had collected the waste, or 'night soil', it would then be transported outside the boundaries of the town or city to whatever waste disposal was established there. As you can imagine, it would hardly have been the most pleasant-smelling job. Thankfully, it eventually became obsolete with the advent of indoor plumbing and more effective disposal systems and sewers.

Gong farmers were decently compensated for the work they did, which is understandable with what they had to endure and the antisocial hours. They charged per cesspit emptied and as most pits were emptied on average every two years, there was a financial incentive to empty as many as you could while waiting for the first one to fill up; there was always a need for such work, so job security was more or less guaranteed. They were also likely to stumble across items such as coins or jewellery that had been dropped into the privies which they could often keep – once it had been fully cleaned of course. They were also liable to be paid in items rather than coin. While they could be compensated as much as 2s per ton of waste moved (approximately £90 a ton today), they could also be paid in food items and one man in the employ of the household of Queen Elizabeth I is reported to have been paid in brandy.

A sad side effect of the job, however, was that they often had to live outside the main centres due to the odour that no doubt emanated from their houses as showers weren't exactly a common occurrence at the time. There were also the inherent health hazards. While an essential service to prevent the build-up of excrement in towns, therefore helping in part to mitigate the spread of some diseases among the population, this did not protect the health of the gong farmers themselves and those who did not die by disease; well, let us put it this way, they worked at night and street lights were not as we know them now to be.

Collecting the waste was not a one-man job, and teams of up to four or five men could be involved (we say men, though there would have been boys apprenticed to the trade or joining the family business) to assist the one whose job it was to climb down into the pit and shovel into the buckets.

As well as the gong farmers clearing out the cesspits, you would also have muckrakers who cleaned the waste left by animals on the street, as well as that left over from the emptying of chamber pots. This was also a physically demanding and antisocial job to be carried out overnight with the excrement again being loaded and carried beyond the town or city limits. Sometimes deals with local farmers were made to sell the human excrement as fertiliser, a practice that has thankfully died out – though since writing this chapter we are certainly looking more suspiciously at the vegetable section in the local supermarket.

While we acknowledge here that the presence of cesspits or latrines and the occupation of the gong farmers were hazardous, sometimes the simple act of going to and from the toilet was as hazardous as actually getting there. Take for example Andrew Maste who, while breaking up his journey with an overnight stay at the Maiden's Head Inn in Kent, went to relieve himself in the night. As he was making his way back to bed he tripped on the stairs and fell, breaking his head, an injury which it took him just over five days to succumb to.

A similar fate befell one Robert Parsuns, our second clergyman in this chapter to die in a toilet-related accident. Unlike the unfortunate later demise of Mr Whalley of Dunstable, Mr Parsons didn't make it to the latrine. Instead, he was on his way in the early hours of 25 November 1508 when he tripped on the stairs, fell and broke his neck, dying almost instantly. The lesson here, it seems, is to either not drink before bed, or keep a chamber pot nearby just in case. Failing that – invest in an en suite without stairs.

It wasn't only human waste removal that could prove problematic to the point of death for those involved; animal waste removal was also hazardous, as John Ryder of Kent found out in 1599 as he was helping to clean out a pigsty alongside Michael Nottingham Junior. As he had finished emptying his shovel, just as Nottingham was using his pitchfork to prepare more, Ryder turned at the wrong moment as Nottingham swung and the pitchfork connected. The injury did not kill Ryder instantly, he lingered for a further fifteen days, so it is more likely that infection from the pig dung got him rather than just a pitchfork to the face.

Waste management may have been a work in progress during the Tudor period, but as stated before it was a necessary process. With the prevalence of plagues and diseases, as well as the somewhat colourful treatments and proposed cures, every little thing helped when it came to hygiene and public health, and it would pave the way for the later inventions that make our modern conveniences so, well, convenient.

One of the most concerning illnesses that spread because of questionable hygiene was dysentery, also known as the bloody flux. Dysentery has been a prevalent disease throughout human history, claiming the lives of at least four known English monarchs, being Henry I, John, Edward I and Henry V and causing issues throughout the religious wars known as the Crusades. Ongoing military campaigns in inclement weather conditions, poor hygiene and tainted sources of drinking water are all contributing factors to this illness.

Symptoms include, but are not limited to, fever, stomach cramps and severe diarrhoea leading to intense dehydration which is often the final cause of death. The alternative name for the disease came from the fact that victims would often start to pass blood in their stool as their bodies eventually succumbed to the illness. With towns and cities, as well as military camps, becoming overcrowded and access to clean drinking water being limited at best, it is hardly surprising that such things as dysentery spread like wildfire.

Dysentery Victims

One notable case of dysentery during the Tudor period was that of Cardinal Thomas Wolsey. Initially a favourite advisor to the king, Henry VIII, following his failure to secure an annulment between the king and his first wife Catherine of Aragon, Wolsey was arrested on charges of treason. The whole ordeal was, understandably, very stressful for him and while travelling from Cawood Castle in Yorkshire back to London he fell ill. The illness, exacerbated by the cold, wet weather and an injury sustained from hitting his head on the royal barge during his journey, turned into dysentery and at Leicester Abbey on 29 November 1530 the cardinal's body eventually gave out.

Another contemporary of Wolsey's and one-time friend of Henry VIII's, the Dutch philosopher and poet Desiderius Erasmus, is also believed to have died after contracting dysentery, though according to contemporary sources his death on 12 July 1536 was peaceful and in the company of friends, which is more than we can say for some of his associates who will be getting honourable mentions in our 'Crime and Punishment' section.

One of the heroes of the fight against the Spanish Armada (or villain if you are on the side of the Spanish), the career of Sir Francis Drake took somewhat of a downturn with a series of defeats along the Spanish and Portuguese coasts. He then sailed west and continued his career along the South American coast, meeting with a similar lack of success against the entrenched Spanish, narrowly avoiding death when a cannonball shot from the battlements of the Castillo San Felipe del Morro (El Morro Castle) passed through the state room of his ship.

While docked at Panama on the trail of Spanish treasure ships, Drake caught dysentery and on 28 January 1596, he died. His body was sealed in a lead-lined coffin, and he was buried at sea where his remains have yet to be found, though marine archaeologists in the area are trying to locate them.

Uesugi Kenshin

Now this case is somewhat of a notable mention as there is some discussion ongoing around the actual cause of his death, however it is certainly worth recording for one of the theories circulated.

Useugi Kenshin, also known as Nagao Kagetora, was a Japanese daimyō (feudal lord) who oversaw the Echigo Province under the nickname the Dragon of Echigo. Known as a very effective military leader overseeing no fewer than thirteen battles or sieges during his career, he also ruled over a period of increased prosperity for his area.

In what is admittedly about to be a vast oversimplification of the situation, a breakdown in relationship with the powerful rival daimyō Oda Nobunaga led to conflict between the two, however Kenshin's health began to deteriorate through suspected oesophageal cancer, which it is suspected to be a main contributor to his death in 1578 when he was on the latrine and suffered a severe stomach ache, wherein he then passed away.

An alternative speculation on how Kenshin died is somewhat more entertaining, though we would suspect not for him. Legend has it that while encamped in preparation for an assault on land owned by Nobunaga, Kenshin was overtaken by a stomach ache and went to relieve himself. Unbeknown to Kenshin, a ninja was concealed in the camp cesspool and when Kenshin arrived, he struck, fatally wounding him. Whether the ninja assassination actually happened, it is a cool story and either way that latrine saw the end of an impressive man who we would certainly encourage readers to learn more about.

In Transit

It was not just the act of cleaning or owning a cesspool that could be a serious risk to life in the sixteenth century. Take the case of Daniel Woodall of Grantchester in Cambridgeshire who was playing near his father James's dung cart which was heavily laden by that point. The cart was stationary and as the animals were not present to pull it, it was being held upright by a piece of wood called a crutch. As Daniel was playing, the crutch gave out, tipping the cart which knocked Daniel to the ground. The contents then poured on top of Daniel, and he suffocated under the weight of all that dung.

Daniel Woodall was not the only one to suffocate under the weight of waste. A similar end befell William Bulleyn of Huntingdonshire who was unloading his dung cart near the dunghill in Hemingford. Bulleyn lost his balance and fell while unloading, causing the cart to tip over with the dung dumping on him in such a way that he was instantly crushed by the weight of it.

Several accidents also occurred during the transit of the collected waste that could prove equally as deadly, if not more so. For example, there is the case of Edmund Dennye of Norwich who was transporting dung along the River Wensum in 1544. As the boat was being unloaded it started to take on water. Attempting to get out before it sank, Dennye grabbed the punting pole and attempted to use it to vault across to the bank but underestimated the amount of sediment at the bottom of the river. Instead of the pole moving forward with him, it stuck upright in the mud, causing Dennye to fall back into the now-polluted water, where he drowned.

Transit on water could therefore be troublesome, but by land was equally risky, with no fewer than forty-six separate deaths being attributed to accidents on or under dung carts recorded in a list of sixteenth-century coroner's inquest reports diligently compiled by Stephen Gunn. This would, therefore, not be an exhaustive list of those who died this way and doesn't cover similar accidents elsewhere in the world.

It wasn't just the case that people were crushed or hit by the carts in question; sometimes it would be the driving that caused the issue, and sometimes the dung did not need to even be on the cart to inflict damage. Thomas Anne was driving his cart in Hampshire in August 1520, the cart being completely empty and the drive being thus far uneventful, when one of the cartwheels went over a large heap of dung in the middle of the track, causing the cart to tip, throwing Thomas out. The cart then collapsed on top of him, giving him an instantly fatal wound to the head. We can't help but wonder what on earth kind of animal left a dung heap so solid that it could violently pitch a cart!

Chapter 10

Weaponry Woes

We are going to say it. War is not fun … for anyone. Yes, we know, understatement of the century but military mishaps can be interesting. Especially when weapons and tactics were not as advanced as they are today. The number of stories of people looking into the barrel of a gun when it had failed to fire is astronomical. You would think it would be common sense to not, but as this chapter will show, common sense is not always that common.

Before we get into the ridiculousness of people, let us first give a brief overview of Tudor military techniques and ongoing wars. The best place to begin is the battle that started it all, well for the Tudors anyway: the Battle of Bosworth. In a nutshell, Henry Tudor defeated King Richard III on the battlefield on 22 August 1485, beginning the end of the Wars of the Roses and kick-starting a dynasty that would live in infamy, even if it did only last 118 years.

Henry, for all intents and purposes, should not have won the Battle of Bosworth. Richard III was king so would have had the bigger, stronger army made up of knights and nobles as well as a large peasant contingent. He had years of experience fighting the Wars of the Roses under his elder brothers George, Duke of Clarence, and King Edward IV. He also has more money at his disposal, but this battle would show Henry at his best and the tactics and techniques that would shape his reign.[1]

Henry VII is known for preferring peace to war and made several successful peace treaties with many prominent powers of the time: Spain, the Holy Roman Empire, France and Scotland, to name just a few. This was done mainly through matrimonial alliances, with his first born and heir Prince Arthur marrying the Spanish Princess Catherine of Aragon[2] and his daughter Mary marrying King Louis XII of France, for example.

His son Henry VIII however was the complete opposite to dear old dad in that he loved a good war. He was battle hungry and would often engage in battles with both France and Scotland. Henry's marriage to Anne Boleyn also caused strife back home on English soil with the breakaway from the Catholic Church and the beginnings of the newly established Church of England, with uprisings and bad feeling growing in the country. The Dissolution of the Monasteries from 1536 did not help matters, neither did changing the country's main religion back to Catholicism under Mary I in 1553 and then back to Protestantism again under Elizabeth I in 1558. The Spanish and Italians would take up arms against the English during these times due to their religious affiliations.

The Tudor period was a time of significant military activity both in Europe and globally. With the fall of the Aztec and Incan empires in the Americas due to the Spanish conquests, the Ottoman Empire was also fighting with the Habsburgs in Hungary and the Safavid Empire of Persia over territories in the Middle East. There were also several civil wars in France occurring during this time as well. The dynamics of war during this era were influenced by territorial ambitions, religious conflicts and the rise of powerful empires. England's involvement in these conflicts helped shape its emerging status as a significant European power by the end of the Tudor dynasty.

After Henry VII was victorious against Richard III at the Battle of Bosworth, Henry knew the army needed to change and under the Tudors the army evolved from medieval feudal levies[3] to a more centralised and professional force. This included the use of archers, billmen, pikemen and later, musketeers and artillery.

The navy under the Tudors, especially Henry VIII, saw significant growth and development, with the construction of larger and more heavily armed ships such as the 600-ton *Mary Rose* and the lesser known smaller and faster 450-ton *Peter Pomegranate*, establishing the foundations of England's future naval dominance.

Coastal defences and fortifications were significantly improved during this period as well, reflecting the increasing importance of protecting the country against invasion while controlling key ports and harbours – which proved particularly useful at the time of the 1558 Spanish Armada, but more on that in our chapter 'Notable Mentions'.

Military campaigns had significant economic and social impacts on England and its people, including high taxation to fund multiple wars and the social disruption caused by military levies and conscription, especially those conflicts that arose under Henry VIII and Elizabeth I. There may seem to have been a lot of fighting, but the Tudor period was also a transformative era for the English military, characterised by significant advancements in naval power, military reforms and key battles that shaped the future of England. However, as impressive as all this seems, there were a lot of blunders and downright ridiculous military mishaps that happened along the way.

Firearm Failures

You did indeed read that correctly, firearms in the sixteenth century. Swords and crossbows were the favoured weapons of choice in medieval England; however, firearms were becoming more common.

The arquebus was an early type of long gun dating from the sixteenth century and was used most notably in Europe and the Ottoman Empire. Initially the arquebus referred to a hook-like projected handgun which was useful for steadying the gun against castle battlements when firing. Adding a shoulder stock, priming pan and matchlock[4] mechanism turned the arquebus into the first ever handheld firearm with a trigger. Rudimental in their make-up, the arquebus would take a painfully long time to reload after it was fired and would more often than not miss its intended target. Just like it did on an autumnal Monday in November 1536.

The first time a coroner's court encountered the novel issue of a fatal shooting accident was in 1519, when a woman in Welton, near Hull, was accidentally shot and killed by a handgun. The perpetrator, a bookbinder from France, aptly named Peter Frenchman, had fired the weapon when the victim, unaware of the noisy device's danger, walked right in front of it, the discharged weapon instantly killing her.

The role of firearms in society was further highlighted in 1557 through an incident involving the Duke of Norfolk. While travelling on a road in

Tottenham, the duke's horse unexpectedly stumbled, leading to an accidental discharge of the duke's gun. While both the duke and his horse were unharmed, it seems that the sudden misfire resulted in the accidental death of one of his nearby servants.

Robert Pakington

Robert Pakington was a notable English merchant and Member of Parliament during the early 1500s, but he is mostly remembered for his untimely and unfortunate death which, to this day, is shrouded in mystery.

It was a brisk morning on 13 November 1536 and Robert Pakington was walking to early morning mass at around 6 am at St Thomas of Acre in Cheapside, London. Robert's journey was a short one, but he carried a lantern and due to the time of year it was still dark and the smoke from a thousand chimneys, mingling with a mist from the Thames, reduced visibility to a mere few paces. His usual route took him past the Great Conduit, a square building in the middle of Cheapside containing the fountain that provided the nearby houses with their water supply, so it was a well-known landmark. As he crossed the street, a single shot rang out and Robert immediately fell dead. Almost as soon as his body hit the floor, a crowd rapidly gathered around him and started asking questions. Why would someone want to kill one of London's most respectable figures? Packington was not only an MP and a prominent merchant, but he was also a leading member of the Worshipful Mercers' Company.[5]

It is important to note that Pakington was a Protestant reformer, which was dangerous in England at this time. Henry VIII had only recently established the Church of England after breaking away from the Catholic Church. The English people were expected to change religions and renounce Catholicism, but most people refused to do so and suffered the consequences. Robert was already a Protestant, and proud of it, but this would not have sat well with his Catholic neighbours or members of the Catholic Church.

It should also be said that handguns were extremely new in England and very rustic in their creation, so shooting on target would be rare for even the best marksman. Arquebuses were even more rudimental and needed both hands to fire. Weapons needed a match to light the gunpowder and would produce a bright light when ignited and fired – so with all that in mind, how was this murderer not seen?

It is stated that Robert Pakington was not only the first person in England to be murdered or killed by a handgun but may also have been the first ever political assassination. Was he murdered because of his religious affiliations, or was he not actually the intended target and was just incredibly unlucky to be in the wrong place at the wrong time? Either way the murderer was never caught and Robert Pakington's death remains a history mystery to this day.

The Battle of Nagashino

You know the infamous saying 'don't take swords to a gunfight' – have you ever wondered where that came from? We do not have definitive proof, but the Battle of Nagashino in 1575 may be a strong contender.

Before this battle, Japan was in the midst of the Sengoku period, also known as the Warring States period. This era, spanning roughly from the mid-fifteenth century to the early seventeenth century, covered a land of fractured political entities and constant warfare, with powerful daimyōs[6] competing for dominance. Oda Nobunaga, through his known strategic brilliance and ruthless ambition, was emerging as a central figure in the quest to unify Japan, along with Tokugawa Ieyasu, another influential daimyō and future shogun of Japan, who controlled the Mikawa Province. The opposition leader Takeda Katsuyori sought to expand his power by attacking the Tokugawa territory.

Takeda Katsuyori was extremely powerful and good at what he did. His Takeda clan, as they were known, were making their way across Japan, conquering towns and cities as they went. The army was made up of some 15,000 battle-hardened samurai warriors and included Takeda's renowned cavalry, which had won numerous battles with its devastating charges.

Takeda Katsuyori had taken over from his father Takeda Shingen when he died. Katsuyori wanted to not only solidify the Takeda clan's dominance in central Japan, but also, he felt that he had something to prove so he decided to besiege Nagashino Castle, a strategic stronghold held by the Tokugawa clan. The castle's defenders were vastly outnumbered and likely could not hold a siege for very long at all. However, in their time of strife an unlikely hero would emerge – Torii Suneemon.

Torii took it upon himself to sneak out of the castle, past the Takeda clan and went straight to Oda Nobunaga and Tokugawa Ieyasu for help, and luckily, they agreed to send some. On his way back, Torii Suneemon was captured by Takeda's forces and upon threat of crucifixion he 'agreed' to help the clan by going back and telling the castle defenders that no help was coming; they even walked Torii to the castle to ensure he delivered the news. In an act of the utmost bravery, Torii instead shouted that help was on its way and they would not be defeated. He was instantly taken down and killed, but he is remembered around Japan as a symbol of loyalty and bravery. His actions not only demonstrated his personal valour but also played a crucial role in the sequence of events that led to the Oda–Tokugawa victory at the Battle of Nagashino. His story is often recounted in Japanese history as an example of the samurai code of honour and self-sacrifice.

The story does not stop there, however. On hearing the news, the castle defenders reinforced what they had, knowing that help was on the way, which it most certainly was. Oda and Tokugawa sent a 38,000-strong army to aid the defenders and on 28 June 1575 the Battle of Nagashino began. You might be thinking it was the fact the attacking army was roughly double the size the defending one that then clinched the victory for Oda Nobunaga and Tokugawa Ieyasu, or maybe it was the fact the opposing army had to defend from the front against the castle and from the rear against the oncoming enemy army so they would be effectively fighting on two fronts: they both helped but were not the deciding factors.

Arquebus firearms had made their way over to Japan approximately twenty years before the battle, but they were not widely used, as most armies stuck to the traditional samurai weapons. This had been working undoubtedly well for the Takeda clan and they continued to believe that this would be the way they would win all wars and seize control of Japan – after all, if it is not broken, don't fix it, right?

The 38,000-strong army sent by Oda and Tokugawa consisted of a lot of well-trained soldiers carrying the arquebus. The tactics implemented for continuous fire and wooden stockades allowed Oda Nobunaga's forces to decimate the charging Takeda cavalry.

The Battle of Nagashino exemplifies the transition from traditional samurai warfare to the adoption of gunpowder weapons in Japan. The strategic use of firearms by the Oda–Tokugawa alliance demonstrated how technological innovation and tactical adaptation could decisively impact the outcome of battles, even against highly skilled and disciplined traditional samurai forces. Who knew that a bullet would beat a sword?

By the 1560s, illustrating the marvels of scientific progress, guns were responsible for more accidental deaths than longbows. However, being struck by an arrow happened more often that you would think.

Hitting the Mark

Arrows, along with bows, are among some of the oldest projectile weapons known to humanity. The exact time of their first introduction is difficult to pinpoint, but archaeological evidence suggests that they have been in use for tens of thousands of years, as far back as the Stone Age.[7] Death by arrows in the mediaeval times was therefore remarkably unremarkable. Being the main weapon for both soldiers and peasants alike, the humble bow and arrow was a fantastic tool, not just for fighting but for hunting and sport too. It is relatively easy to practise and aim for the perfect shot with a bow and arrow or indeed a crossbow, but it is also very easy for things to go very wrong, very quickly.

Just as happened on 30 June 1501, in a garden in Southwark, Surrey, when Mr Edward Taylour was standing approximately twelve feet away from a practice mark where various people were shooting arrows, just having a drink and catching up with friends. William Davy, a cooper[8] from London, aimed at the mark; however, Davy was not as steady as he could have been and missed his mark, his arrow veering away from the target and striking a branch of a cherry tree, causing it to richocet approximately twelve feet in the wrong direction, hitting poor Edward Taylour. The arrow hit the right side of Taylour's neck just below the ear, causing a wound of around two inches deep. Taylour bravely fought to recover from the injury for almost three weeks until he could hold out no longer and died on 19 July. It was ruled that the incident was a case of accidental death, and no charges were brought against Davy, though he may perhaps have thought again before attempting archery in a public place.

This next accident takes the word 'unlucky' to a whole new level. On 20 July 1507, in Almondbury, Yorkshire, John Kay shot an arrow known as a 'prykshaft'[9] at a sign known as a 'bracken bush' ('bracanboske'). Due to the inherent lightness of the arrow, a strong wind blew it approximately 100 feet off course, causing it to fall into a large gathering of people. The arrow struck one Mr William Shaw on the forehead, causing quite a significant wound. Shaw suffered for around six weeks from the injury until 3 September 1507, when he finally succumbed.

Picture this: it is a lovely, sunny Friday afternoon in May, where you are just relaxing in your own home, going about your business and suddenly, in flies an arrow … through the wall. On 19 May 1511, in Sutton-upon-Derwent in Yorkshire, Elizabeth Smyth was inside her house, doing just that while Thomas Egglesfeld was practising archery by shooting arrows at a white mark painted on the wall of the house, blissfully unaware of Elizabeth's presence inside. It was not his house; it was just a house that had a specific mark that he decided to aim at that day. One of his arrows went through the wall – it must have been thin – and struck Elizabeth on the left side of her body, inflicting a mortal wound that caused her instant death. The coroner's inquest into the death of Elizabeth was held. Thomas Egglesfeld was later pardoned on 28 February 1512 due to the incident being ruled as accidental.

Accidental deaths by bow and arrow were unfortunately common and most of the time nothing could have been done to have prevented the death. Sometimes, people are just ridiculous human beings, or extremely unlucky.

For example, on 27 May 1504, in Horsley, Gloucestershire, a group of friends were taking part in some archery practice. William Cassy, John Snowe and Thomas Perselo often joined each other to relax and practise with their bows. Cassy, the first archer, shot his arrow and then took himself over to stand by the target. This was, unsurprisingly, not the most practical place to stand, so the other participants shouted at him to move back from the target, which he did, because he decided to be sensible. However, just as Thomas Perselo released his arrow, John Snowe decided he was going to move in front of the target instead and, to what we are sure will be nobody's surprise, was struck in the throat, causing a wound that went to an inch deep, killing him instantly.

It is interesting to find out in this next account that the recklessness of teenage boys is not a modern concept. Richard Halle, a 17-year-old labourer from Spot Acre, near Spotgate in Stoke-on-Trent, was practising archery by shooting at various targets in a field on 2 June 1512, in nearby Stone, Staffordshire. As John Wryghte walked through the field, he called out to Halle, challenging him to aim for his belly. Taking up the challenge, Halle shot an arrow that did not hit the intended mark. Even if it had, we are not really sure what the boys expected to happen, other than Wryghte dying and ending his life in a lot of pain. What happened, however, was quicker but also far worse. The arrow missed his belly and struck Wryghte directly in the right eye, penetrating his brain, unfortunately not quite killing him instantly as Wryghte was alive for seven hours before he eventually died. We know the saying 'boys will be boys' but we are sure that Wryghte will agree, that was another level of daft.

In Little Langford, Wiltshire, Francis Stourton was out hunting rabbits on 5 August 1548, using his longbow in a place called 'dunshatt'. Stourton was carrying a barbed arrow known as a 'broad arrow' in his left hand, which was a type he favoured as the barbed aspect meant that once an animal had been hit, the arrow could not then easily fall out, meaning that if the arrow itself did not kill, the resulting blood loss from the arrow being torn out would. While running at high speed, however, Stourton stumbled and fell in such a way that the arrowhead penetrated the right side of his chest, causing a wound that resulted in his instant death. It is for this kind of reason that quivers (the device often used for storing arrows, sometimes worn slung over the back) are recommended – though nothing is completely foolproof to a sufficiently talented fool.

Henry Pert

The death of Henry Pert is proof, if it were needed, that you can have all the money in the world, but you cannot buy common sense. Henry Pert was a gentleman and a member of the English gentry from Welbeck, near Worksop in Nottinghamshire. In 1552, he met a tragic, unusual and quite frankly ridiculous end caused by his own arrow and his own stupidity.

Pert was practising archery, a common way the gentry passed the time. As he was drawing his bow to shoot, something went terribly wrong. Some historical accounts suggest that the bowstring might have snapped, or the arrow might have been improperly nocked (placed on the bowstring), which was again, common in archery. As a result, the arrow became somehow lodged in the bow and did not fly towards the target as Pert had intended. Unsure as to what was happening, he moved his arms to look at the bow which meant that the arrow was now pointing at his own face. At this exact moment his fingers moved, and the arrow dislodged itself, leaving the bow and striking Henry Pert with enough force to inflict a fatal wound to the head that knocked him over, causing what was later ruled as death by misadventure.

Henry Pert's death was a notable event of its time, given the unusual circumstances and his standing in society. It would have been widely discussed among his contemporaries and probably used as a cautionary tale, as apparently one was needed, to not look directly into a loaded weapon.

The 'Butte' of the Joke

It is not just the archers who need to take precautions when taking part in archery practice. There is a very important role that is usually undertaken by a servant, and that is in the buttes. We still have butts on a modern shooting range, but with guns being used more often than bows and arrows. Working the buttes meant that you were, in theory, behind the target where you were far enough away from it to not be hit; then when firing had finished, you gathered up the arrows and took them back to the participants. Simple enough, when everyone is paying attention at least.

But what happens if not everyone *is* paying attention? On 26 May 1506, in Southwark, John Waller was digging and collecting 'Turfez vel Tussetez for a larke'[10] behind an archery target, a 'butte'. Meanwhile, Robert Myssilden of Croydon, a yeoman, was practising archery with a group of other men. Unaware of Waller's presence behind the target due to the fact he did not actually make himself known to them and indeed was not even supposed to be there, Myssilden accidentally shot an arrow over the butts, striking Waller. The arrow struck the right side of the head just above the ear near the temple. Despite the nature of the injury, Waller did not actually die immediately; instead he suffered for a good few hours before succumbing later that same day.

You would think that people would understand that you should maybe be a bit vigilant when people are firing sharpened objects at high speed in your general vicinity, but perhaps not. As in Wendover, Buckinghamshire, on 9 June 1506, John Barweke was standing near an archery target, observing Thomas Doyly of Great Marlow shooting at the butts. As Barweke watched, he turned and leaned in such a way that his head ended up in the corner of the target area, which it could be argued was his first rookie mistake. At that exact same moment, in a move of pure bad luck straight out of a *Final Destination* movie, the sleeve of Thomas Doyly's shirt fell without him noticing, which affected the flight of his arrow. The released arrow curved slightly mid-air and struck John Barweke in the left side of his throat and jaw, causing a one-inch-deep wound. Due to the swift and immediate care given, Barweke initially survived the injury until 21 June when he succumbed.

Again, on 18 April 1507, this time over in Surrey, Nicholas Digon thought it would be a good idea to lie down near an archery target with other boys, watching butcher John Underhill shooting with his neighbours. Unfortunately, Underhill misfired and accidentally struck Nicholas Digon with his arrow on the left side of his head, not quite killing him instantly but a few hours later. A word to the wise: if you plan to engage in archery, 18 April is not a lucky day to do so, avoid if possible.

Axe-identally Dead

When we talk about the Tudors and the axe, your mind automatically goes to beheadings and usually Henry VIII, but what about those poor souls who found themselves felled by an axe of their own? The axe was a common household tool. Used for chopping wood, animal carcasses and a myriad of other things, it unfortunately does lend itself to some ridiculous and rather gruesome deaths.

John Kynge from Maders, Cornwall, found himself on the wrong side of an axe at home on 5 July 1516 thanks to Ralph Kynge, who was using a 'Fyllyngaxe',[11] to make firewood. Ralph cut a piece of wood and then threw the axe against it to further cut it into smaller pieces of wood. Unfortunately, he was no Captain America and could not rip it apart with his bare hands. The axe struck a knag (a knot in the wood) causing it to bounce back and, rather unluckily, hit John square in the middle of his forehead, penetrating straight to his brain. Surprisingly he did not die straight away; instead it took as long as three days for John to pass away, in what we can only imagine to be the most horrendous pain.

To cut a big trunk of wood into logs for domestic use requires quite a lot of force. You can appreciate that it would be near to impossible to hit the same mark twice (as shown by Rose in the handcuff scene in the movie *Titanic*) and this unfortunate circumstance meant that many limbs were hurt or chopped off. Just like what happened to Robert Byrde of Ashmore in Dorset, who managed to relieve himself of the burden of his right foot while trying to cut some wood for a friend, John Coke, using said friend's axe.

Again, in Hampton Bishop, Herefordshire, a carpenter named John Crompe was squaring a piece of wood with an axe when he slipped and hit himself in the left leg, severing his femoral artery and dying instantly, and messily. You might think as a carpenter he should know how to handle such a weapon, but experience breeds complacency.

It always seems a little more exciting, shall we say, when we find a local incident that we can include, and this one is quite the doozy. On 30 September 1535, in King's Lynn, Norfolk, John Chase was chopping firewood at the house of his master William Pers. Robert Forsett of Wiggenhall St Peter approached him, took his axe in frustration due to the amount of time being taken by Chase to complete his task, and struck one of the billets (a smaller piece of wood used for firewood) with as much force as he could manage. Unable to split the wood due to an unseen knot, the axe ricocheted and struck Chase, who was now standing nearby, in the left shin, slicing it to the bone. The wound, one inch wide, became badly infected and despite hanging on for seven or eight days, Chase lost his life at the end of September. According to the coroner's report, the perpetrator, Robert Forsett, had a grey gelding (a castrated male horse with a coat colour ranging from white to dark grey) worth ten shillings which remained in his custody. Mr Forsett's horse had absolutely nothing to do with the death of John Chase, it was only mentioned in the report to show Robert Forsett's wealth. But what would happen if the horse was accidentally the axe murder?

On a sunny late August afternoon in 1541 a Mr Robert Belyndon was riding his horse from the fields of Billington to Leighton Buzzard in Bedfordshire, with an axe attached at his belt. While passing through a place called Colake, Robert's horse tripped, causing him to fall off and hit the ground in such a way that he landed on his axe, fatally injuring the left side of his body.

Axes, while apparently a fairly regular instrument of doom, are not always the direct cause of a person's untimely end. An axe sometimes has the tendency to start a domino effect if a person lacks sufficient forethought. Laurence Hymon was involved in a tragic accident while helping with a building project in Alice Hymon's barn in Purton, Gloucestershire. He was assisting with the placement of a piece of timber, referred to as 'a couple of a house',[12] and while trying to secure the timber with an axe, the beam fell and struck him on the right side of his head, resulting in a fatal injury, with Hymon being pronounced dead on 31 August 1509.

In Sussex on 23 or 24 May 1508, an accident occurred involving young Daniel Carpynter. It was early in the morning, around 6 am, and Daniel was helping his father William cut down a beech tree with an axe on the family plot. All seemed to be going well, until young Carpynter was struck by a falling branch, hitting him on the left side of his head, causing an instantly fatal wound. Maybe trees really do fight back, and with some gross and unbelievable consequences.

A prime example occurred on 20 January 1520, in Newington, Kent, when yeoman John Marchall was injured while felling an aspen tree with an axe. We agree, the story starts like many others: man cuts down a tree with an axe and said tree falls on him and he dies a few days later, but it would seem this tree had it in for Mr Marchall in particular. As he worked, John was struck on the back of his head by a bough from the tree with such force that it in fact knocked him down, causing such a severe injury that his brain came out through his nostrils. Yes, this poor man was hit from behind by a tree so hard it quite literally brained him and forced it out of his nose. The most shocking part is that John Marchall did not finally die until six days later, on 26 January.

On 25 January 1513, in Bagborough, Somerset, a man called William Smale was felling an oak tree in the nearby Bagborough Wood with an axe – again a fairly standard activity for the time. During the process, the oak could not completely fall as an ash tree was in the way that prevented the oak from cleanly hitting the ground. The ash tree began to bend under the weight of the felled tree, forming an arch. To release the oak, Smale this time struck the ash tree a few times with his axe. This was a bad move as suddenly, the ash tree shattered and a piece of it struck Smale in the head, penetrating his brain. It took William three days to succumb to his injuries, dying on 28 January.

Knives Out, or In

When researching for this book, we were constantly finding ourselves astounded by the ridiculous ways that humans met their maker. Each time we found what we thought was *the* most ridiculous one, we would only need look in another book or journal and the previous 'winner' would be beaten. This is never more accurate when reading about the damage a simple kitchen knife can do.

Take the death of servant girl Alice Bate, who on 14 June was undertaking her usual day-to-day activities for John Brouger, the master of the house.

She was fetching Mr Brouger's bay horse from the pasture and when she reached the gate, she found the horse and tied it to the horse she was riding, so that she could control both as she had done numerous times before. As Alice attempted to remount her horse, assuming the saddle was securely attached, she accidentally stabbed herself in the belly with a knife she was holding in her left hand. The wound, located just under the navel was an inch and a half deep and proved fatal.

On 20 February 1508, in Yeovilton, Somerset, John Gaytt was playing football when he fell onto a knife hanging from his belt. The fall caused a fatal wound to his body, and he died instantly. Just going to throw it out there … maybe don't play sports with knives hanging from your clothing.

A couple of friends from Barking, Essex, proved why you should always leave your work tools at work. William Dale, a goryngman (someone involved in butchery or tailoring), and John Phelippe, a servant of the abbess[13] of Barking Abbey, were arm-wrestling in jest, to see who was the strongest. Phelippe held a trencher knife (a sturdy sharp knife used for cutting thick slices of bread and meat) which he had been using to cut the abbess's bread just before Dale's arrival. During their match, William fell, presumably being unsteady after losing the arm wrestle and unfortunately landed on the tip of John's knife, which penetrated his stomach, causing a fatal injury.

On 17 October 1535, in Horsham St Faith, Norfolk, two teenage boys were working together when boredom kicked in and a one small decision for fun had disastrous consequences. John Shremplyng, aged 15, was in a mill when George Leche, a 14-year-old labourer from Rackheath, arrived to grind a measure of grain. In jest Shremplyng took a handful of flour and threw it into Leche's face and eyes, temporarily blinding him. He then jumped onto his back. There was a brief struggle as Leche tried to get Shremplyng off his back and in the midst of this, Shremplyng accidentally cut himself with Leche's knife. He suffered a three-inch-deep, one-inch-wide wound to his right leg, dying two hours later from the injury.

While hunting a goshawk (a medium–large bird of prey) Nicholas Samborne was trying to build a perch to get a better view by cutting down a small oak with his wood knife. Halfway through cutting, he finished with the knife and threw it on the ground with the tip pointing upwards. As

Nicholas pulled the oak downwards, a rotten branch he was holding suddenly broke off, causing him to fall … straight onto the upturned knife. The knife caused a deep wound to his thigh that extended through to his stomach, measuring twenty inches long, resulting in instant death.

The point of a mediaeval entertainer in the sixteenth century was to be funny. Court jesters were highly skilled and could be well paid, if they were funny enough. Henry VIII loved one of his jesters, Will Sommers, so much his courtiers and privy council would have him deliver the king bad news as he was known to take it better when coming from him. One Tudor entertainer let the 'fame and fortune' go to his head so much, however, that he made a stupid mistake that would cost him his life.

Ironically, there are no records of this particular Tudor entertainer's name, and he may well have vanished into obscurity had it not been for the nature of his death. Night after night this man would go onstage in front of hundreds of people and plunge a dagger into his chest. Blood would gush forth, but he would not die. The crowd loved this, he wooed them with his apparent immortality and they would shower him with applause and money. His trick was that he would be wearing a concealed stab-proof vest that had a bag of pig's blood in the middle, that gave the impression he was in fact bleeding. This continued every evening for a good few months where he would put his vest on, stand on a stage and plunge a dagger into his heart. He was very successful, raking in the money, until one fateful night when, with his usual flourish he plunged the long, shiny dagger into his chest – only this time he had forgotten to put on his all-important vest, and he dropped dead on stage. The crowd cheered, not knowing this was real and assuming his act was extra dramatic that evening. Suffice it to say, his final curtain would end up being one to remember.

Getting the Point

Have you ever held a sword? A proper one, that is, not a wooden one or a toy sword; we mean an actual fighting sword. Those things are no laughing matter. Not only are they obviously sharp, but they are deceptively heavy! In the sixteenth century swords had evolved from the arming sword, with its broad, double-edged blade to the two-handed long sword which featured a longer blade and grip, allowing for powerful strikes and more versatile techniques.

Due to the expense involved in creating one, swords were not a common weapon owned by many and were often a sign of social standing with some being passed down through a family for generations. Usually, knights and other members of the nobility were given a sword either when they were appointed to their position or as a child as a rite of passage, being taught how to use them from an early age, so if the average person were to come across a sword and they were not familiar with how to wield one, it could end badly.

One such example happened in Nottingham at around 11 pm on 4 December 1508. Alan de Sables, a furrier (someone who specialises in the preparation, design and sale of furs), was playing with a sword belonging to William Hall, a cartwright from Gunthorpe. During their play, William Hall accidentally struck Alan de Sables with the point of the sword, inflicting a wound to his stomach that penetrated the intestines. The wound was an inch deep, causing a severe injury from which the contents of his intestines flowed. Alan unfortunately could not be saved and died the next day. To give an idea of how expensive they could be, the sword was valued at twelve shillings and the incident was deemed an accident caused by William Hall.

At Stratford-upon-Avon, some fifty years before the birth of its most famous inhabitant, William Shakespeare, William Wilson was resisting arrest by John Barbour, the local constable. There are no records of what he was being arrested for but in 1509 the most common reasons to be arrested were theft, begging, debt, witchcraft and of course religious nonconformity (one of these is not like the others). In the struggle, William tried to defend himself with a shield and a sword but during the altercation, by some ironic misfortune, William struck and penetrated his own left shin with the sword, inflicting a fatal wound.

The honour of the British gentleman is portrayed in many a film or TV show, sometimes to show how ridiculously far we tend to take our politeness and chivalry. This next unfortunate incident will prove this in all its glory. On 5 June 1517, in Bridgwater, Somerset, John Bartelet and John Trevet of Wendon were engaging in a friendly show of swordsmanship (get your mind out of the gutter). While unsheathing his sword, Bartelet accidentally caused his buckler (a small, round shield) to fall to the ground. Trevet, intending to help his acquaintance, placed his left hand on the buckler and held his sword peaceably in his right hand. Mr Bartelet, not wanting Trevet to have to pick up his shield, slammed his left foot on the buckler to pin it in place. In doing so, this resulted in unexpectedly impaling his lower left leg on the point of Trevet's sword, causing a wound so deep that Bartelet could not recover and he died four days later. The incident was deemed a foolish accident.

'All accidents are preventable' is an infamous line said by Kevin Bush (Emily's father) whenever anyone has a clumsy moment, which means he says it pretty much daily. Clumsiness cannot always be prevented though; sometimes bad things happen to good people for no rhyme or reason and other times you find yourself scratching your head at the stupidity of people.

In Gillingham, Kent, on 23 April 1521 Richard Chelliffeld, a labourer, was with John Coksegge also a labourer, in a local church courtyard. To pass the time they were playing with their swords when Chelliffeld's arm malfunctioned and his sword suddenly and involuntarily fell out of his hand and onto his right leg, causing a wound half an inch deep. The wound bled so much and so quickly that no medical care would help, and he died shortly after. The death was deemed accidental and not caused by any malice from John Coksegge.

Imagine going to a weekend of town games, taking a broken sword as you absolutely did not intend using it, let alone causing anyone harm with it, only for circumstances to be taken out of your control. This is what happened to Thomas Ive from Swavesey in September 1530. Ive, along with a large number of people from Huntingdonshire, Cambridgeshire, and other local counties gathered to watch or participate in various games and competitions, commonly referred to as 'Game of [faded]tyng and other masteryes'. [14] While standing next to an unknown man, Ive noticed that his new companion had a sword in a broken scabbard, intended to show that he meant no harm. The crowd was densely packed, leading to many falling to the ground. In the chaos, Thomas lost his balance and stumbled into the man with the sword, which pierced his thigh, causing a wound from which he could not be saved, and he died that day. The incident was determined to be accidental, with the unknown man bearing no malice or intent to harm. Maybe next time you have no intention of using a sword, do not bring a sword.

Weapons in the sixteenth century were in the process of evolving from swords, axes and longbows to arquebuses and handguns. The many different uses for gunpowder were spreading through the western world, meaning warfare was changing at an alarming rate, and sadly the stupidity of people was keeping pace. If this chapter has taught us nothing else, it is to never underestimate the deadly nature of the humble kitchen knife.

Chapter 11
Notable Mentions

In possibly one of the most human aspects of this entire book, we found during our research that there were certain people and situations that failed to fit neatly into any one of our chapters. There are some that we managed to include in the best fitting place but referenced elsewhere; however, here we have a collection of the stubborn few that would not be labelled.

Hans Steininger

We can guarantee that if you do any online search for strange ways that people have died, along with the inevitable reference to the execution of George, Duke of Clarence,[1] you will likely find reference to Hans Steininger. Regrettably there is not a great deal known about the life of Hans Steininger, and even his year of birth (1508) is an approximation. He lived in the village of Braunau am Inn in Austria, on the Bavarian border. He was apparently quite beloved by his fellow townsfolk as records indicate he was elected governor six consecutive times, which is impressive for any period really. What else was impressive about Steininger was his beard, measuring in at a staggering four feet in length.

Under normal circumstances, Steininger would go about his daily business with his beard rolled up and neatly tucked into a pocket in his clothing. However, on 28 September 1567 a fire broke out in the town and Governor Steininger jumped to the rescue. In the panic, he neglected to roll up and secure his beard and, while coming down the stairs of his home, tripped on the hair and stumbled and fell, breaking his neck in the process. His epitaph at the Braunau parish church depicts Steininger with his beard loose and flowing. As for the beard itself? It has been carefully preserved and passed down through generations of Steininger's descendants before being gifted to the District Museum Herzogsburg where it is on display to this day, a visual acknowledgement of one of the most famous residents of the town. Considering the next most famous resident would be Adolf Hitler, it is understandable why they would be keen to promote one and not the other.

King Charles VIII of France

We have already covered the demise of one king of France, Henry II, in our chapter 'Kill or Cure' due to the employment by his physicians of the wait-and-see method. Fine if you have a cold, not so fine if you took a lance to the eye. Henry II was not the first king of France who met with an avoidable end during the sixteenth century however, as he was beaten to that title by Charles VIII, the last of his branch of the royal House of Valois. Also known as Charles the Affable,[2] he was the only surviving son of his predecessor Louis XI and was reportedly an unwell child and although likeable, perhaps not well suited to the office of a king. When his father died in 1483, Charles inherited the crown aged around 13 and his older sister Anne, along with her husband Peter of Bourbon, stood as regents until he came of age to rule alone.

Despite an earlier betrothal to Margaret of Austria, daughter of the man who would become Holy Roman Emperor Maximilian I, Charles went on to make a political match with Anne of Brittany. A treaty was still made with Emperor Maximilian, however, and with Henry VII of England.[3] Conflict was not to be avoided, and following power struggles in Italy around the infamous Borgia family and its patriarch Pope Alexander VI, Charles was goaded into military action to invade Italy to claim the Kingdom of Naples, which had been offered to him by the previous pope, Innocent VIII.

The French army met with a good deal of success in their campaign, remaining largely unopposed as they marched south, successfully subduing the Republic of Florence and then taking Naples, with Charles being crowned King of Naples on 22 February 1495. The remaining Italian rulers were startled by the success of the French troops and, together with Pope Alexander VI, formed the League of Venice and began the First Italian War in March 1495. The geographical positions of the members of the League meant that it would be difficult for Charles and his troops to leave Italy and return to France without crossing into hostile territory. Somehow, he managed to do it, though it was not without cost and a lot of the riches gained during his campaign were lost in the journey. After the French withdrew from Italy, the forces of Ferdinand II of Aragon swept in and took Naples back, so in the end the French invasion achieved very little except as a show of force.

Despite repeated attempts to take Naples, due to excessive debts at home, Charles was unable to do so before he died. On 7 April 1498, Charles VIII, then aged around 27, was at the Château d'Amboise in the Loire Valley when he decided to watch a game of *jeu de paume*, an early precursor to modern tennis played with the hands instead of racquets and more notably, though more concerningly for the furniture and windows, played indoors. This has earned it the nickname of 'real tennis' compared to the later racquet and lawn versions that we have come to know. While in a hurry on his way to the game, Charles struck his head on the lintel above a door. While this may have hurt, there seemed to be no further cause for concern. Several hours later, however, after the game had finished and he was due to return to his quarters, Charles suddenly collapsed.

The physicians who attended him insisted that the king should not be moved and instead he was carefully placed on a makeshift bed where he was monitored. According to a second-hand account featured in the memoirs of Philip de Commines, Charles started to speak a total of three times, but his powers of speech did not exceed a few words of alleged prayer and nine hours after he had collapsed, Charles VIII died. The widely accepted cause of death is head trauma; however, this is being reviewed by some scholars who believe that the impact with the lintel may not have been enough to cause a terminal head injury and that there may have been an underlying cause at play. Either way, we would certainly suggest paying attention to 'mind your head' signs when passing through doorways, just in case.

Making the Jailhouse Rock

For those who have been fortunate enough to visit a moderately preserved castle or dungeon that functioned during the sixteenth century, it can reasonably be assumed that we agree on one thing – the prison area would not have been a pleasant place to stay. So, it is little wonder that some people tried, with varying degrees of success, to escape incarceration. Our chapters on 'Extracting a Confession' and 'Crime and Punishment' will give you a little more indication as to why, as well as what happened when they failed to escape. In December 1502, twenty-eight prisoners being held together in a single cell in Colchester Castle jail made a valiant attempt to escape, that did not end well for them at all.

Somehow, while under the watch of jailer John Onger, the prisoners managed to smuggle in all the equipment necessary to create fire, including sulphur and a fire source itself. How they managed to sneak this past a guard fire of any kind is a mystery, but somehow, they did. They managed to break the chains securing the prisoners, known as bayards, to enable mobility around the cell, then they placed the fuel against the thick wooden door and set it alight. We can only assume that the plan was for the door to burn down sufficiently to enable the prisoners inside the cell to storm out and then make their way to freedom. What was not factored in, however, was the thickness of the door and the stone walls around them, providing insulation for the fire.[4] Soon the heat became intense and the cell began to fill with smoke; as they had set fire to their only means of exit, all twenty-eight suffocated in the smoke.

Under the Weather

The British weather is renowned as one of our main sources of complaint as well as our main conversation opener. Throughout history the weather in and around the British Isles has proven to be an effective weapon against invaders, holding back the Spanish Armada and the German Luftwaffe.[5] It can, however, also be damaging to the people living on the Isles.

In possibly one of the most dramatically poetic deaths we have encountered (which in the post-Renaissance era of courtly love and poetry is saying something), servant John Potter of Wiltshire was having quite a bad day of it when in February 1505 he was using his master's horse to carry oats to Salisbury. As he came through an area called Charlton Down the heavens opened and pelted poor Potter. Being completely alone in the field aside from the horse and seeing no end to the wind and the rain, Potter 'gave up his spirit gasping' (Gunn, 2017). It isn't documented how long Potter was in the field before being found, but his death was so beautifully dramatic that it seemed worthy of special mention. John Potter was not the only soul to have expired due to exposure in a storm; the same fate befell Isabel Burngate in 1534 as she was walking home from market in Cumberland, Edward Wyn in 1542 in Yorkshire, too.

It wasn't just the wind and rain that would have a fatal effect, though. Weather during the sixteenth century and then into the seventeenth century took somewhat of a strange turn, starting with intense summer heat that caused drought, turning to extreme flooding and including a period that has been termed the Little Ice Age.[6] Temperatures began to rise across Europe, starting in February 1540. Records show that in the period between February and September of that year the city of London only experienced rain six times. Streams and rivers began to dry up and the situation became so extreme that the River Thames was depleted to the extent where seawater was able to come on a tidal flow past London Bridge. The influx of seawater polluting the main water supply to the city led to an outbreak of cholera and dysentery, killing thousands. Over in Paris the water level of the River Seine flowing through the heart of that city had dropped so much that in some parts people were able to walk across from one bank to the other. The heat caused crops to either ripen too early or fail entirely across Europe, leading to mass famine, death of livestock en masse and drought. The ancient city of Rome in Italy went without a single drop of rain falling in approximately nine months. Winters remained too warm for snow and rain to fall; by mid-1541 there appeared no end in sight, with much of Europe in serious trouble due to drought, famine, disease and the often-materialising risk of forest fires.

But with the water evaporating across the continent, what goes up must come down and in October 1541 the proverbial dam finally broke and the heavens opened. People rejoiced at first, but by 1542 the scale had tipped in the other direction. Flooding hit most of England, the parched land unable to absorb the deluge, causing equal mayhem, not to mention being the perfect conduit for dysentery-causing bacteria. The damp was followed by cold and storms, causing the River Thames to flood in 1551 and battering port towns along the North Sea, particularly along the Dutch coast.

The weather then seemed to be on a pendulum over the next decade, swinging between excessive heat and drought to violent storms and flooding. It is little wonder why people such as John Potter found themselves giving up on life when caught in a storm. Winters grew colder and more severe, with rivers icing over enough that sports and games came to be enjoyed on them, most notably the court of Elizabeth I at Westminster in 1564 where football and other sports were played, with even the queen herself on the ice. It wouldn't be until 1607 that the 'Great Winter' occurred, but winters towards the end of the sixteenth century were starting to claim lives.

In 1542 Thomas and Jane Crabtree, husband and wife from Derbyshire, were killed along with their young son Otwell, when a large snowdrift collapsed against the side of their house, knocking loose masonry that fell on the family. In December of the same year an additional seven people were recorded as having been found in the snow, with cause of death being listed as exposure due to a sudden storm.

The Spanish Armada

The Spanish Armada was a formidable fleet of approximately 130 ships, assembled by King Phillip II of Spain with the aim of invading England to re-establish Catholicism. It was one of the most ambitious naval endeavours of its time and vastly outweighed the English fleet. However, due to a series of unfortunate events, for the Spanish anyway, the English would defeat the Armada not once but twice, with ease.

The Armada carried around 30,000 men, including sailors, soldiers, officers and support staff, with 8,000 sailors to man the ships and 19,000 soldiers intended for the land invasion of England. There were 2,500 cannons on board of various sizes and each soldier was armed with equipment such as muskets, pikes and swords. The Armada was also intended to rendezvous with an additional fleet carrying the Duke of Parma's army from the Spanish Netherlands, adding more troops and supplies to the invasion force. Everything was set for an easy Spanish victory. But there was something so big, so unpredictable that the Spanish didn't count on, something they rarely had to worry about, with being that much closer to the equator ... the British weather.

Uncertain how the weather will behave hour by hour let alone day by day, the British skies like to make fools of us all, being incredibly warm and sunny one minute to a raging thunderstorm the next. During the initial encounters with the English fleet in the English Channel, the weather was relatively calm, which allowed the English to effectively use their superior manoeuvrability and long-range cannons against the slower, less-agile Spanish galleons. On 29 July 1588, the decisive Battle of Gravelines took place. Although the weather was fair during the battle, the subsequent stormy weather played a significant role in scattering the Spanish fleet. The Armada attempted to retreat northward around Scotland to then return to Spain by sailing down the west coast of Ireland. This route was chosen to avoid further confrontation with the English fleet. However, the Armada encountered severe unforeseen storms in the North Sea, causing significant damage and forced many Spanish ships off course, leading to shipwrecks along the rugged western coast of Ireland. It is estimated that around a total of twenty-four ships were wrecked on the Irish coast, and thousands of Spanish sailors and soldiers perished as a result. The Armada had few opportunities to find safe harbour due to the continuous storms. Out of the original 130 ships in the Armada, only sixty-seven made it back to Spain.

The severe weather conditions that plagued the Spanish Armada have often been referred to as the 'Protestant Wind', a term coined to describe the belief in England that divine intervention favoured the Protestant English cause over the Catholic Spanish invasion.

If you think unforeseen weather is ridiculous enough to have taken out the fearsome Armada, there was one other very simple yet effective strategy that the English used. They took dilapidated ships, set them on fire and pointed them towards the enemy fleet. As the English fleet engaged the Spanish Armada in the English Channel, they sought ways to disrupt and scatter the tightly packed Spanish ships anchored off the coast of Calais. Two of Queen Elizabeth's most trusted advisors and favourites, Lord Charles Howard and Sir Francis Drake, devised a plan to use fire ships to break the defensive crescent formation of the Armada. On the night of 28 July 1588, the English prepared eight old, expendable vessels to serve as fire ships. These vessels were filled with pitch, tar, gunpowder and other flammable materials, set on fire and allowed to drift with the tide towards the anchored Spanish fleet. The sight of the burning ships approaching in the darkness must have been something to behold and created immediate panic among the Spanish, which forced the Spanish to cut their anchor cables to avoid the inferno.

The defeat of the Spanish Armada in 1588 was a result of a combination of innovative English tactics and adverse weather conditions. The strategic use of fire ships by the English effectively disrupted the formidable Spanish formation, causing panic and disarray that left the Armada vulnerable . This tactical brilliance was compounded by severe storms, which scattered the retreating Spanish ships and resulted in significant losses due to shipwrecks and harsh conditions.

The once-feared Spanish Armada, with its grand ambitions, was rendered powerless by the ridiculous effectiveness of these combined factors. Together, these elements decisively thwarted the Spanish invasion attempt, marking a pivotal moment in naval warfare. The victory not only safeguarded England from invasion but also signalled the decline of Spanish maritime dominance and the rise of England as a global naval power.

Game, Set, Match

Sport could be a dangerous business in the sixteenth century. Aside from the more martial pastimes like jousting and tournaments, football was a sport enjoyed by many. Admittedly it was not like the modern version we know now. First, it was played between two opposing towns and the goalposts were the town gates, or equivalent markers. Add to this the fact that teams consisted of as many from either town who wanted to join in and knives were allowed on the 'pitch', and it is little wonder that after approximately seven deaths throughout his reign from the not-so-beautiful game, Henry VIII made it illegal in 1540 and this was not overturned until the following century. It is worth noting that football had already been banned previously by Edward III, but it seemed that the love of the game would just not die, unlike some of the players.

Another game that often had violent results was Prisoner's Base, similar in form to the game known variably as Tag or Tig, but where, when a player from the opposing team ventures out of their base, the other team have to chase, capture and imprison them.[7] On 1 January 1545 Louis Rugge was playing Prison Base in Worcestershire and as he was running to capture someone from the opposing team, he lost his footing and fell, giving himself an injury to which he succumbed six days later. A similar accident happened later that same year when William Warter was engaging in a game in April and was making to chase and capture Richard Harwood of the opposing team when Warter slipped and fell over onto his back. He possibly would have been fine, with only his pride wounded, except that as Warter had left his base he became fair game for the opposing team to capture, and Harwood was making for him at the same time as Warter was coming to make a capture. Harwood did not see Warter go down until it was too late, and caught his foot on the fallen man, tripping and falling onto him, crushing him against the stony road surface and causing a fatal injury to his back and kidneys.

Games that were played one on one could easily be just as troublesome as team sports, even ones made up in the spur of the moment for a laugh. This was tragically understood far too late by John Ruyley when he was standing in a courtyard next to the building where one William Gosworth was making tiles, accompanied by his father's servant, Alice. Gosworth took a lump of tile-making clay and threw it at Alice, attempting to be playful, however his aim was off and he missed her. The lump of clay instead flew past Alice and hit Ruyley on the side, causing him a serious injury from which he died later that same day. Gosworth did not stick around to see what came from his misfire, as he is alleged to have fled the scene.

A more genteel pastime could be found during country celebrations in the late spring where the tradition of dancing around the maypole lived on. This too was not without its dangers however, as Thomas Alsopp of Coventry found out when, in April 1558, he was standing in the grounds of the Greyfriars cemetery when a maypole in a neighbouring field fell over, hitting the cemetery wall and sending loose stones flying straight at his head, killing him instantly. Something similar also happened to a boy called Thomas Wylkes in Oxfordshire who was playing in May 1543 near a maypole that was about to be taken down as the celebrations for were over for the year. As the pole was ready to fall, one of the gentlemen responsible for removing it called out to warn those around. Young Thomas tried to run but tripped, and the pole fell on his back.

Deadly Workloads

It is alleged that cleanliness is next to godliness, but there are some who perhaps took that a little too literally, inadvertently using chores to meet their maker. This was the case for Alice Malyne who, in March 1576, found herself washing laundry in one of the ponds at Earith in Huntingdonshire. Among the items to be cleaned was a large linen sheet, which was proving cumbersome to carry. To transport this back with the rest of her linen, Malyne came up with the bright idea of wearing the sheet across her shoulders like a cape and pinned it in place. On any other day this would, indeed, have been a good idea, but as fate would have it, a strong wind picked up and caught in the sheet, whipping it up around Malyne's head so that she was temporarily blinded. While struggling to get free, she staggered too close to a nearby pond and fell in still tangled in the sheet and drowned.

Risky Kisses

We know from the exploits of Henry VIII and some of his courtiers that the realm of courtly love could be a risky one, but the deadly aspects of romance were not just the remit of the upper classes. Jerome Snouke, a servant in a household in Somerset, had been turning his attentions for a while towards Grace Wyseman, with every intention of soon making her his wife and it seems his affections were returned. One day in December 1565, Snouke spied Wiseman walking by, and ran up to her with the hope of stealing a kiss. Wiseman was accommodating to his wishes, but it seems that both had underestimated the length of a willow rod she was holding. Snouke did not underestimate it for long though as, when reaching his beloved and going in for the kiss, the rod poked him hard in his left eye, leaving a deep wound from which he would die four days later. It is worth noting for all the ardent lovers out there, check first if your partner is holding a pointed object before going in for a kiss – advice that works for many other situations too.

Pronged Problems

While we toyed with including these in the chapter entitled 'Weaponry Woes', it was felt that accidents involving pitchforks would be better suited here as they weren't technically a military weapon, though in some frays we know that peasant-based militia used whatever they could get their hands on. But here we are and here are some of the ways in which people fell afoul of the pronged menace.

John Hammyng of Hertfordshire kept his demise short, sharp and simple when, in September 1524, he fell backwards onto a pitchfork and stabbed himself in the right buttock, causing a two-inch-deep wound that must have been either infected or hit a main blood vessel as he died not long after. William Love of Fleggburgh in Norfolk met a bit more of a dramatic end as he decided it would be a good idea to carry a pitchfork while riding a horse – what could go wrong? Well, quite a few things actually if you've managed to read this far into the book. In this instance Love lost his grip on the horse and fell, catching himself with the pitchfork and wounding himself in a very intimate area which according to the coroner's inquest was around ten inches deep. The wound was quite rapidly fatal, so a lesson was very much learned there.

Sticks and Stones

Sometimes all a person needed to do in the sixteenth century to fall victim to misfortune was to simply go for a walk and fate would find them. We have all seen those sketches on television of a poor, unsuspecting person walking underneath a piano that is being lifted into a building when the rope snaps. Jane Morton of Staffordshire was prey to something similar while walking in late January 1508 when a rock that was being held up by a rope suddenly came loose somehow and fell on her head, causing her an injury that she would succumb to two days later. The coroner in his report felt that it was important to note that the rock was of no value, though we are not sure that particular thought would have mattered much to Jane Morton as it plummeted towards her.

A second person to fall victim to a particularly vicious stone was John Massey of Shropshire who, in 1599, was minding his own business leaning against a large stone when he slipped and fell. The stone, clearly deciding to pay like for like, proceeded to fall on top of him, squashing Massey flat. In this instance, the stone had worth, being valued at 2s 6d.

Twenty years after the batfowling incident mentioned in 'Food Fatalities' where Thomas Gadge met his end, John Shorte was out with Arthur Fayerfaxe at 11 pm trying to flush out wildfowl. Fayerfaxe started to beat the hedge from one side with a staff while Shorte went round to the other side to flush the birds out from there. Fayerfaxe became a bit too vigorous with his staff and, not knowing where Shorte was, he struck him in the head, mortally wounding him as Shorte did not survive through the next day.

History Mystery

Christopher Marlowe, an influential playwright, poet and William Shakespeare's best friend (this is an assumption, but they would have known each other) is surrounded by a fascinating historical mystery. Marlowe's life and more importantly death are shrouded in intrigue.

Born in Canterbury, in 1564, the same year as William Shakespeare, Marlowe's exact date of birth is unknown, but he was baptised on 26 February 1564. He attended the King's School in Canterbury and later received a scholarship to study at Corpus Christi College in Cambridge. He earned a Bachelor of Arts degree in 1584 and a Master of Arts degree in 1587, despite initial opposition due to suspicions about his activities, perhaps arising from his frequent absences, or speculation that he had converted to Roman Catholicism and would soon attend college elsewhere. These suspicions were put to rest, or at least dismissed, when the Queen's Privy Council sent a letter declaring that he was now working 'on matters touching the benefit of his country', and he was awarded his master's degree on schedule.

Marlowe's role as a spy is well documented but not thoroughly understood. He was reportedly recruited while at Cambridge and worked for Sir Francis Walsingham's intelligence network for the Elizabethan government. His assignments and the exact nature of his work remain largely speculative, adding to the mystery, and possible reason for his murder.

After leaving university, Marlowe began writing and his ability to turn the 'blank page' into complex works of art laid the foundation for playwrights to follow. However, Marlowe's writings often challenged contemporary norms and religious doctrines. For example, the play *Doctor Faustus* deals with themes of ambition, sin and damnation, and he was known for his atheistic and controversial ideas, which might have put him at odds with the authorities. Being an atheist and blasphemous were serious charges at the time. These accusations, along with his association with radical thinkers, may have contributed to his dangerous position.

Marlowe died on 30 May 1593, in Deptford, London at the age of just 29 under very suspicious circumstances. On the day of his death Marlowe spent the day at a Miss Eleanor Bull's house in Deptford, with Ingram Frizer, Nicholas Skeres and Robert Poley. These men were all connected to the Elizabethan court and intelligence networks. According to the official inquest, the men had been eating and drinking throughout the day. In the evening, a quarrel broke out between Marlowe and Frizer over the bill, referred to as 'the reckoning'. During said altercation, Marlowe allegedly attacked Frizer with a dagger. Then, in self-defence, Frizer struck Marlowe above the right eye with the dagger, resulting in Marlowe's death.

Frizer was arrested and put on trial for Marlowe's death. The inquest, led by the coroner, concluded that Frizer acted in self-defence, and he was subsequently pardoned by the queen herself just a month later. This swift pardon and the circumstances of the inquest have led to suspicions and conspiracy theories about whether Marlowe's death was a premeditated murder orchestrated by political enemies or part of a larger cover-up.

There have been several conspiracy theories over the death of Marlowe, each more mysterious then the last, but all possible. Well, nearly all:

- Espionage/spy connections – Marlowe's involvement in espionage for the Elizabethan government would have made him a likely target. His connections with high-profile figures and his potential knowledge of sensitive information could have led to an assassination by political enemies.
- Atheism and blasphemy – Marlowe was accused of atheism and heresy, serious charges in the sixteenth century. Some scholars have since suggested that his death was orchestrated to silence him and prevent the spread of his controversial ideas.
- Escape from prosecution – Some theories propose that Marlowe's death was actually staged to allow him to escape imminent arrest and prosecution, but no reports state what he could have been arrested for, however. This theory is supported by the mysterious and somewhat convenient nature of the inquest and Frize's quick pardon.
- Accepted narrative – The official account remains that Marlowe's death was the result of a drunken brawl over a petty dispute. While many find this explanation unsatisfactory given the backgrounds of those involved, it is the narrative supported by historical records.

The craziest and most radical of all the speculative theories must be the one where Christopher Marlowe is actually William Shakespeare. This suggests that Marlowe faked his own death but continued to write under the pseudonym William Shakespeare. Supporters of this theory point to similarities in writing styles and themes between Marlowe's known works and Shakespeare's early plays. Ignoring the fact that we have records of Shakespeare's baptism, county of birth being completely different, his school records, his family history etc., personally, we don't think this one has much credence.

Despite his short life, and the mystery that surrounds it, you can't argue that Marlowe's impact on literature was profound. He is often credited with transforming English drama, and he remains one of the most intriguing figures of the Elizabethan era.

Chapter 12

Ridiculous Survivals

When writing a book that is all about death you can find yourself becoming a little despondent with life. There is only so much you can read about misfired arrows, people drowning in poo and 'suddenly cow' before it all starts to get to you, so we thought we would add a chapter celebrating the absolutely ridiculous ways people have survived what should have otherwise definitely have killed them.

From being shipwrecked on a deserted island, sold into slavery and beaten to flooding entire provinces, eating leather to survive and befriending your indigenous captors – were these people the epitome of human resilience or were they helped by fate and just a little divine intervention? Either way the human mind, body and soul can endure more than we might think possible. To paraphrase the immortal words of Iago (the parrot from Disney's *Aladdin*) it is surprising what you can live through.

Not So Plain Sailing

The sea is a cruel mistress, and if not treated with respect and care she will bite back. That has always been the case, but in the sixteenth century ships were nowhere near as robust as they are today, and even now we have several sunken ships and issues on board sailing vessels. When things went wrong on boats made of wood and nails, they went very wrong but the persistence and determination of the human body to survive in the toughest of elements can be extraordinary.

Álvar Núñez Cabeza de Vaca

Álvar Núñez Cabeza de Vaca's journey is one of the most remarkable survival stories of the age of exploration. He and four shipmates should not have made it through another day, let alone survive for years.

Born around 1490 in Jerez de la Frontera, Spain, Cabeza de Vaca came from a noble family whose surname origin ('cow's head' in Spanish) is not known, unfortunately. He embarked on the ill-fated Narváez expedition in 1527, aiming to explore and conquer Florida. The expedition, led by Pánfilo de Narváez, set sail from Spain with about 600 men on board. His military service to the Spanish crown then and later during a brief civil war in Spain (May 1520–April 1521) won Cabeza de Vaca the appointment as treasurer and first lieutenant of said expedition. Their goal was to establish colonies and find riches in the New World, as were several other explorers from all over the known world. After a series of unfortunate events including bad weather and navigation errors, the expedition landed somewhere near present-day Tampa Bay, Florida, in April of 1528. However, with their ship wrecked, things for the team would not get any easier from there.

The Native Americans already settled there were not best pleased when random people from other countries started to claim land that did not belong to them, so the explorers met quite a lot of indigenous resistance. Along with dense forests, swamps and unfamiliar terrain, their supplies and morale were quickly depleted.

The leadership struggled with internal conflict and poor decision-making, that led to a feeling of mistrust within the group, thus creating further complications with their efforts to find a sustainable route or to establish a colony. As time went on and starvation and disease took their toll, the men decided to leave and constructed makeshift rafts to escape by sea. This decision led to further disaster as the rafts were then separated by currents and storms.

Álvar Núñez Cabeza de Vaca's raft washed ashore on what is now Galveston Island, Texas. So decimated by sickness were the crew due to the unknown natures of this new country that by spring 1529 only thirteen Spaniards and an African slave remained alive. Cabeza de Vaca then ventured into the interior of mainland, but he soon became seriously ill during the winter and as he had been absent for so long, he was believed dead. As a result of this, twelve of the fourteen survivors headed down the coast toward Mexico when the weather warmed, which seems sensible. Spoilers – it was not. Out of the dozen who left, nine would die from mishaps or attacks by natives; the three still alive were Alonso del Castillo, Andrés Dorantes de Carranza and his slave, the African Estevanico, plus Cabeza de Vaca … somewhere. All survived by becoming slaves of Coahuiltecan Indians—specifically Mariames and Yguaces – and adopting their indigenous customs and languages. Due to his quick thinking and abilities Cabeza de Vaca became known as a healer among the different tribes, where he used both new (to the natives) European techniques as well as indigenous ones he learned along the way to treat the sick. He also engaged in trading, which provided some level of mobility and improved his relations with the natives, demonstrating the level of trust he had built in that time.

Eventually he was reunited with the other survivors and after eight long years, they managed to escape, embarking on an epic 2,400-mile trek across the American Southwest, travelling through present-day Texas, New Mexico, Arizona and eventually reaching the Gulf of California. In 1537 Cabeza de Vaca returned to Spain and published his account of the expedition, entitled *La Relación*, that detailed his experiences of the geography and the indigenous tribes.

From surviving disastrous seas, starvation and disease, to being held captive for eight years and walking 2,400 miles to freedom, Álvar Núñez Cabeza de Vaca's story is a testament to human endurance, quick thinking and sheer stubbornness.

Pedro Serrano

Pedro Serrano hailed from a seafaring community in Spain, and likely received training and experience in navigation, seamanship and survival skills from a young age. During the early sixteenth century, Spain was a dominant maritime power, with many of its coastal settlements being hubs of naval activity. Very little is known about Serrano's life but given the period's focus on exploration and military campaigns, it is probable that Serrano had participated in previous naval and military endeavours, so it is doubtful that his last was also his first, especially considering how he was able to survive.

Around 1526, Pedro Serrano was part of a Spanish expedition navigating the treacherous waters of the Caribbean Sea. The specifics of the shipwreck are unclear, but it is believed that Serrano's ship either ran aground on a reef or was wrecked by a storm. Either way, the ship sank, and Serrano was washed ashore. He found himself completely alone on a small, uninhabited island in the Caribbean that was totally barren, with no freshwater sources, vegetation or animal life to provide any kind of food, water or shelter. Things were looking beyond bleak for Pedro; he needed to figure something out otherwise he would be dead; it was as simple as that.

From his apparent extensive training and experience Serrano quickly began putting a plan in motion. He found shells, rocks and any remnants from the ship to catch and store rainwater. With no other sources of food, Serrano needed to rely on the sea with fish becoming his primary diet, using makeshift tools fashioned from debris or even his bare hands to catch them. In addition to fish, when possible, Pedro would find shellfish such as clams and crabs, and occasionally even caught sea turtles which were common in the Caribbean. It's not nice to think of him killing and eating a turtle but he was in a precarious situation and needs must.

Shelter was an extremely important aspect to his survival. He used any materials he could find. This may have included driftwood, parts of the wrecked ship, and other debris washed ashore, but it would have been few and far between.

One of the biggest challenges Serrano faced would have been the psychological impact of complete isolation. He had zero human contact for years. Maintaining somewhat of a routine and clinging to any small amount of hope of a rescue would have been critical to Serrano's mental well-being and kept him alive just as much as the food, water or shelter.

Serrano spent around eight years on the island before a passing Spanish ship spotted him. The Spanish sailors were initially wary of Serano due to his wild appearance and outlandish claims, but they eventually took him aboard, ending his prolonged isolation. After his rescue, Serrano returned to Spanish-controlled territory where his story of survival became famous and was documented in a variety of sources such as Spanish chroniclers and historians.

Richard Wood

On 5 February 1566, a fisherman named Richard Wood and his two sons Thomas and Edward were out in their small boat, a 'dredging cock', at Bartlett Creek, near Gillingham, in the Medway marshes. They were dredging for oysters, a common activity for fishermen given the high demand in London, and they would make a pretty penny for a few hours' early work. By 11 am their boat was filled with oysters, and so they began their journey back to the bank of the Thames.

However, the wind began to pick up, causing the boat to take on water faster than they could bail and eventually the boat filled to the point where it finally capsized, throwing all three into the creek. Due to the cold water and the strong currents the situation quickly turned perilous, especially for the two boys. Fortunately, two other fishermen, Edward Geere and John Grygg, were moored nearby. They, along with what the jurors at the time described as the 'favour of God', managed to rescue Richard and Edward from the water. Despite their best efforts, however, Thomas Wood drowned.

The story of Richard, Edward and Thomas Wood exemplifies both survival and devastating loss. While Richard and Edward were lucky enough to survive with the help of fellow fishermen Geere and Grygg, Thomas's death serves as a sobering reminder of the dangers faced by those who made their living from the sea in the sixteenth century.

Sir Hugh Willoughby and Richard Chancellor

Sir Hugh Willoughby's expedition to find the Northeast Passage is a tale of exploration and the enduring human will to survive. While the crew, including Hugh Willoughby, did in fact perish in the extreme conditions of the Arctic, Willoughby's journals and diaries show an exceptional group of men with such a desire to live, coupled with the determination of Richard Chancellor, who by sheer luck steered his ship in a different direction, to survive, and spent his life making sure his men weren't forgotten.

During the mid-sixteenth century, European nations were keen to find new trade routes to and from Asia. The Northeast Passage, a sea route along the northern coast of Europe and Asia, was one such route that promised direct access to China and the East Indies, bypassing the long and often perilous journey around Africa. The previous route began in a major European port such as Lisbon, London or Amsterdam, down the Atlantic sailing routes, along the west coast of Africa before crossing the Indian Ocean to eventually reach Asia. This would take approximately six to twelve months, depending on weather conditions, ships' conditions, etc. The new Northeast Passage route would typically begin in a European port, such as Arkhangelsk in Russia or ports in Scandinavia, sail past the northern coast of Russia, continue through the Bering Strait that separates Russia and Alaska before entering the Pacific Ocean and ending in Asia. This route would take twenty to thirty days, which is considerably shorter and thus more cost effective. However, the route is a lot more treacherous and in unknown territory with conditions many European sailors would likely not have endured before.

Formed in 1551, the Muscovy Company, also known as the Company of Merchant Adventurers to New Lands, was established to find this most northern route to Asia with Sir Hugh Willoughby chosen to lead the company's first expedition. The expedition consisted of three ships: the *Bona Esperanza*, commanded by Willoughby; the *Edward Bonaventure*, commanded by Richard Chancellor; and the *Bona Confidentia*. Just two years later, on 10 May 1553 the fleet set sail, northward through the North Sea without any issues, navigating past the Shetland Islands with ease. However, in August, the ships encountered a severe storm near the coast of Norway which caused the fleet to become separated, with Chancellor's ship, the *Edward Bonaventure*, continuing its own path. A stroke of luck that would turn out to be the difference between life and death.

Continuing their course, Willoughby's ships, the *Bona Esperanza* and the *Bona Confidentia*, became trapped in ice when the Varzino River in the Kola Peninsula of Russian Lapland, in the Arctic region, froze over. As the harsh Arctic winter set in, Willoughby and his seventy-strong crew faced extreme cold like never before, as well as starvation, and scurvy.[1] They were ill-equipped, with no suitable clothing or experience for these types of conditions. They attempted to find food and shelter, but the severe weather made survival impossible.

In the spring of 1554, a group of Russian fishermen discovered the frozen bodies of Willoughby and his crew. The ships had been abandoned, and the crew had succumbed to the elements. Among the remains, the fishermen found Willoughby's extensive journals and logbooks. These detailed documents provided a comprehensive and grim record of their struggle to survive. The early entries describe the fleet's separation from Richard Chancellor and his ship due to the storms off Norway. Willoughby documents the landscapes, weather conditions and any notable geographical features they encountered. He then journals how the ships became trapped in ice and the moment he and the crew realised they would be unable to proceed until the ice thawed. The entries describe the crew's efforts to find food and shelter such as hunting local wildlife and attempting to make their living conditions more bearable, vividly depicting the severe cold and how it affected the crew. Willoughby wrote how they tried to ration the remaining food and how malnutrition was exacerbated by the harsh environment.

The later entries reflect a sense of hopelessness as the crew's condition worsened. Willoughby's handwriting becomes more sporadic, brief and to the point, indicating his declining health and morale. The final entries are poignant, documenting the last few days of the crew. Willoughby's last recorded words express heartbreak of acceptance of their fate, acknowledging that they were unlikely to survive.

While Hugh Willoughby and his crew's fate was tragic, Richard Chancellor managed to navigate the *Edward Bonaventure* safely to the White Sea. He travelled overland to Moscow, where he established trade relations with Tsar Ivan IV (better known as Ivan the Terrible), laying the groundwork for future successful Anglo-Russian trade. Chancellor ensured that Willoughby's story was told and used to highlight the dangers and challenges of Arctic exploration. The knowledge gained from the failed expedition informed future attempts to navigate the Northeast Passage and doubtlessly saved many more lives than were lost on that voyage.

Some forty years later, in 1596, Dutch explorer Willem Barentsz attempted to find the Northeast Passage. Unsurprisingly, his ship became ice-bound near Novaya Zemlya, and Barentsz and his crew were forced to spend the winter in the Arctic. They built a cabin out of the ship's timber and survived the extreme cold by hunting polar bears and using driftwood for fuel. Barentsz himself did not survive the return journey, but many of his crew did thanks to his quick thinking and leadership.

Grace O'Malley – The Pirate Queen of Ireland

You could call her the first twenty-first-century feminist ... in the sixteenth century. Known in Irish as Gráinne Ní Mháille, Grace O'Malley is a remarkable figure in Irish history, renowned for her prowess as a pirate, chieftain and leader, which is an amazing show of survival not only insofar as having dangerous jobs that are usually held by men, but that she was also a high-powered woman in a patriarchal society. Her life and legacy are steeped in adventure, resistance and defiance against the English.

Grace O'Malley was born around 1530 into the O'Malley clan, a powerful seafaring family from County Mayo on the west coast of Ireland. Her father Eoghan Dubhdara Ó Máille was the chieftain of the clan, which controlled the coastlines and engaged in both legitimate trade and piracy. She would have been taught the art of seafaring and been familiar with the seas around her from childhood. Despite the traditional gender roles of the time, Grace was determined to follow in her beloved father's footsteps. She is said to have cut her hair short and dressed as a boy to convince her father to take her on his sea voyages, earning her the nickname 'Gráinne Mhaol' (bald Gráinne)

When she was of age, Grace married Dónal an Chogaidh Ó Flaithbheartaigh (Donal of the Battles) from the powerful O'Flaherty clan, uniting two influential families. They had three children, and upon Dónal's death in battle, Grace returned to her family's territory. She later married Richard 'Iron Richard' Burke, aligning herself with yet another powerful family. This marriage was both strategic and brief, as Grace reportedly divorced him after a year but retained control of his castle on Clare Island

After the death of her father, Grace commanded a fleet of ships, engaging in piracy against English and Spanish vessels. She also conducted legitimate trade, using her deep knowledge of the western coast of Ireland to her advantage. Her leadership extended to defending her territories from rival clans and conducting raids on English-controlled lands. Her reputation as a fierce and cunning leader grew, earning her respect and fear from allies and enemies alike.

As English influence in Ireland expanded under Elizabeth I, Grace effectively resisted their incursions with ease. She supported Irish rebellions and used her naval power to disrupt English shipping and supply lines. In 1577, she was captured by the English governor of Connacht, Sir Richard Bingham, and imprisoned in Dublin Castle. However, due to her connections and the strategic importance of maintaining some level of local control, she was swiftly released.

Her biggest and most notable achievement is her private in-person meeting with Elizabeth I. In 1593 she made a bold move by sailing to England to petition Queen Elizabeth I. She sought the release of her sons and half-brother, who had been captured by the English and imprisoned in the Tower. She also sought the alleviation of the oppressive policies imposed by Sir Richard Bingham. The meeting between these two formidable women took place at Greenwich Castle in 1593 and was conducted in Latin, as neither spoke the other's native language. Grace's charisma and political acumen impressed Elizabeth so much that it led to a negotiation that secured her family's release as well as some minor concessions, though English pressure on her territories continued.

During the 1595–97 rebellion by Hugh O'Neil, Earl of Tyrone, County Mayo suffered much devastation during the uprising. Grace's fleet was able to be put to sea once again unchallenged, but she was now in her twilight years and could no longer sail the seas as she once did. Grace O'Malley died sometime in 1603, but her legacy as a courageous and powerful woman lives on, immortalised in Irish folklore, songs and literature, highlighting her as a trailblazing female leader in a male-dominated world.

She had strongholds on her headlands.
And brave galleys on the sea
And no warlike chief or Viking
E'er had bolder heart than she.

Chambers, 1979

The Mary Rose

The famous warship of the English Tudor navy, the *Mary Rose*, was named after Henry VIII's favourite sister Mary and the humble rose, the emblem of the Tudor dynasty. She was launched in 1511, and served the navy for 34 years, participating in several naval engagements against the French, winning all but one.

On 19 July 1545, during the Battle of the Solent,[3] the *Mary Rose* faced the French fleet, not an uncommon occurrence based on previous battles. The ship had approximately 600 men on board as well as equipment and many gun ports. The gun ports would open, and the cannons would be lined up to fire out of them.

The French fleet, seeking to invade England, posed a serious threat, prompting the English to mobilise their navy, which included the *Mary Rose*. Due to possibly the weight of everything onboard, the open gun ports or the sudden change in wind direction the *Mary Rose* sank suddenly and quickly. The crew barely had time to react with all but thirty-five men going down with the ship. The reason this is a more significant event is because her sinking was actually seen by Henry VIII as he watched the battle from Southsea Castle.

The *Mary Rose* lay on the seabed undisturbed for over four centuries until its discovery in 1971 by marine archaeologist Alexander McKee and a team of divers and researchers. The human remains of more than 179 individuals were found, aged between 18 and 40. Some remains showed signs of traumatic injuries, either sustained during the sinking or from previous battles. However, many of the crew likely drowned when the ship rapidly filled with water, which makes the survival of the thirty-five men even more extraordinary. In 1982, a complex salvage operation, becoming one of the most significant maritime archaeology projects, raised the remains of the ship. The hull was preserved and eventually placed in the Mary Rose Museum in Portsmouth Historic Dockyard.

Extraordinary Escapes

John Smith

Have you heard of the tale of Pocahontas, whether that be the true historical account or, yes, even the 1995 Disney movie of the same name? If you have, you will know the name John Smith, basically the quintessential English name, with the moniker used in many a movie or TV shows. Doctor Who even uses it as one of his many aliases. However, John Smith was a real person and is best known for his role in establishing the Jamestown Colony, just as depicted in the Disney movie, but his earlier life was equally as adventurous and marked by extraordinary experiences.

Born in Lincolnshire in January of 1580, Smith displayed a strong desire for adventure and exploration from an early age, always wanting to see the world and learn as much as he could about it, so it was no surprise to his parents that in 1596 at the age of just 16, Smith left England to fight for Dutch independence from Spain during the Eighty Years' War. This experience not only provided him with experience and vital skills, but it also gave him a taste for adventure.

Realising that the best way to see the world was being part of the military, Smith travelled to Eastern Europe and joined the army of the Holy Roman Empire to fight the Ottoman Turks advancing into Europe. By his own accounts, he defeated and beheaded three Turkish officers in a single battle, earning significant accolades and a promotion to the rank of captain. It was while fighting this same army again in 1602 that Smith was captured, taken prisoner and sold into slavery.

John Smith was sold to a Turkish nobleman in Constantinople (now Istanbul) and was presented by his master as a gift to his fiancée, Charatza Tragabigzanda. According to Smith's own account, Charatza became infatuated with him, and apparently to convert Smith to Islam, she sent him to work for her brother Tymor Bashaw, who ran an agricultural station in present-day Russia, near Rostov. She was so in love she instructed her brother to show kindness and win him over to their faith so they might marry. However, Bashaw instead mistreated him by shaving his head, placing a heavy iron ring around his neck, giving him very little to eat and often severely beating him. Smith could not see a way out other than death and was becoming increasingly desperate. During one particularly brutal beating, something came over Smith, possibly adrenaline-fuelled anger, and he overpowered Bashaw, killing him and fleeing his enslavement using Bashaw's horse and clothing.

Travelling for days, unsure of where he was or where he was going, Smith was befriended by a Russian and his wife Callamatta, whom Smith called this 'good lady'. With their assistance Smith was able to regain his strength and begin a two-year solo adventure back home to England. It would take him approximately 11,000 miles across Russia, Ukraine, Germany, France, Spain and Morocco. In 1604 the captain was finally home, but not for long. In 1606 Smith joined the expedition to establish the Jamestown Colony in Virginia, the first permanent English settlement in North America.

His story after landing in Jamestown is legendary but would not have been possible without his tenacity and self-belief. Plus, had fate not intervened and made him cross paths with the Russians, he surely would not have survived.

John Knox

John Knox was a Scottish minister and one of the leading figures in the Protestant Reformation, in times when that was a rather dangerous thing. The fact that he was born in 1514 in Haddington, Scotland, is about all the records show of Knox's early life and next to nothing is known until around 1540. He was trained as a priest in the Roman Catholic Church, having received his religious orders by 1540, and in 1543 there are records showing he was practising as an apostolic notary in the Haddington area.

However, Knox later embraced Protestantism under the influence of reformers such as George Wishart. Wishart began a preaching tour in the Lothians in December 1545 and shortly after, Knox wrote to him detailing his full conversion to the Protestant faith. In a mostly Catholic country like Scotland, this did not go down well and in March 1546 George Wishart was burned at the stake by David Beaton, Archbishop of St Andrews, and became one of the first martyrs for the Protestant cause in Scotland.

Three months after Wishart's death, Beaton was murdered by Protestant conspirators, and Knox, along with said conspirators, took refuge in St

Andrews Castle, which had been seized by Protestant rebels. They held up there for the best part of the year before, in July 1547, the castle was besieged by French forces allied with the Catholic regent of Scotland, Mary of Guise (mother to Mary, Queen of Scots) The siege ended with the surrender of the castle, and Knox, along with other defenders, was taken prisoner. Knox was condemned to serve as a galley slave on French ships, a harsh and gruelling punishment.

Galley slaves endured brutal conditions, including physical hardship, malnutrition and exposure to the elements. Slaves were often chained to their oars and required to row for long hours with little rest. Despite these extreme conditions, Knox maintained his Protestant faith, reportedly preaching to his fellow slaves and defying his captors' attempts to force him to attend Catholic mass. Although his time as a galley slave was horrendous, Knox does recount one rather humorous incident. At times the Scottish prisoners were 'threatened if they didn't give reverence to the Roman Catholic mass and sometimes asked to partake in idolatry', which they refused to do. Knox continued that once when they arrived in Nantes, a wooden, painted image of a lady was brought to the Scots prisoners who were told to kiss the feet of the statue. Knox told them: 'Trouble me not, such an idol is accursed and therefore I will not touch it.' But he was told, 'Thou shalt handle it' and the statue was violently thrust in his hands. Knox looked about then said, 'Let our Lady now save herself; she is light enough let her learn to swim.' He then threw it over the side of the ship into the water. He states that after that 'was no Scottish man again urged with that idolatry'.

Knox's exact route to freedom is unclear, much like a few chunks of his life. However, it is known that he was released in early 1550, possibly as part of a broader prisoner exchange or diplomatic negotiation between France and England. What we do know is that upon his release, Knox travelled to England, where he found refuge during the reign of the Protestant King Edward VI (youngest son of Henry VIII). He served as a minister and preacher in various locations, including Berwick, Newcastle and London, gaining recognition for his fervent preaching and strong Protestant convictions.

Knox settled for about three years, thinking all was safe and well, but not for long. Following the accession of the Catholic Queen Mary I, after the sudden death of Edward VI in 1553, Knox fled again, this time to continental Europe to escape religious persecution. He initially went to Frankfurt where he became involved in a dispute over the form of worship in the English exile congregation as people were still following the Catholic faith from before the Reformation in 1536. In 1556 Knox moved on once more, to Geneva, where he found a welcoming environment under the leadership of John Calvin, the prominent Reformation theologian. In Geneva, Knox thrived, contributing to the Reformation movement through his writings and teachings. He also began writing his most influential works, including *The First Blast of the Trumpet Against the Monstrous Regiment of Women*, a polemic against female monarchs, and *The History of the Reformation in Scotland.*

In 1559 Knox returned to Scotland and played a key role in the Scottish Reformation, leading to the establishment of Presbyterianism as the national religion. With a life involving daring escapes, demonstrations, reformations and hate books against women, you must admit, John Knox had gumption.

Siege What We Can Do

This is the mediaeval times; sieges are commonplace. Most of the time one side will win, and it is usually the side on the outside looking in, with the bigger army, better supplies and most importantly, ways to get more of each. The resilience of the people on the inside of those sieges can sometimes be so surprising and unexpected, however, that the opposition have no choice but to wave those white flags and retreat.

The Siege of Vienna

The Siege of Vienna in 1529 is remembered as a critical moment in the struggle between the Ottoman Empire and European powers. It showcased the strategic importance of fortifications, the value of strong leadership and the impact of logistical and environmental factors on military campaigns. The defence of Vienna became a symbol of resistance against Ottoman expansion and played a crucial role in shaping the future of European geopolitics. It also showcases the resilience of people and what they can live through.

In the spring of 1529, Sultan Suleiman the Magnificent assembled a massive army, estimated at between 120,000 and 200,000 men, which included the Janissary infantry,[2] cavalry, artillery and various auxiliary troops, so the Sultan really was covering all his bases. The Ottomans advanced through the Balkans, easily overcoming resistance and many logistical challenges, but Vienna was their ultimate target. Due to being considered the gateway to Western and Central Europe, controlling Vienna would provide the Ottoman Empire and indeed Sultan Suleiman with a direct route into Europe.

The people of Vienna knew that the Ottoman army was heading their way, so took early action to mount a defence. Led by Count Niklas Salm and Wilhelm von Roggendorf, they stockpiled food, weapons and other supplies. They reinforced their mediaeval walls with additional earthen ramparts and bastions effective in absorbing and deflecting cannon fire. They only had a defending force of about 16,000 troops, a stark contrast to the 200,000 men in the Sultan's army. A win for the Viennese did not seem likely but they were most definitely not going down without a fight.

Orchestrated by Suleiman, the siege began in late September with the Ottomans establishing a perimeter around the city and beginning their assault with an intense artillery bombardment aimed at weakening Vienna's walls and creating breaches, which it did not. To combat this, they next attempted to undermine the walls by digging tunnels and placing explosives to create breaches, but again this did not work as the defenders were adept at countermining, detecting and neutralising such efforts.

The attacks were, however, ruthless and seemed never-ending and if they wanted a chance at winning this thing, Salm and Roggendorf knew they needed to come up with a plan of attack that would hit the Ottomans where it hurt. They launched frequent sorties to disrupt the besiegers' operations. These small-scale attacks targeted Ottoman siege equipment, supplies and labour forces with devastating effect. Call it luck or divine intervention, but the siege was also hampered massively by unseasonably wet and cold weather. Rain and mud made it difficult to move heavy artillery and supplies, and as the Ottomans were not accustomed to it, many fell ill. The weather also made it difficult for supplies to get through, so food and equipment shortages occurred.

The prolonged siege, combined with the adverse weather as well as effective and continued resistance by the defenders, began to take a toll on Ottoman morale. Attack after attack was repulsed by Salm and his army, who picked off the Ottoman troops with arquebuses from the high city walls and forced back those who scaled the walls with long pikes, so much so that in late October, Suleiman ordered one last all-out assault. It was to be big, to throw everything the Ottoman army had at its disposal, but alas this was also repulsed. Suleiman then ordered a retreat, which turned into even more of a disastrous ordeal as winter snows came early causing many deaths and the loss of the remaining artillery. Defeat at Vienna forced Suleiman back into Ottoman Hungary and, after a second failure to take Vienna in 1532, he abandoned thoughts of conquering Europe.

So, two relatively inexperienced men, one city and an army less than a fifth of the size of the enemy, managed to secure victory over one of the most feared, powerful and ambitious rulers of the Ottoman Empire.

The Siege of Leiden

The Eighty Years' War took place from 1568 to 1648, primarily fought between the Spanish Empire and the Dutch provinces, with the latter seeking independence from Spanish rule. The conflict was driven by religious tensions (Protestantism vs. Catholicism), a desire for political autonomy and economic issues. The war ultimately resulted in the recognition of the independence of the Dutch Republic with the Treaty of Münster in 1648, part of the larger Peace of Westphalia that ended the Eighty Years' War. The Siege of Leiden is one of the most dramatic and pivotal events of those wars.

Leiden, located in the then province of South Holland, was a significant stronghold for the Dutch rebels, which made it a key target for the Spanish to launch their attacks to subdue the rebellion. The Spanish, led by Francisco de Valdez, laid siege to Leiden in October 1573 and this formed part of a broader strategy to recapture rebel-held cities.

The Dutch, however, said nay (or *nëe*), and Leiden was well prepared for the siege with robust fortifications and a determined populace. The first initial months saw the city effectively resisting all Spanish assaults; however, as the siege was almost a year old, supplies were dwindling and the situation inside the Leiden walls were growing desperate. The inhabitants faced starvation and were reduced to eating anything they could find, including dogs, cats, rats and even leather. (brings whole new meaning to the term, tough as old boots). Malnutrition, overcrowding and weakened immune systems led to outbreaks of disease, further exacerbating the suffering of the population. To add to the trouble, beer was in such short supply that people were forced to drink dirty, disease-ridden canal water. It is estimated that 6,000 people died out of the 15,000 inside the city.

The Dutch, led by William of Orange, made several attempts to break the siege, but these were in vain. The Spanish easily repelled these efforts, maintaining their stranglehold on Leiden. William of Orange knew he needed to do something and soon, as the people would not be able to hold out much longer under such conditions. He offered up a pretty crazy solution, but the people were so desperate they would try anything.

His solution was to break the dykes, flooding the entire region. This drastic measure was intended to turn the geography against the Spanish. It was swiftly decided and so in early October of 1574, almost a year to the day after the siege began, the dykes were breached, and the waters of the North Sea and the rivers began to inundate the land around Leiden. This action created a temporary shallow sea, rendering Spanish siege positions untenable, but it gave Willam of Orange's 'Sea Beggars' (a small fleet of flat-bottomed boats) the chance to sail through the flooded waters and bring supplies and food to the starving townspeople. The arrival of the relief fleet was met with overwhelming joy and relief, bringing the morale boost the Dutch forces needed to continue. They would not have to hold out for too long though, as the Spanish, unable to hold their positions in the flooded landscape, withdrew in disarray.

This Dutch victory marked a turning point in the Eighty Years' War, showcasing the determination and resilience of the Dutch people, so much so that William of Orange founded the University of Leiden in 1575 in its honour, as a symbol of Dutch resistance and perseverance.

The date of 3 October is still celebrated annually in Leiden as 'Leidens Ontzet' (Relief of Leiden), a day of thanksgiving and festivity to remember the resilience and ingenuity of the Dutch during their struggle for independence, a testament to the ability to survive against seemingly insurmountable odds.

Chapter 13

End of an Era

The Tudor era, spanning from 1485 to 1603, was marked by a blend of grandeur and absurdity. It featured a parade of larger-than-life monarchs like Henry VIII, who notoriously married six times and established the Church of England to divorce his first wife. The era was rife with dramatic politics, such as the ruthless execution of rivals and the volatile reign of Mary I, known as 'Bloody Mary', for her persecution of Protestants. The court was a stage for opulent displays of wealth juxtaposed with brutal enforcement of loyalty, while the societal obsession with lineage and power often led to extremely convoluted claims to the throne. Despite the period's remarkable cultural achievements, including the flourishing of the arts under Elizabeth I, it was also a time of extravagant excess, intense intrigue and ridiculous deaths.

In this book we hope we have transported you to the sixteenth century and guided you through the weird and wonderful world that was Tudor England. We'd like to think that we have demonstrated through our various chapters that ways in which people have left this earth can be more stupid and ridiculous than you could ever imagine. We hope you can use the misfortune of our deceased friends as life lessons of what to do or not do, but here is a list of recommendations taken from their greatest hits:

1. Do not give knives to babies – they are sharp, and children have no concept of danger.
2. Don't run, walk, climb, ride or even stand with pointed weapons.
3. If an arrow doesn't fire, DO NOT hold it to your face to have a look.
4. Archery ranges are not suitable places for nap time.
5. Don't wash your sheep in rivers; in fact stay away from rivers altogether.
6. Be extra careful when nature calls.

7. Don't imagine, plan or attempt the death of a monarch.
8. Don't catfish a monarch (looking at you Anne of Cleves) and certainly don't flirt with them.
9. Don't take swords to a gunfight.
10. Beware the maypole.
11. Respect the British weather, she takes no prisoners.
12. Always read the food labels; flour and arsenic are in fact different.
13. Remember that cows are always watching.

Notes

Introduction

1. The Battle of Bosworth is often cited as being the end of the Wars of the Roses, but it didn't technically end until the Battle of Stoke Field in June 1487.
2. Frances Brandon married Henry Grey, 3rd Marquess of Dorset, and had three children. One of them was the nine-day queen, Lady Jane Grey.
3. It is estimated in seventeenth-century France that approximately 40 percent of children born died in infancy.
4. Some scholars dispute the claims of her mental ill health as there was a good deal of financial and political gain for others in her being considered incompetent or incapable of ruling.

Animal Accidents

1. The focus on exploration and territorial expansion would lead to the introduction of new crops and livestock types as the sixteenth and seventeenth centuries progressed.
2. Based on an estimate provided in an article on the history of the English wool trade, T*udor Times*, 2018
3. A variant of the bovine genus bred specifically for work such as pulling carts or ploughing with predominantly males used for this, whereas your more traditional cow was bred for meat and milk.
4. In this context, a way of saying a piece of land that he owned or rented, not to be confused with the building type of tenement which is a single building divided into multiple occupancy homes, rooms or flats.
5. A brutal 'sport' where a captive bear would be chained by either leg or neck to a stake in the middle or a pit and then a pack of dogs would be released into the pit to fight it while spectators took bets on the victor.

Crime and Punishment

1. A liminal space in between the realm of the living and the eventual afterlife that a person is destined for. In purgatory a soul would wait until either they were ready for judgement, or the living had said enough masses and prayers for their souls to be released to heaven. This was not a part of formal Catholic doctrine until the Second Council of Lyon in 1274 made it so.
2. To paraphrase the definition given by Merriam Webster, a seneschal is the steward or acting agent in charge of an estate or manor within a feudal system, in

charge of the day-to-day running of the estate and dealing with minor disputes in the absence of the lord.

3. Anything more than minor could be considered heretical and would warrant a much harsher punishment.
4. It was even considered treason following the introduction of the Treason Act to imagine the death of the king, queen or heir apparent. Though how that could be proven in court is somewhat of a mystery and it leaves a lot of room for interpretation.
5. We acknowledge in hindsight that a family tree of the monarchs of Europe would have been beneficial to our readers, but confess we do not have the time, mental endurance or space on paper to create this.
6. The central keep of the overall fortification of the Tower of London, constructed in the 1070s by William the Conqueror as a show of his power following the Norman Conquest of 1066.
7. The *pro ecclesiasticae unitatis defensione*, a pamphlet published in response to correspondence received from Henry VIII which denied the royal supremacy of the king and called for the deposing of the king.
8. An act of law that names someone as guilty of a crime and sentences them, often without a trial.
9. In his *Description of Elizabethan England, 1577*
10. The act of renouncing or abandoning a religion or belief system.
11. Harrison's book would suggest 13.5d as a minimum; more than this would warrant the death penalty, less an alternative punishment.
12. It is believed that the word *gala* derives from the Anglo-Saxon word for gallows, and therefore going to a gala could mean going to the gallows to watch an execution. A potentially stark beginning for something that is now synonymous with charity events or strange celebrity fashions,
13. Heads that were displayed on spikes at places like London Bridge in London or Micklegate Bar in Yorkshire would be dipped in tar to preserve them for longer and potentially dissuade scavengers and bugs from getting to work on them too soon.
14. Executions were often a public affair to act as a deterrent against the behaviour that had led the accused to this position. For the most part, they provided a day out for the whole family, where picnics and pop-up stalls were not an uncommon sight.

Extracting A Confession

1. An act drawn up at the beginning of the reign of Elizabeth I, like the one created for her father Henry VIII in 1534, which restored to the crown all jurisdiction over ecclesiastical and spiritual matters within the kingdom, making the monarch again the Supreme Head of the Church in England. While certain sections of the act have since been repealed and now only section 8 remains in force.

2. The seemingly miraculous conversation of the elements of the eucharist (being the wafers and wine) into the body and blood of Jesus Christ, to be given out among the faithful at mass.
3. Defined by John Hopkins Medicine as an injury that has stemmed typically from neck trauma, damaging the brachial plexus nerves in the shoulder responsible for carrying sensory signals to the arms and hands. This injury can cause pain, weakness and numbness. In the most severe cases it can result in a loss of limb function without surgery to attempt to repair the damage.
4. Also known as the Eighty Years' War.
5. Rat torture continued to be used as an interrogation method in parts of the world until the mid-twentieth century.
6. John Kincaid, also known as the Witch Pricker, was a Scottish witch hunter who lived outside the century that we are focusing on, having been active in his profession from around 1649–65, but who was eventually found guilty by the Privy Council of fraud.
7. Often interchanged in popular culture with a voodoo doll, both being used as a representation of a person or amulet in what is known as sympathetic magic.
8. She was allegedly turned to stone after holy water was thrown on her by a monk from the nearby Glastonbury abbey who came to use the power of prayer to rid the area of the witch.
9. Based on an estimate of 17,000 in 2018 from Rewilding Europe.
10. Interestingly, lycanthropy is categorised by the *Encyclopedia Britannica* as a mental disorder.
11. Succubae and incubi are a classification of demons in female and male form respectively that are often known for sexually assaulting their victims while they sleep or engaging in such acts with willing persons as part of demonic pacts.

Food Fatalities

1. Another word for gallows, taken from the French variation and were used for displaying the bodies of executed criminals as a warning to others and that came in several different types.
2. The Medici family, a powerful and influential dynasty in Renaissance Florence, were prominent bankers and patrons of the arts, significantly contributing to the cultural and political landscape of Italy from the fifteenth to the seventeenth centuries. Their support of artists like Michelangelo and Leonardo da Vinci and their establishment of the Medici Bank solidified their legacy in history.
3. His nose was long believed to be silver, but an exhumation of Tycho's corpse in 2010 revealed that it was made from brass.
4. Bat fowling is an old method of catching birds at night. It involves the use of a light source, such as torches or lanterns, to dazzle or confuse roosting birds, making them easier to catch.

Kill or Cure

1. Celestial bodies, also known as astronomical objects, are naturally occurring physical entities that exist in the observable universe outside the Earth's atmosphere. e.g. stars, planets, moons

Perils and Plagues

1. It is believed that prior to the outbreak of the Black Death the global population was around 450 million, and that following the pandemic it was reduced by almost half, with the greatest toll being taken on the populations of southern Europe.
2. According to research done by J. K. Taubenberger and D. M. Morens for their paper, 'Pandemic influenza – including a risk assessment of H5N1' featured in the National Library of Medicine. They composed a list of historic influenza pandemics from 1510 onward.
3. Germ theory was not discovered until late into the nineteenth century with the work of Louis Pasteur and Robert Koch.
4. A coastal city on the north coast of central Japan.
5. The story around this is that he was covered in viscera during the battle, which has led some scholars to question whether it was leprosy or perhaps syphilis.
6. A shogun, according to the *Cambridge Dictionary* definition, was a military governor in feudal Japan prior to 1867, who answered to the emperor. The system they would govern over was known as a shogunate and this would often be hereditary but could also be acceded to by right of conquest.
7. Full name: Hernán Cortés de Monroy y Pizarro Altamirano, of Medellin in Castile.
8. They referred to themselves as the Mexhicah. The name Aztec is believed to have been coined by the Spanish as the word Azteca, based on the mythical land that the people of the region believed their ancestors came from, known in the native tongue of Nahuatl as Aztlan, and the people from there were therefore the Aztecah.
9. For orientation purposes, the Mayan civilisation came from what is now South-eastern Mexico and Guatemala, whereas the Incan empire spread across what is now Chile and Peru.
10. This is known as lymphadenitis and would have been incredibly painful to live with, as well as being quite unsightly.
11. This idea originated in Italy, in the port city of the Republic of Venice where ships and their crews were made to stay on an outer island such as Poveglia Island for forty days before being allowed into the main ports. The Venetian word *quarantena* means forty days.
12. A poultice is a soft, damp mass of material, often heated, spread on a cloth, and applied to the skin to treat an inflamed sore or injured area. More commonly made from natural substances such as herbs, grains or other plant materials, which are believed to draw out infection, reduce inflammation and relieve pain.

13. August de Augustinis of Venice, who also became the personal physician to Henry VIII following the downfall and later death of Thomas Wolsey.
14. Defined by the Cambridge online dictionary as meaning an everyday or ordinary thing.

Ruthless Religion

1. Being a belief or opinion that goes against the established or popular beliefs and principles of a certain culture or religion.
2. This decree being the Act of Supremacy, 1534
3. The Dissolution of the Monasteries was a process begun within the reign of Henry VIII in 1536 as part of the Reformation. This involved the suppression of sale of monasteries and monastic land, as well as convents, abbeys and religious houses. Accusations were levelled against those living in such institutions of corruption, heresy, sodomy and other immoral behaviours. The former residents of such places would be turned out and while some were given pensions, others were forced to resort to begging to survive. For those who refused to comply or leave, imprisonment, execution or both often followed.
4. An old rivalry that was not helped by the trickery and resultant military actions of Edward I, also known as the Hammer of the Scots, and that would arguably culminate in the Jacobite uprisings of the eighteenth century.
5. This was also one of the initial reasons for the Dissolution of the Monasteries, to try and refill the royal coffers after years of conflict and often extravagant royal spending.
6. Historians who have read the document in its entirety have noted a bias towards the noble-class rebels within the demands and it is believed that pilgrims of common birth may have been omitted from the meeting.
7. Clifford's Tower is now owned by English Heritage and stands today atop a mound near the York Castle Museum and the York Crown Court.
8. The stereotypical sailing ship, consisting of three to four masts and often equipped with guns on the broadside – being the side of the ship on which the cannon were kept. These marked the galleon out as a vessel of war as much as transportation.
9. Governed by King Philip II of Spain following a succession crisis in Portugal which weakened the country and paved the way for conquest by the Spanish in 1580.
10. The Ottoman Empire at this point encompassed most of South East Europe including Hungary, the Balkans and Greece as well as the Middle East and parts of North Africa and the Arabian Peninsula.
11. Followers of a variation of Sharia law.
12. Translated to Reconquest this is the period between 772 CE to 1492 CE when Christian forces fought a bitter rebellion to retake Muslim-controlled Spain and led to the founding of the Kingdom of Portugal, ending with the surrender of Emir Mohamed XII in January 1492.

13. A variant of the Inquisition, known as the Roman Inquisition, which answered directly to the Pope was never disbanded, although it follows a very different layout in modern times, often being used to investigate crimes within the Catholic Church or questions around doctrine.
14. Property disputes is one of the reasons believed to be behind some of the accusations made during the Salem Witch Trials in 1692, particularly in the case of John Proctor.

Weaponry Woes

1. Henry VII reigned from 1485 until his death in 1509.
2. Catherine of Aragon would marry King Henry VIII and is the mother of Queen Mary I.
3. The system by which vassals (landowners) and knights, bound by the feudal contract to their lords, provided military service when called upon. This obligation was typically in exchange for land and protection.
4. Meaning they used a slow-burning match to ignite the gunpowder in the touchhole.
5. The Mercers' Company is a livery company focused on being a philanthropic force for good, still in effect today giving more than £10 million to charity each year.
6. A daimyō is a private landowner who held both political and military power.
7. Evidence of archery has been found in some archaeological sites in South Africa dating back over 60,000 years, with further evidence of archery existing in Europe around 17,000 years ago – Blackwell et al, 2018.
8. A cooper is a mediaeval craftsman who made barrels, buckets, baskets out of wood.
9. A 'prykshaft' is a specifically designed arrow intended for target practice of the smallest and precise targets. They were typically longer and slimmer than war/hunting arrows, with less fletching (feathers) and a smaller, sharper arrowhead designed for accuracy over moderate distances rather than for penetration and damage.
10. Quoted from the coroner's report, meaning John Waller was digging and collecting patches of grass or small clumps of vegetation for a laugh.
11. A 'fyllyngaxe' is a type of axe specifically designed for cutting down trees. It has a sharp, thin blade designed to make deep, clean cuts into the wood, making it easier to chop through the trunk of a tree.
12. 'A couple of a house' is a pair of timber beams that form part of the roof structure. These beams are usually angled and work together to support the roof.
13. The abbess was the female head of a nunnery, specifically the Barking Abbey Benedictine nunnery in this case.
14. The phrase 'Game of [faded]tyng and other masteryes' refers to medieval or Tudor-era games and competitions, showing off both physical- and mental-based challenges.

Notable Mentions

1. Executed, legend has it, by being drowned in a vat of Malmsey wine in 1478, sadly nearly a decade outside of the remit for this book.
2. The French and Frankish people have also given us such varied monikers as Charles the Bold, Charles the Fat, Pepin the Short, Louis the Pious and Philip the Fair.
3. Charles VIII was initially a supporter of the pretender to the English Throne, Perkin Warbeck, who claimed to be Richard, Duke of York, one of the famous 'Princes in the Tower'. He later renounced this support following a show of force by Henry VII.
4. The cell that they were in was approximately 30 feet (9.14 metres) long, 14 feet (4.27 metres) wide and 12 feet high (3.66 metres), and the walls were seven feet (2.13 metres) thick and made of solid stone.
5. Adverse weather caused delays through the latter half of August 1940, reducing the activities that the Luftwaffe were able to undertake and potentially saving many lives from reduced bombing capability.
6. A term coined by the Dutch American Geologist F. E. Matthes in around 1939 to describe the period of cold from the mid-fourteenth to mid-nineteenth centuries, when glaciers at various points of the world expanded considerably.
7. Variations of prisoners' base continue to be played into the modern day, though with less frequent dangerous consequences.

Ridiculous Survivals

1. Scurvy is a disease caused by a serious vitamin C deficiency. Not eating enough fruits and vegetables is the main cause and if left untreated, scurvy can lead to bleeding gums, loosened teeth and bleeding under the skin. Scurvy was a significant problem for sailors during long sea voyages when fresh produce was not available.
2. The Janissary Infantry were the first modern standing army, and perhaps the first infantry force in the world to be equipped with firearms.
3. The Solent is a strait separating the Isle of Wight from mainland England, a strategically important area for naval defence.

Bibliography

The Tudor Period: A Quick Tour

Brain, J. (2024, 17 April). *Mary Tudor, Princess of England and Queen of France.* Retrieved from Historic UK: www.historic-uk.com/HistoryUK/HistoryofEngland/Mary-Tudor-Queen-Of-France/

Deary, T. (1996). *Horrible Histories: Slimy Stuarts.* London: Scholastic Children's Books.

Deary, T., & Tonge, N. (1993). *Horrible Histories: Terrible Tudors.* London: Scholastic Children's Books.

Forcen, F. (2014). The Tragic Story of Joanna the Mad. *The Journal of Humanistic Psychiatry, 2*(2). Retrieved from Medievalists: www.medievalists.net/2015/12/the-tragic-story-of-joanna-the-mad/

Friehs, J. T. (n.d.). *An encyclopaedia of the Monarchy.* Retrieved from The World of the Habsburgs: www.habsburger.net/en/chapter/encyclopaedia-monarchy

Harrison, W. (2010, 30 May). *A Description of England.* (L. Withington, Editor) Retrieved from Project Gutenberg: www.gutenberg.org/files/32593/32593-h/32593-h.htm#CHAPTER_XXIV

Jackson-Laufer, G. M. (1999). *Women rulers throughout the ages: an illustrated guide.* California: Santa Barbara ABC-CLIO.

Myers, A. R. & Morrill, J. S. (2024, 20 June). *Henry VII.* Retrieved from Britannica: www.britannica.com/biography/Henry-VII-king-of-England/Foreign-policy

oeta, S. (2007). The Hispanic and Luso-Brazilian World: From Mad Queen to Martyred Saint: The Case of Juana La Loca Revisisted in History and Art on the Occastion of the 450th Anniversary of Her Death. *Hispania, 90*(1), 165–72. Retrieved from www.jstor.org/stable/20063477

Ponti, C. (2023, 11 August). *Who Were the Six Wives of Henry VIII?* Retrieved from History: www.history.com/news/henry-viii-wives

Stollberg-Rilinger, B. (2018). *The Holy Roman Empire: A Short History.* (Y. Mintzker, Trans.) Princeton, New Jersey: Princeton University Press. Retrieved from www.jstor.org/stable/j.ctvc778tr

The Mercers' Company. (n.d.). *Livery Companies.* Retrieved from The Mercers' Company: www.mercers.co.uk/about-the-company

Thulin, L. (2019, 4 December). *The Distinctive 'Habsburg Jaw' Was Likely the Result of the Royal Family's Inbreeding.* Retrieved from Smithsonian Magazine: www.smithsonianmag.com/smart-news/distinctive-habsburg-jaw-was-likely-result-royal-familys-inbreeding-180973688/

Vivid Maps. (2016, 1 December). *The Holy Roman Empire*. Retrieved from Vivid Maps: https://vividmaps.com/holy-roman-empire/

Animal Accidents

Andrews, E. (2023, 3 October). *The Gruesome Blood Sports of Shakespearean England*. Retrieved from History: www.history.com/news/the-gruesome-blood-sports-of-shakespearean-england

Carter, K. (n.d). *The Rise and Fall of a Tudor Wool Factory*. Retrieved from English Heritage: www.english-heritage.org.uk/visit/places/baconsthorpe-castle/history/tudor-wool-factory/

Glatz, K. (2024, 11 July). *Ox vs Cow: What Are the Differences?* Retrieved from A–Z Animals: https://a-z-animals.com/animals/comparison/ox-vs-cow/

Grau-Sologestoa, I. & Albarella, U. (2018, 5 October). The 'long' sixteenth century: a key period in animal husbandry change in England. *Archaeol Anthropol Sci, 11*, 2781–803. Retrieved from https://link.springer.com/article/10.1007/s12520-018-0723-6

Johnson, B. (2015, 13 March). *History of the Wool Trade*. Retrieved from Historic UK.

Overton, M. (2011, 17 February). *Agricultural Revolution in England 1500–1850*. Retrieved from BBC: www.bbc.co.uk/history/british/empire_seapower/agricultural_revolution_01.shtml

Oxford English Dictionary. (2023, December). *Tenement*. Retrieved from Oxford English Dictionary: www.oed.com/dictionary/tenement_n?tab=meaning_and_use&tl=true#18911685

Tudor Times. (2018, 9 February). *The English Wool Trade*. Retrieved from Tudor Times: https://tudortimes.co.uk/politics-economy/the-english-wool-trade/economics-of-sheep-farming

Widdall, C. (2020). *Expansion of the Wool Trade – sixteenth century Onwards*. Retrieved from Kirklees Cousins: https://kirkleescousins.co.uk/16th-century/

Crime and Punishment

Aanmoen, O. (2020, 3 August). *The night 19 Ottoman princes were killed by their brother*. Retrieved from Royal Central: https://royalcentral.co.uk/asia/the-night-19-ottoman-princes-were-killed-by-their-brother-146628/

Abbott, G. (2007). *What a Way to Go: The Guillotine, the Pendulum, the Thousand Cuts, the Spanish Donkey, and 66 Other Ways of Putting Someone to Death*. Chicago: St Martin's Publishing Group.

Abbott, G. (2023, 14 July). *Boiling*. Retrieved from Encyclopedia Britannica: www.britannica.com/topic/boiling-punishment

Abbott, G. (2024, 17 May). *Burning at the stake*. Retrieved from Britannica: www.britannica.com/topic/burning-at-the-stake

Anonymous. (2008, 22 May). *Question from Caila – Humphrey Lisle*. Retrieved from Tudor History.org: Questions and Answers Blog: https://queryblog.tudorhistory.org/2008/05/question-from-caila-humphrey-lisle.html

Ardill, T. (2022, 21 October). *City of Gallows: mapping London's execution landscape.* Retrieved from Museum of London Docklands: www.museumoflondon.org.uk/discover/city-gallows-mapping-londons-execution-landscape-docklands

Bilyeau, N. (2013, 27 May). *1541: Margaret Pole, Countess of Salisbury.* Retrieved from Executed Today: www.executedtoday.com/2013/05/27/1541-margaret-pole-countess-of-salisbury/

Brigden, J. (2024). *That Takes Guts: 7 Gory Execution Methods from Tudor England.* Retrieved from Sky History: www.history.co.uk/articles/that-takes-guts-7-gory-execution-methods-from-tudor-england#Wheel_of_Misfortune_%E2%80%93_Death_by_The_Breaking_Wheel

Britain Express. (no date). *The Oxford Martyrs.* Retrieved from Britain Express: www.britainexpress.com/cities/oxford/oxford-martyrs.htm

Brown, S. (2018, 11 December). *Treason law in England from 1351 to the present.* Retrieved from Doing History in Public: https://doinghistoryinpublic.org/2018/12/11/treason-law-in-england-from-1351-to-the-present/

Cambridge Dictionary. (n.d.). *Shogun.* Retrieved from Cambridge Dictionary: https://dictionary.cambridge.org/dictionary/english/shogun#google_vignette

Clark, R. (1995). *The history of judicial hanging in Britain 1735–1964.* Retrieved from Capital Punishment UK.

Clark, R. (1995). *Timeline of capital punishment in the UK.* Retrieved from Capital Punishment UK: www.capitalpunishmentuk.org/timeline.html#:~:text=Some%20320%20people%20were%20executed%20as%20a%20result.,The%20men%20being%20mainly%20hanged%2C%20drawn%20and%20quartered.

Clark, R. (n.d.). *Confirmed Executions at the Tower of London.* Retrieved from Capital Punishment UK: www.capitalpunishmentuk.org/tower.html

Davies, C. S. (1966). Slavery and Protector Somerset: The Vagrancy Act of 1547. *The Economic History Review, New Series, Vol. 19*(3), 533–49. doi:2593162

Encyclopedia.com. (2024, 10 July). *Crime and Punishment in Elizabethan England.* Retrieved from Elizabethan World Reference Library: www.encyclopedia.com/humanities/news-wires-white-papers-and-books/crime-and-punishment-elizabethan-england

Fan, R. (2021, 9 May). *The Wheel: One of History's Cruelest Forms of Torture.* Retrieved from Medium: https://medium.com/frame-of-reference/the-wheel-one-of-historys-cruelest-forms-of-torture-880ecaf8200b

Hanson, M. (2015, 6 February). *The Pilgrimage of Grace 1536 Summary & Information.* Retrieved from English History: https://englishhistory.net/tudor/the-pilgrimage-of-grace-1536/

Harvey, A. (2023, 13 April). *The Agonizing History of the Breaking Wheel: One of History's Cruelest Execution Methods.* (J. Kuroski, Editor) Retrieved from All That's Interesting: https://allthatsinteresting.com/breaking-wheel

Head, D. M. (1982, Winter). 'Beyng Ledde and Seduced by the Devyll' – The Attainder of Lord Thomas Howard and the Tudor Law of Treason. *The Sixteenth Century Journal, 13*(4), 3–16. doi:10.2307/2540006

Higginbotham, S. (2016). *Margaret Pole: The Countess in the Tower.* Gloucestershire: Amberley Publishing Limited.

Hilts, C. (2022, 26 October). *City of Gallows: tracing the human stories behind London's history of public executions.* Retrieved from The Past: https://the-past.com/feature/city-of-gallows-tracing-the-human-stories-behind-londons-history-of-public-executions/

History Maps. (2022, 22 August). *Dozsa's Rebellion.* Retrieved from History Maps: https://history-maps.com/story/Kingdom-of-Hungary-Late-Medieval/event/Dozsa%27s-Rebellion

Hotle, C. (2022). The Outlaw, Sir William Lisle: A Case Study in Anglo-Scottish Border Affairs. Retrieved from Sir William Lisle, Outlaw: www.academia.edu/93509555/The_Outlaw_Sir_William_Lisle_A_Case_Study_in_Anglo_Scottish_Border_Affairs

Hubball, B. (2024, 10 February). *The Brutal Execution of Gyorgy Dozsa.* Retrieved from The Dark History Files: https://thedarkhistoryfiles.com/2024/02/10/gyorgy-dozsa/

Ingram, D. (2017, 10 March). *Carnal Knowledge: Regulating Sex in England, 1470–1600.* Retrieved from University of Oxford: Faculty of History: www.history.ox.ac.uk/carnel-knowledge-regulating-sex-in-englabd-1470-1600#:~:text=Offenders%20arraigned%20and%20found%20guilty%20by%20the%20magistrates,from%20their%20wards%20or%20from%20the%20city%20itself.

Kovacs, Z. (2018, 30 August). *The martyr criminal of Hungarian history and the peasants' revolt led by him.* Retrieved from Daily News Hungary: https://dailynewshungary.com/the-martyr-criminal-of-hungarian-history-and-the-peasants-revolt-led-by-him/

Lipscomb, S. (2022, 8 August). *The 1600s Were a Watershed for Swear Words.* Retrieved from History Today: www.historytoday.com/archive/explicit-content

Mckenzie, A. (2005). 'This Death Some Strong and Stout Hearted Man Doth Choose': The Practice of Peine Forte et Dure in Seventeenth- and Eighteenth-Century England. *Law and History Review*, 279–313. Retrieved from Archive.Today: https://archive.ph/TwZn

Medieval Times & Castles. (n.d.). *The Rack Torture.* Retrieved from Medievality: www.medievality.com/the-rack-torture.html

Merriam-Webster. (2024, 22 July). *In forma pauperis.* Retrieved from Merriam-Webster Dictionary: www.merriam-webster.com/dictionary/in%20forma%20pauperis

Merriam-Webster. (2024, 22 July). *Seneschal.* Retrieved from Merriam-Webster: www.merriam-webster.com/dictionary/seneschal

Miller, H. (1982). Pakington, Robert (by 1489–1536), of London. In S. Bindoff (Ed.), *The History of Parliament: the House of Commons 1509–1558.* Martlesham, Suffolk: Boydell & Brewer. Retrieved from www.historyofparliamentonline.org/volume/1509-1558/member/pakington-robert-1489-1536

O'Connor, L., Werner, Z. & Barnard, J. (2024). More Than A Nick: Male Surgical Castration Throughout History. *The Journal of Sexual Medicine, 21*(Supplement 1). Retrieved from https://doi.org/10.1093/jsxmed/qdae001.263

Reggio, M. H. (2024, 7 June). *History of the Death Penalty*. Retrieved from PBS: www.pbs.org/wgbh/frontline/article/history-of-the-death-penalty/

Ridgway, C. (2023, 17 April). *April 17 – A Stolen Head*. Retrieved from Tudor Society: www.tudorsociety.com/april-17-a-stolen-head/?utm_content=cmp-true

Screti, Z. (n.d.). *Margaret Clitherow, the Pearl of York*. Retrieved from Historic UK: www.historic-uk.com/HistoryUK/HistoryofEngland/Margaret-Clitherow

Sky History. (n.d.). *Seven Sadistic Sultans from the Ottoman Empire*. Retrieved from Sky History: www.history.co.uk/articles/seven-sadistic-sultans-from-the-ottoman-empire

Spurr, J. (2018, 29 June). *'Damn your blood': Swearing in early modern English*. Retrieved from History Extra: www.historyextra.com/period/medieval/damn-your-blood-swearing-in-early-modern-english/

Swart, E. (2012). *Strategy, Tactics and Organisation of Dutch Rebel Troops, ca. 1566–1590* (unpublished). Retrieved from Academia: www.academia.edu/34589168/Strategy_tactics_and_organisation_of_Dutch_rebel_troops_ca_1566_1590

The Anne Boleyn Files. (2010, 27 May). *The Execution of Margaret Pole, Countess of Salisbury*. Retrieved from The Anne Boleyn Files: www.theanneboleynfiles.com/the-execution-of-Margaret-pole-countess-of-Salisbury/

Thoson, A. S. (2022, 7 August). *Sir Humphrey de Lisle*. Retrieved from Geni: www.geni.com/people/Sir-Humphrey-de-Lisle/6000000018600990887

Topkapi Palace. (n.d.). *What's Inside the Topkapi Palace*. Retrieved from Istanbul Tourist Information: Topkapi Palace: https://topkapipalace.gen.tr/inside/

Tracy, L. (2023). *Castration and Culture in the Middle Ages*. Suffolk: Boydell & Brewer.

Wayback Machine. (2009, 14 March). *The Research of Ishikawa Goemon*. Retrieved from Wayback Machine: Internet Archive: https://web.archive.org/web/20090314112133/www.page.sannet.ne.jp/s-koshi/misc/goemon2.html

Xu, R. (2021, 17 September). *Spectatorship and the Consumption of Dying at Public Executions*. Retrieved from The Coalition of Master's Scholars on Material Culture: https://cmsmc.org/opeds/spectatorship-and-the-consumption-of-dying

Extracting A Confession

Acts of the English Parliament. (1991). Act of Supremacy 1558 – Whole Act. *Actos of the English Parliament*. United Kingdom. Retrieved from www.legislation.gov.uk/aep/Eliz1/1/1

Ankeny, A. (Director). (2024). *Suranne Jones: Investigating the Witch Trials* (Motion Picture).

Castelow, E. (2015, 29 May). *Witches in Britain*. Retrieved from Historic UK: www.historic-uk.com/CultureUK/Witches-in-Britain/

Cowie, A. (2021, 20 October). *Germany's Brutal Werewolf Belt and The Gut-Wrenching Execution of Peter Stumpp*. Retrieved from Ancient Origins: www.ancient-origins.net/history/german-werewolf-009397

Crowther, D. (n.d.). *Anne Askew, Martyr And Author*. Retrieved from The History of England: https://thehistoryofengland.co.uk/resource/anne-askew-martyr-and-author/

Encyclopaedia Britannica. (2024, 21 June). *Lycanthropy*. Retrieved from Britannica: www.britannica.com/science/lycanthropy

English Heritage. (n.d.). *A Journey into Witchcraft Beliefs*. Retrieved from ENglish Heritage: www.english-heritage.org.uk/learn/histories/journey-into-witchcraft-beliefs/

Franco, S. (2023, 5 January). *The Judas Cradle Torture Device: How the 'Judas Chair' Used a Pyramid to Torture and Kill Its Victims*. Retrieved from The Vintage News: www.thevintagenews.com/2023/01/05/judas-cradle-one-of-the-most-painful-torture-devices-in-history/

Guilford, G. (2018, 24 January). *Germany was once the witch-burning capital of the world. Here's why*. Retrieved from Quartz: https://qz.com/1183992/why-europe-was-overrun-by-witch-hunts-in-early-modern-history

Hindley, C. (1862). *The life, prophecies and death of the famous Mother Shipton. Being not only a true account of her strange Birth and most important passages of her life; but also all her Phrophesies, now newly collected and historically explained [...]*. Brighton: J. Buck. Retrieved from The John Hopkins University Sheridan Libraries, et al.: www.jstor.org/stable/community.35015652?seq=26

Jackson, S. T. & Rafferty, J. P. (2024, 4 July). *Little Ice Age*. Retrieved from Britannica: www.britannica.com/science/Little-Ice-Age

John Hopkins University. (2024). *Brachial Plexus Injury*. Retrieved from Hopkins Medicine: www.hopkinsmedicine.org/health/conditions-and-diseases/brachial-plexus-injuries

Johnson Lewis, J. (2020, 20 February). *A Timeline of Witch Hunts in Europe*. Retrieved from ThoughtCo.: www.thoughtco.com/european-witch-hunts-timeline-3530786

Kramer, H. (2018). *The Hammer of Witches: Malleus Maleficarum*. (M. Summers, Trans.) Virtual: e-artnow.

Larison Danz, S. (2010). *The History of Mother Shipton: A Legendary Myth or a Legendary Woman?* Retrieved from Mother Shipton: www.mothershipton.com/history.html

Lechene, R. (2024, 4 June). *The Gutenberg Press*. Retrieved from Britannica: www.britannica.com/topic/printing-publishing/The-Gutenberg-press

Ledger, S. E., Rutherford, C. A., Benham, C., Burfield, I. J., Deinet, S., Eaton, M. … McRae, L. (2022). *Wildlife Comeback in Europe: Opportunities and challenges for species recovery*. London: Rewilding Europe.

Lee, A. (2020, 1 January). *A History of the Wolf*. Retrieved from History Today: www.historytoday.com/archive/natural-histories/history-wolf

Machielson, J. (2019). The Making of a Teen Wolf: Pierre de Lancre's Confrontation with Jean Grenier (1603–1610). *Folklore, 130* (3), 237–57. Retrieved from https://orca.cardiff.ac.uk/id/eprint/116724/3/Jean%20Grenier%20-%20Article%20REVISED%20%281%29.pdf

McDonald, MA, MSc, J. (2010, 1 October). *Medieval Torture*. Retrieved from Medieval Warfare: www.medievalwarfare.info/reference.htm

Moore, J. (2021, 5 October). *The 5 Most Gruesome Tudor Punishments and Torture Methods*. Retrieved from History Hit: www.historyhit.com/the-most-gruesome-tudor-punishments/

Morbid Kuriosity. (2023, 31 May). *Rat Torture, Its Origins, and Usage in History*. Retrieved from Morbid Kuriosity: https://morbidkuriosity.com/rat-torture-its-origins-and-usage-in-history/

Mother Shipton's. (n.d.). *The story of England's most famous Prophetess*. Retrieved from Mother Shipton's: www.mothershipton.co.uk/the-story/

O'Byrne Mulligan, E. (2022, 24 May). *Agnes Sampson: What happened to the Scottish healer burned as a witch explored in Lucy Worsley Investigates*. Retrieved from https://inews.co.uk/culture/television/agnes-sampson-what-happened-scottish-healer-witch-lucy-worsley-investigates-1648016?ico=related_stories

Redd, W. (2023, 23 April). *The Gruesome History of Rat Torture, from Medieval London to 20th-Century South America*. Retrieved from All That's Interesting: https://allthatsinteresting.com/rat-torture-method

Rojas, R. E. (2016). *Bad Christians and Hanging Toads: Witch Trials in Early Modern Spain, 1525–1675*. Retrieved from Duke University Libraries: https://dukespace.lib.duke.edu/items/716bc611-c869-40a0-986b-962611f9b61b

Roth Pierpont, C. (2008, 8 September). *The Florentine*. Retrieved from New Yorker: www.newyorker.com/magazine/2008/09/15/machiavelli-the-prince-florence

Rowley, M. (n.d.). *Weather in History 1500 to 1599 AD*. Retrieved from WeatherWebDotNet: https://premium.weatherweb.net/weather-in-history-1500-to-1599-ad/

Rowley, M. (n.d.). *Weather in History 1600–1649 AD*. Retrieved from WeatherWebDotNet: https://premium.weatherweb.net/weather-in-history-1600-to-1649-ad/

Ruickbie, L. (2022). Chapter Three – Was a Real Teenage Werewolf: The Seventeenth-Century Witchcraft Trial of Jean Grenier. In L. Ruickbie, S. Bacon & L. Ruickbie (Eds.), *The Cultural Construction of Monstrous Children: Essays on Anomalous Children from 1595 to the Present Day* (pp. 53–70). Cambridge: Anthem Press. Retrieved from www.cambridge.org/core/books/abs/cultural-construction-of-monstrous-children/was-a-real-teenage-werewolf-the-seventeenthcentury-witchcraft-trial-of-jean-grenier/7540B40B8C57F581AE6EA0C690228170

Sedgwick, I. (2022, 25 June). *Shady Meg: The Burning Witch of King's Lynn*. Retrieved from Icy Sedgwick: www.icysedgwick.com/shady-meg-kings-lynn/

Thadeusz, F. (2010, 28 October). *A Fresh Look at Torture in the Middle Ages*. Retrieved from Spiegel International: www.spiegel.de/international/zeitgeist/purification-through-pain-a-fresh-look-at-torture-in-the-middle-ages-a-725629.html

The Harvard University Center for Italian Renaissance Studies. (2013, 15 February). *The banishment and arrest of Niccolo Machiavelli*. Retrieved from The Harvard

University Center For Italian Renaissance Studies: https://itatti.harvard.edu/news/banishment-and-arrest-niccol%C3%B2-machiavelli

Willumsen, L. H. (2020). Witchcraft against Royal Danish Ships in 1589 and the Transnational Transfer of Ideas. *The International Review of Scottish Studies, 45*. Retrieved from www.irss.uoguelph.ca/index.php/irss/article/view/5801

Food Fatalities

Bauer, P. (2024, 10April). *Dancing plague of 1518*. Retrieved from Encyclopedia Britannica: www.britannica.com/event/dancing-plague-of-1518

Eggen, O. J. (2024, 3 July). *Tycho Brahe*. Retrieved from Encyclopedia Britannica: www.britannica.com/biography/Tycho-Brahe-Danish-astronomer

Henry 8th Boiled to Death. Retrieved from Owlcation: https://owlcation.com/humanities/richard-roose-the-cook-that-king-henry-8th-boiled-to-death

Hayle, J. (2023, 6 September). Richard Roose: The Cook that King Henry 8th Boiled to Death. Owlcation. Available at: https://owlcation.com/humanities/richard-roose-the-cook-that-king-henry-8th-boiled-to-death

Haynes, A. (1972, 5 May). Pietro Aretino. *History Today, 22*(5). Retrieved from www.historytoday.com/archive/pietro-aretino#

Historica. (n.d.). *Richard Roose*. Retrieved from Historica: https://historica.fandom.com/wiki/Richard_Roose

Jana, R. (2022, 13 May). *The people who 'danced themselves to death'*. Retrieved from BBC Culture: www.bbc.com/culture/article/20220512-the-people-who-danced-themselves-to-death/

Marabini, L. (2021, 25 September). *Clement VII, when food is deadly*. Retrieved from New Daily Compass: https://newdailycompass.com/en/clement-vii-when-food-is-deadly#:~:text=He%20died%20in%20excruciating%20pain,themselves%20initially%20as%20severe%20gastroenteritis

Taylor Tillman, N. & Staniforth, E. (2023, 21 June). *Tcyho Brahe: Colorful life, accomplishments and bizzare death*. Retrieved from Space.com: www.space.com/19623-tycho-brahe-biography.html

The Frick Collection. (n.d.). *Pietro Aretino*. Retrieved from The Frick Collection: www.frick.org/exhibitions/parmigianino/aretino

Kill or Cure

Cavendish, R. (2009, 7 July). Henry II of France Dies of Tournament Wounds. *History Today, 59*(7). Retrieved from History Today: www.historytoday.com/archive/henry-ii-france-dies-tournament-wounds#:~:text=Henry%20II%20was%20fatally%20injured,died%20on%20July%2010th%2C%201559.&text=Born%20in%201519%2C%20the%20future,were%20both%2014%20years%20old

Davis, M. (2023, 14 July). *The bizarre story of the deadly 'dancing plague' of 1518*. Retrieved from Big Think: https://bigthink.com/the-past/dancing-plague-middle-ages/

Felson Duchan, J. (2023, 29 May). *Astrology and Medicine in Medieval Times.* Retrieved from Judy Duchan: www.acsu.buffalo.edu/~duchan/new_history/middle_ages/astrology_and_medicine.html

Fischer, K. (2022, 28 October). *What Is Ergostim?* (D. Pathak, Editor) Retrieved from WebMD: www.webmd.com/first-aid/what-is-ergotism

The Editors of Encyclopaedia. (2024, 11 July). *Clement VII.* Retrieved from Encyclopedia Britannica: www.britannica.com/biography/Clement-VII-pope

Trueman, C. (2015, 17 March). *Tudor Medicine.* Retrieved from History Learning Site: www.historylearningsite.co.uk/tudor-england/tudor-medicine/

Tudor Times. (2021, 21 September). *Elizabeth I: Life Story. Chapter 8: Scandal, Smallpox and Succession.* Retrieved from Tudor Times: https://tudortimes.co.uk/people/elizabeth-i-life-story/scandal-smallpox-and-succession

Wear, A. (2015, 20 June). Making us as cruel as dogs: plague in the 16th and 17th century England. *The Art of Medicine, 385*(9986), 2456–2457. Retrieved from www.thelancet.com/journals/lancet/article/PIIS0140-6736(15)61129-1/fulltext

Zanello, M., Charlier, P., Corns, R., Devaux, B., Berche, P. & Pallud, J. (2015). The death of Henry II, King of France (1519–1559). From myth to medical and historical fact. *Acta Neoruchir (Wein), 157(1)*, 145–149. Retrieved from https://pubmed.ncbi.nlm.nih.gov/25421951/

Perils and Plagues

Barberis, I., Bragazzi, N., Galluzzo, L. & Martini, M. (2017). The history of tuberculosis: from the first historical records to the isolation of Koch's bacillus. *J Prev Med Hyg, 58*, E9-E12. Retrieved from https://pdfs.semanticscholar.org/d384/614ebf701fc78219074f935796065d48e73b.pdf

Basham, P. (2015, 24 April). *The 'beak doctors'.* Retrieved from Royal College of Physicians: https://history.rcplondon.ac.uk/blog/beak-doctors

Cambridge University Press. (n.d.). *Quotidian.* Retrieved from Cambridge Dictionary Online: https://dictionary.cambridge.org/dictionary/english/quotidian

Center for Disease Control. (2021, 1 May). *History of Smallpox.* Retrieved from Center for Disease Control: www.cdc.gov/smallpox/history/history.html

Center for Disease Control. (2024, 2 July). *About Influenza A in Animals.* Retrieved from Center for Disease Control: www.cdc.gov/flu-in-animals/about/index.html

Center for Disease Control. (2023, 18 October). *Tuberculosis (TB).* Retrieved from Center for Disease Control: www.cdc.gov/tb/worldtbday/history.htm#:~:text=In%201943%2C%20Selman%20Waksman%2C%20Elizabeth,%2C%20and%20rifampin%20(1966)

Crespo-Lopez, M. E., Augusto-Oliviera, M., Lopes-Araujo, A., Santos-Sacramento, L., Souza-Monteiro, J. R., Farias da Rocha, F. & de Paula Arrifano, G. (2022). Chapter Eight – Mercury neurotoxicity in gold miners. (R. G. Lucchini, M. Aschner & L. G. Costa, Eds.) *Advances in Neurotoxicology, 7*, 282–314. doi:10.1016/bs.ant.2022.04.003

Encyclopedia. (2024, 10 July). *The Appearance of Syphilis in the 1490s*. Retrieved from Science and Its Times: Understanding the Social Significance of Scientific Discovery: www.encyclopedia.com/science/encyclopedias-almanacs-transcripts-and-maps/appearance-syphilis-1490s

Famous Fix. (n.d.). *16th-century deaths from tuberculosis*. Retrieved from Famous Fix: https://m.famousfix.com/list/16th-century-deaths-from-tuberculosis

Fontanilla, J.-M., Barnes, A. & Fordham von Reyn, C. (2011, 15 September). Current Diagnosis and Management of Peripheral Tuberculous Lymphadenitis. *Clinical Infectious Diseases, 53*(6), 555–62. doi:10.1093/cid/cir454

Galley, C. (2023). *Infant Mortality in England 1538–2000*. Local Population Studies Society. Retrieved from www.localpopulationstudies.org.uk/wp-content/uploads/GALLEY-Infant-mortality-book.pdf

Gunderman, R. (2019, 19 February). *How smallpox devastated the Aztecs – and helped Spain conquer an American civilization 500 years ago*. Retrieved from The Conversation: https://theconversation.com/how-smallpox-devastated-the-aztecs-and-helped-spain-conquer-an-american-civilization-500-years-ago-111579

Hammond, E. (1975). Doctor Augustine, Physician to Cardinal Wolsey and King Henry VIII. *Medical History, 19*(3), 215–49. doi:10.1017/S0025727300020251.

Harper, D. (2022, 2 October). *Etymology of Aztec*. Retrieved from Online Etymology Dictionary: www.etymonline.com/word/Aztec

Haub, C. (2011, October). *How Many People Have Ever Lived on Earth?* Retrieved from Wayback Machine: https://web.archive.org/web/20130424014209/www.prb.org/Articles/2002/HowManyPeopleHaveEverLivedonEarth.aspx

Henry, F. P. (1892, 13 January). Remarks on the Diagnosis of Influenza. (L. H. Adler, Ed.) *Proceedings of the Philadelphia County Medical Society, 13*, 11–13. Retrieved from https://books.google.co.uk/books?id=FQqgAAAAMAAJ&pg=PR1&source=gbs_selected_pages&cad=1#v=onepage&q&f=false

History In Numbers. (2024). *Black Death Facts*. Retrieved from History In Numbers: https://historyinnumbers.com/events/black-death/facts/

History Skills. (n.d.). *Medieval Plague Doctors: Masked saviours or grim harbingers of impending death?* Retrieved from History Skills: www.historyskills.com/classroom/year-8/plague-doctors/

Katz, B. (2018, 14 May). *Did Leprosy Originate in Europe*. Retrieved from Smithsonian Magazine: www.smithsonianmag.com/smart-news/did-leprosy-originate-europe-180969061/

Langdon, G. (2006). *Medici Women: Portraits of Power, Love and Betrayal.* Toronto: University of Toronto Press Incorporated.

Minato Tsuruga Yama Museum. (n.d.). *Otani Yoshitsugu: Owner of Tsuruga Castle*. Retrieved from Minato Tsuruga Yama Museum: https://tsuruga-yama-museum.jp/english/ootani-yoshitsugu/

Nash, J. E. & Kearns, S. C. (2024, 23 July). *Leprosy*. Retrieved from Britannica: www.britannica.com/science/leprosy/History

National Park Service. (2022, 5 October). *Chapter 3: Battle of Sekigahara*. Retrieved from National Park Service: www.nps.gov/articles/000/battle-of-sekigahara.htm

Nunez, K. & Hammond M.D., N. (2021, 19 May). *What Is Mad Hatter Disease (Erethism)?* Retrieved from Healthline: www.healthline.com/health/mad-hatter-disease

O'Neill, A. (2020, April). *Estimates of the Black Death's death toll in selected European cities from 1347 to 1351*. Retrieved from Statista: www.statista.com/statistics/1114273/black-death-estimates-deaths-european-cities/

Razzell, P. & Spence, C. (2007). The History of Infant, Child and Adult Mortality in London 1550–1850. *The London Journal*, 271–92. doi:10.1179/174963207X227578

Riccardi, N., Canetti, D., Martini, M., Diaw, M., DI Biagio, A., Codecasa, L. ... Besozzi, G. (2020, 30 April). The evolution of a neglected disease: tuberculosis discoveries in the centuries. *J Prev Med Hyg, 31*(1 (Suppl 1)), E9–E12. doi:10.15167/2421-4248/jpmh2020.61.1s1.1353

Robin, D., Larsen, A. R. & Levin, C. (2007). *Encyclopedia of Women in the Renaissance*. Bloomsbury Academic.

Roger, E. (2019, 5 December). *Living with leprosy in late medieval England*. Retrieved from The National Archives: https://blog.nationalarchives.gov.uk/living-with-leprosy-in-late-medieval-england/

Roser, M. (2023, 11 April). *Mortality in the past: every second child died*. Retrieved from Our World In Data: https://ourworldindata.org/child-mortality-in-the-past

Samurai Archives. (n.d.). *Otani Yoshitsugu*. Retrieved from Samurai Archives: https://samurai-archives.com/w/index.php?title=Otani_Yoshitsugu&action=edit

Science Museum. (2023, 8 November). *The History of Syphilis Part Two: Treatments, Cures and Legislation*. Retrieved from Science Museum.

Shimizu, K. (1997, October). History of influenza epidemics and discovery of influenza virus. *Nihon Rinsho, Japanese Journal of Clinical Medicine, 55*(10), 2505–11. Retrieved from https://pubmed.ncbi.nlm.nih.gov/9360364/

Taubenberger, J. K. & Morens, D. M. (2010, April). Influenza: The Once and Future Pandemic. *Public Health Reports, 125* (Suppl 3), 16–26. Retrieved from www.ncbi.nlm.nih.gov/pmc/articles/PMC2862331/

Taubenberger, J. & Morens, D. (2009, April). Pandemic Influenza – including a risk assessment of H5N1. *Rev Sci Tech, 28*(1), 187–202. doi:10.20506/rst.28.1.1879

The Editors of Encyclopaedia. (2023, 12 October). *Encyclpedia Britannica*. Retrieved from Britannica: www.britannica.com/science/puerperal-fever

The Editors of Encyclopaedia. (2024, 3 July). *Smallpox*. Retrieved from Britannica: www.britannica.com/science/smallpox

Thomas, D. (2023, 7 Apri). *Notable Cases of Leprosy*. Retrieved from News-Medical: www.news-medical.net/health/Notable-Cases-of-Leprosy.aspx

Thompson, T. (1852). *Annals of Influenza or Epidemic Catarrhal Fever in Great Britain from 1510 to 1837*. (T. Thompson, Ed.) London: The Sydenham Society. Retrieved from https://play.google.com/books/reader?id=vUEJAAAAIAAJ&pg=GBS.PR6&hl=en

Vogt-Luerssen, M. (2021, 7 September). The True Faces of the Daughters and Sons of Cosimo I de' Medici. *Medicea – Rivista interdisciplinare di studi medicei, 10*, 74–95. Retrieved from Kleio: www.kleio.org/en/books/true_faces_medici/artikel/

Watsons Health Hub. (n.d.). *Quotidian Fever*. Retrieved from Watsons Health Hub: https://watsonshealth.com.ph/quotidian-fever/#1547099972315-4dcee210-1847

World Mapper. (n.d.). *Population Year 1500*. Retrieved from World Mapper: https://worldmapper.org/maps/population-year-1500/

Ruthless Religion

Barry, P. (2024). *The Penal Laws*. Retrieved from Eternal Word Television Network: www.ewtn.com/catholicism/library/penal-laws-1704

Baumgartner, F. J. (2011, 13 November). Selim I ('the Grim') (1465–1520). *The Encyclopedia of War*. Retrieved from https://onlinelibrary.wiley.com/doi/abs/10.1002/9781444338232.wbeow562

Cambridge University Press. (n.d.). *Heresy*. Retrieved from Cambridge Advanced Learner's Dictionary & Thesaurus: https://dictionary.cambridge.org/dictionary/english/heresy

Cypa, E. H. (2017). *The Making of Selim: Succession, Legitimacy, and Memory in the Early Modern Ottoman World*. Indiana University Press: Indiana University Press.

Dalton, J. (2021, 13 January). *10 Facts About the Inquisitions*. Retrieved from History Hit: www.historyhit.com/facts-about-the-inquisitions/

Dash, M. (2012, 22 March). *The Ottoman Empire's Life-or-Death Race*. Retrieved from The Smithsonian Online Magazine: www.smithsonianmag.com/history/the-ottoman-empires-life-or-death-race-164064882/#:~:text=Capital%20punishment%20was%20so%20common%20in%20the%20Ottoman,the%20royal%20family%20and%20their%20most%20senior%20officials.

Encyclopaedia Britannica. (2020, 12 October). *Spanish Inquisition Key Facts*. Retrieved from Encyclopaedia Britannica: www.britannica.com/summary/Spanish-Inquisition-Key-Facts

Encyclopaedia Britannica. (2024, 8 April). *Selim I: Ottoman Sultan*. Retrieved from Britannica: www.britannica.com/biography/Selim-I

Executed Today. (2008, 5 February). *1597: The 26 Martyrs of Japan, for God and trade routes*. Retrieved from Executed Today: www.executedtoday.com/2008/02/05/1597-the-26-martyrs-of-japan/

Foxe, J. (1563). *Foxe's Book of Martyrs*. London. Retrieved from https://archive.org/details/foxesbookofmartyrs_201708/page/n3/mode/2up?view=theater

Freeman, S. (2008, February). *How the Spanish Inquisition Worked*. Retrieved from How Stuff Works: https://history.howstuffworks.com/historical-figures/spanish-inquisition3.htm

History Hit. (2017, 9 January). *What Was the Reconquista and Why Did It Last So Long?* Retrieved from History Hit: www.historyhit.com/1492-reconquista-iberia-completed/

History Skills. (n.d.). *What was the Spanish Reconquista*. Retrieved from History Skills: www.historyskills.com/classroom/ancient-history/anc-spanish-reconquista-reading/

History.com Editors. (2018, 7 May). *Printing Press*. Retrieved from History: www.history.com/topics/inventions/printing-press

Johnson, B. (n.d.). *Dissolution of the Monasteries*. Retrieved from Historic UK: www.historic-uk.com/HistoryUK/HistoryofEngland/Dissolution-of-the-Monasteries

Jokinen, A. (2007, 13 April). *Robert Aske (d. 1537)*. Retrieved from Luminarium: Encyclopedia Project: www.luminarium.org/encyclopedia/aske.htm

Kasteel Radboud. (2024). *Diederik Van Sonoy (*1529)*. Retrieved from Kasteel Radboud: https://kasteelradboud.nl/en/diederik-van-sonoy/

Lempinen, E. (2022, 20 July). *The tortures of the Spanish Inquisition hold dark lessons for our time*. Retrieved from Berkeley News: https://news.berkeley.edu/2022/07/20/the-tortures-of-the-spanish-inquisition-hold-dark-lessons-for-our-time/

Mingren, W. (2017, 23 February). *Eliminating the Competition: Selim I, A Grim Conqueror Who Vastly Extended the Ottoman Empire*. Retrieved from Ancient Origins: www.ancient-origins.net/history-famous-people/eliminating-competition-selim-i-grim-conqueror-who-vastly-extended-ottoman-021240

Nalle, S. (2018, 25 September). *Spanish Inquisition*. Retrieved from Oxford Bibliographies: www.oxfordbibliographies.com/display/document/obo-9780195399301/obo-9780195399301-0150.xml

New World Encyclopedia. (n.d.). *Spanish Inquisition*. Retrieved from New World Encyclopedia: www.newworldencyclopedia.org/entry/Spanish_Inquisition

Nichols, S. (2015, 25 June). *The Spanish Inquisition*. Retrieved from Ligonier: www.ligonier.org/learn/articles/spanish-inquisition

Perez, J. (2005). *The Spanish Inquisition: A History*. New Haven: Yale University Press.

Rawlings, H. (1997, 1 December). *The New History of the Spanish Inquisition*. Retrieved from Historical Association: www.history.org.uk/publications/resource/500/the-new-history-of-the-spanish-inquisition

Rawlings, H. (2006). *The Spanish Inquisition*. Oxford: Blackwell Publishing.

Ray, M. (2018, 3 April). *Timeline of the Spanish Inquisition*. Retrieved from Encyclpedia Britannica: www.britannica.com/list/timeline-of-the-spanish-inquisition

The Editors of Encyclopaedia. (2024, 14 June). *Galleon*. Retrieved from Britannica: www.britannica.com/technology/galleon

Trueman, C. N. (2024, 22 July). *The Pilgrimage of Grace*. Retrieved from History Learning Site: www.historylearningsite.co.uk/tudor-england/the-pilgrimage-of-grace/?utm_content=cmp-true

Ward, D. P. (2017, April 8). *Punish the Non-Believers: 6 Cruel Torture Methods of the Spanish Inquisition*. Retrieved from History Collection: https://historycollection.com/snap-crackle-pop-torture-methods-of-the-spanish-inquisition/

Wayback Machine. (n.d.). *List fo the 26 Martyrs of Japan in Nishizaka, Nagasaki*. Retrieved from Wayback Machine: Internet Archive: https://web.archive.org/web/20100214135648/http://www1.bbiq.jp/martyrs/ListEngl.html

World History Edu. (2022, 4 December). *Spanish Inquisition: Meaning, Torture Methods, Deaths and Shocking Facts*. Retrieved from World History Edu: https://worldhistoryedu.com/spanish-inquisition-meaning-torture-methods-deaths-shocking-facts/

World History Edu. (2024, 12 July). *History of Ottoman Sultan Selim I: Why was he called 'the Grim'?* Retrieved from World History Edu: https://worldhistoryedu.com/history-of-ottoman-sultan-selim-i-why-was-he-called-the-grim/

The Final Gong

Gunn, S. (2017). Sixteenth-century English accident inquests. (Data Collection). Colchester, Essex, UK. Retrieved from https://dx.doi.org/10.5255/UKDA-SN-852155

Gunn, S. & Gromelski, Tomasz. (2012). For whom the bell tolls: accidental deaths in Tudor England. *The Art of Medicine*, 1222–23.

Weaponry Woes

Alpha History. (n.d.). *1552: Gent dies after looking down a loaded longbow*. Retrieved from Alpha History: https://alphahistory.com/pastpeculiar/1552-gent-dies-loaded-longbow/

Backwell, L., Bradfield, J., Carlson, K. J., Jashashvili, T., Wadley, L. & d'Errico, F. (2018). The antiquity of bow-and-arrow technology: evidence from Middle Stone Age layers at Sibudu Cave. *Antiquity, 92*, 289–303. doi:10.15184/aqy.2018.11.

Discover Middle Ages. (n.d.). *The Medieval Sword*. Retrieved from Discover Middle Ages: www.discovermiddleages.co.uk/medieval-weapons/the-medieval-sword

English Heritage. (n.d.). *Tudors: War*. Retrieved from English Heritage: www.english-heritage.org.uk/learn/story-of-england/tudors/war/#:~:text=CONSTANT%20FIGHTING&text=Matchlock%20muskets%20and%20calivers%20replaced,warfare%2C%20with%20few%20large%20battles

Glenn, C. (n.d.). *The Battle of Nagashino: Samurai matchlock guns and armor*. Retrieved from Aichi Now: www.aichi-now.jp/en/columns/detail/135/

Great Castles. (2024). *Medieval Weapons*. Retrieved from Great Castles: https://great-castles.com/weapons.html

Municipal and provincial archives of Vienna. (n.d.). *The Period of the Turkish Sieges (1529 to 1683)*. Retrieved from City of Vienna: www.wien.gv.at/english/history/overview/turks.html

Reid, A. D. (2018, 28 May). *Medieval Monday: Making Barrels and Wooden Vessels*. Retrieved from Allison D Reid: https://allisondreid.com/tag/medieval-cooper/

This Is London. (n.d.). *The Murder of Robert Pakington*. Retrieved from This Is London: https://thisislondontown.wixsite.com/thisislondon/single-post/2017/09/06/the-murder-of-robert-pakington

Wiltshire Museum. (n.d.). *Barbed and tanged arrowheads*. Retrieved from Wiltshire Museum: www.wiltshiremuseum.org.uk/?artwork=barbed-tanged-arrowheads#:~:text=These%20barbed%20and%20tanged%20arrowheads,from%20the%20loss%20of%20blood

Notable Mentions

BBC. (2011, 14 June). *10 strange ways Tudors died*. Retrieved from BBC: www.bbc.co.uk/news/magazine-13762313

Biography. (2023, 16 August). *Christopher Marlowe*. Retrieved from Biography: www.biography.com/authors-writers/christopher-marlowe

Cellania, Miss. (2018, 27 January). *Visit a Beard That Killed Its Owner*. Retrieved from Neatorama: www.neatorama.com/2018/01/27/Visit-a-Beard-That-Killed-Its-Owner/

de Commynes, P. (1855–56). *The memoirs of Philip de Commines, Lord of Argenton: containing the histories of Louis XI, and Charles VIII, Kings of France, and of Charles the Bold, duke of Burgundy; to which is added the Scandelous chronicle, or, Secret history of Louis XI.* London: H. G. Bohn. Retrieved from https://archive.org/details/memoirsofphilip02commiala/page/284/mode/2up

History.com Editors. (2019, 6 September). *Spanish Armada*. Retrieved from History: www.history.com/topics/european-history/spanish-armada

Inglis, S. (n.d.). *The history of football in England*. Retrieved from English Heritage: www.english-heritage.org.uk/visit/inspire-me/the-history-of-football-in-england/

Kingsmen Premium. (n.d.). *Killed by His Beard: Hans Steininger*. Retrieved from Kingsmen Premium: https://kingsmenpremium.com/blogs/beards-in-history/killed-by-his-beard-hans-steininger

Larson, R. (2016, 3 February). *Ways to Die During the Tudor Period*. Retrieved from Tudors Dynasty: https://tudorsdynasty.com/ways-to-die-during-the-tudor-dynasty/

Lyken-Garner, A. (2011, 6 May). *Strange Death, Anyone?* Retrieved from Kuriositas: www.kuriositas.com/2011/05/strange-death-anyone.html

NADS Admin. (2015, 5 November). *History of Football in England*. Retrieved from NADS: www.nads.org.uk/football-history/history-of-football-in-england/

Nobbs, P. (2022, 18 July). *6 of the most catastophic weather events in British history*. Retrieved from History Extra: www.historyextra.com/period/medieval/catastrophic-extreme-weather-events-british-history/

Poetry Foundation. (n.d.). *Christopher Marlowe*. Retrieved from Poetry Foundation: www.poetryfoundation.org/poets/christopher-marlowe

Potts, R. (2007, 30 November). *Jurassic Tennis*. Retrieved from The Smart Set: www.thesmartset.com/article11300701/

Royal Museums Greenwich. (n.d.). *The history of the Spanish Armada*. Retrieved from Royal Museums Greenwich: www.rmg.co.uk/stories/topics/spanish-armada-history-causes-timeline

The Economic & Social Research Council. (2024, July). *Everyday Life and Fatal Hazard in Sixteenth-Century England*. Retrieved from Tudor Accidents: https://tudoraccidents.history.ox.ac.uk/?page_id=177

The Editors of Encyclopaedia. (2009, 6 November). *Prisoner's Base*. Retrieved from Britannica: www.britannica.com/topic/prisoners-base

The Spitfire Society. (n.d.). *August 1940 Day by Day*. Retrieved from Battle of Britain: www.battle-of-britain.org.uk/history/august-1940-day-by-day

Zanello, M., Roux, A., Gavaret, M., Bartolomei, F., Huberfeld, G., Charlier, P. … Pallud, J. (2021). King Charles VIII of France's Death: From and Unsubstantiated Traumatic Brain Injury to More Realistic Hypothesis. *World Neurosurgery, 156*, 60–67. doi:10.1016/j.wneu.2021.09.056.

Ridiculous Survivals

Blankesteijn, H., & Hacquebord, L. (1993, 3 April). *God and the Arctic Survivors*. Retrieved from New Scientist: www.newscientist.com/article/mg13818674-500-god-and-the-arctic-survivors/

Briffett, E. (2022, 10 October). *What caused the Mary Rose to sink?* Retrieved from History Extra: www.historyextra.com/period/tudor/why-did-mary-rose-sink/

Bunting, T. (2017, 28 March). *Siege of Vienna*. Retrieved from Britannica: www.britannica.com/event/Siege-of-Vienna-1529

Chipman, D. E. (2022, 9 November). *Cabeza de Vaca, Alvar Nunez (ca. 1490–ca. 1559)*. Retrieved from Texas State Historical Association: www.tshaonline.org/handbook/entries/cabeza-de-vaca-lvar-nunez

Farren, J. (Producer) & Gray, J. (Director). (2010). *Digging for Britain: The Tudors* (Motion Picture).

Gordon, E. C. (1986). The Fate of Sir Hugh Willoughby and His Companions: A New Conjecture. *The Geographical Journal, 152*(2), 243–47. doi:10.2307/634766

Hardiman, J. (1979). Irish Minstrelsy, vol. II. In A. Chambers, *Granuaille: The Life and Times of Grace O'Malley*. Appendix 1, 189–93. Dublin.

Historic Jamestowne. (n.d.). *John Smith*. Retrieved from Jamestown Rediscovery: Historic Jamestowne: https://historicjamestowne.org/history/pocahontas/john-smith/

Humanities Texas. (n.d.). *Alvar Nunez Cabexa de Vaca*. Retrieved from Humanities Texas: www.humanitiestexas.org/programs/tx-originals/list/alvar-nunez-cabeza-de-vaca

Kauffman, M. (n.d.). *The salvage crew of the Mary Rose*. Retrieved from Future Learn: www.futurelearn.com/info/courses/black-tudors/0/steps/224736

Leslie, E. E. (1988). *Desperate Journeys, Abandoned Souls: True Stories of Castaways and Other Survivors*. New York: Houghton Miffin Company.

McEwan, J. S. (2024, 4 July). *John Knox*. Retrieved from Britannica: www.britannica.com/biography/John-Knox

Museum De Lakenhal Leiden. (n.d.). *Seige and Relief of Leiden 1573–1574*. Retrieved from Musem De Lakenhal Leiden: www.lakenhal.nl/en/story/siege-and-relief-of-leiden-oud

National Park Service. (2022, 4 September). *Captain John Smith*. Retrieved from Historic Jamestowne: www.nps.gov/jame/learn/historyculture/life-of-john-smith.htm#:~:text=Captain%20John%20Smith%20was%20an,English%20settlement%20in%20North%20America

Reformed Presbyterian Church of Scotland. (2022, 7 April). *John Knox as Galley Slave*. Retrieved from Reformed Presbytarian Churhc of Scotland: www.rpcscotland.org/2022/04/07/john-knox-as-galley-slave/

The Mary Rose. (n.d.). *The life of the Mary Rose*. Retrieved from The Mary Rose: https://maryrose.org/discover/history/life-of-the-mary-rose/#:~:text=The%20Mary%20Rose%20and%20Peter%20Pomegranate&text=These%20ships%20would%20become%20the,is%20now%20Portsmouth%20Historic%20Dockyard

Trowbridge, B. (2016, 16 June). *Meeting Grace O'Malley, Ireland's Pirate Queen*. Retrieved from The National Archives: https://blog.nationalarchives.gov.uk/meeting-grace-omalley-irelands-pirate-queen/

Whitney, C. (2024, 22 July). *John Smith's True Story Is Way Better Than the Fictional Tale*. Retrieved from How Stuff Works: https://history.howstuffworks.com/historical-figures/john-smith.htm

Acknowledgements

As this was a collaborative project there are several people that each of us wished to thank, so we have separated it out in the first instance.

Emily would like to thank her incredible family. My mum Sally for spending countless hours aiding with G.C.S.E history revision and coming up with random sayings and songs to help them stick in my brain, which still work today. My dad Kevin for letting me and Carrie talk to him for ages about something historical that we think is cool, even if it's not, and for trying his best to keep us on track. My sisters Mary and Maddy for being the biggest cheerleaders, telling me exactly what I need to hear (whether I want to hear it or not) and for being there for me in ways they don't even know. My brothers-in-law Gary and Luke, always there with a joke and jibe at my expense but my bodyguards if needed and the very best of men that I could wish for my sisters. To my niece and nephew, Amelia and Henry – be prepared to know more about history than you ever thought possible; I'm the nerdy aunt! My partner John, our first 'editor'. Thank you for coming into my life and turning it upside down in the very best of ways. For making us endless cups of tea, coffee and telling us your true thoughts as only you can: I love you. The Reeds – Karla, Steve and Liam, my Uncle Mark, Auntie Lesley, Naomi, Jamie and Isabella, Nanny Val and Grandad Barrie – the best of family who never fail to make us all laugh. The Ingram-Gettins for all your support and guidance. My girls Natalie, Jaffa and Breanne for supporting and being there for me always, whether it's a huge Chinese, a drink or a hug, I adore you all. Lastly to my person, Carrie, my ride or die. The one who genuinely believes I can do anything that I start to believe it myself. I can't quite get over the fact that our humble little podcast gave us an opportunity like this and there is no one else I would rather have by my side, through his and everything past, present and future. Here's to the next adventure, my Dean.

Carrie would like to thank her mother Theresa for being a source of strength and inspiration, as well as her brother Joe and sister-in-law Patrice for accepting having a history nerd in the family, and to the Bush clan who took me in and helped me to make Norfolk my home. I would also like to thank Kevin for putting up with my endless rants and excited conversations about the most morbid of subjects, and for reminding me to take a break every so often. Thanks go to Carly and Chantelle, my dearest ladies and constant support through all aspects of life, Claire and Carl for teaching me to accept who I am, and to the Jacksons: Steve, Michelle and Maddie (Stringbean), for embracing me in all my weirdness. I love you all. Additionally, thanks go to my many other friends and colleagues who have supported me through this and tried to keep me as sane as it is possible for me to be, especially Claire, Carl, Vicky, Zoe, Mandy, Anita, Sally, Ali, Tom G, Tom P, Dave S, Mark W, Alison R, Ben S, Ashley and many, many more – you know who you all are and your words of encouragement will never be forgotten and can never be underestimated. Last of all, my thanks go to Emily, my partner in historical crime, without whom this would never have come about. I'm very proud of what we have achieved here and of you; thank you for taking this risk with me and for seeing this through despite everything I have watched you endure. Here is to the next adventure, my Sammy. Finally, we would both like to thank six people who together with author Terry Deary fuelled our passion for history to an almost addictive level: Mathew Baynton, Ben Willbond, Laurence Rickard, Martha Howe-Douglas, Simon Farnaby and Jim Howick. What your madcap sketches did for making history accessible and enjoyable to audiences of all ages is more than we could aspire to do here. We would also like to thank our friends and highly dysfunctional family at Watlington Players whose support and love is as unending as their talent, and our Nerd Collective: Matt, Liam, Tobias and Dave, for keeping us going and keeping us grounded. To Dave (Dad), James, Nanny Ann, Grandad Peter and Kelly for watching over us, you're never far from our thoughts, hope we made you proud. We of course would like to thank the team at Pen & Sword for their dedication, help and support throughout this process, especially Sarah-Beth, who listened to our podcast and took a chance on us, and Lucy and Chris who no doubt had their work cut out with us; we have no words, we are so grateful for this opportunity and for the chance to work with you all. Thanks also go to the team at Middleton Hall in Tamworth for the image use and the fascinating conversation. Last and by no means least we must thank our listeners of A Nice Cup of Histortea. Who would have thought that a podcast started in 2018 in Emily's kitchen would lead to this. It has already taken us beyond our wildest expectations. With a global listenership and now a book deal, I can't wait to see what's in store next for next for us, but we'll never forget the day this all started. It's our history, right?